Product Planning Essentials

Product Planning Essentials

SECOND EDITION

Kenneth B. Kahn

Yes Dee Publishing Pvt Ltd
Publishing Par Excellence

ISBN: 978-93-80381-21-3
Indian Reprint, 2012

Kenneth B. Kahn, *Product Planning Essentials, Second Edition*
(Armonk, NY : M.E. Sharpe, 2011)

**Authorized Reprint Edition, for sale in India, Pakistan, Bangladesh,
Nepal and Sri Lanka only.**

Published by
Yes Dee Publishing Pvt Ltd
New No. 16, Old No. 18/A,
Govindan Street, Ayyavoo Colony,
Aminjikarai, Chennai – 600 029.
Tamil Nadu, INDIA.

+91 44 4508 2085
suresh@yesdee.com
www.yesdee.com

Printed at Shakthi Printers, Triplicane, Chennai-5.

Contents

Preface

The first edition of *Product Planning Essentials* was written because of the need for a book that covered both product development and product management topics in a way that was not too quantitative or general. The expressed aim was for the book to be broad and interdisciplinary in nature in order to serve as a good primer on the topic of product planning.

This second edition of *Product Planning Essentials* has a similar aim: to be a useful and welcomed primer on the topic of product planning. Akin to the first edition, this second edition outlines the product planning endeavor by describing the various initiatives that are necessary for successful product planning. Also akin to the first edition, the second edition illustrates various tools and techniques for managing product planning efforts, and in such a way that the reader might readily apply these tools and techniques.

The second edition differs from the first edition in several respects. Two new chapters on design and legal considerations have been added. The discussion of global considerations has been expanded to introduce sustainable product development and base of the pyramid (BoP) product development. The final chapter has been expanded to present product planning best practices from recent noteworthy studies. Analytical discussion of various techniques has been simplified to improve comprehension; and typos in the previous edition have been resolved. The hope is that the reader—whether an undergraduate student, graduate student, or professional—will find the second edition of *Product Planning Essentials* a desktop reference and business topics primer of choice on the basics of product planning.

I wish to thank Harry Briggs of M.E. Sharpe, who encouraged me to pursue this second edition, and Elizabeth Granda and Henrietta Toth, who provided keen editing of this book and guided me through the publication process. Appreciation further goes to Azin Lofti and Tom Walsh, principals at Ice Miller, LLP, in Indianapolis, Indiana, who presented to my classes on intellectual property and company entity formation and provided a basis for the "Legal Considerations" chapter. Sincere appreciation is expressed to colleagues both in academia and in industry who read through draft manuscripts and offered their constructive criticism as well as support for this book. Naturally, the process of writing a book cannot be accomplished successfully without the support of family. My loving appreciation to Mary Kay, Alex, and Michael for their somewhat quiet patience in allowing me to complete this second edition of *Product Planning Essentials*.

Product Planning Essentials

1 Introduction to Product Planning

Scanning today's marketplace reveals a cornucopia of products. A deeper look reveals that each product available for purchase has undergone considerable planning, consumed ample resources, and required appropriate execution of strategy just to make it to the marketplace. That process through which a product is conceived, brought to market, and managed across the life cycle is called "product planning"—the focus of this book.

Product planning is very important to a company because, when done properly, it can reduce resource expenditures, drive revenues, and generate profitability. New product profitability is often a key objective and driver for product planning because it directly corresponds to the company's bottom line. Just as important, a product reflects the company's reputation, and thus a company will be intent on launching only those products that enhance its image and reputation. Other objectives such as company awareness, customer satisfaction, and market share attainment are also product planning objectives and underlie a company's long-term viability and competitiveness. The nature of these objectives exemplifies the strategic implications that product planning poses for a company in pursuit of successful new products. Product planning will not guarantee 100 percent success, but it does increase the likelihood of achieving success.

Product Planning Defined

The company process called "product planning" is formally defined as the process of envisioning, conceptualizing, developing, producing, testing, commercializing, sustaining, and disposing of organizational offerings to satisfy consumer needs and wants and achieve organizational objectives. By this definition, product planning is certainly a broad and complex endeavor, comprising numerous issues and activities—many of which are cross-disciplinary in nature.

To clarify understanding of the topic, product planning can be characterized as comprising the two processes of product development and product management. Product development represents the up-front process, where the

3

product or service is conceived, conceptualized, developed, produced, and tested. All these activities occur prior to the formal offering of the product or service to the marketplace, which is termed the "launch."

Product management represents the back-end process, where the product or service is commercialized, sustained, and eventually disposed. Product management includes the launch endeavor along with all activities that occur after the launch.

While distinguishing product planning as product development and product management simplifies the product planning endeavor, separating the two processes can lead to some unfortunate circumstances. For one thing, the separation of product development and product management implicitly assumes a break between the two processes, which overlooks the necessary transition between them. Various new product offerings have failed to reach their potential because product development was not properly linked to the product management team and misunderstanding about the new product offering abounded. Separating the two processes also implies that product development has a stopping point, which is not really true. Even after launch, product developers should work with product managers to broaden the brand or product line. Conversely, product management should not be seen as just a launch and postlaunch activity. In fact, product managers can work with product developers to delineate market trends and customer needs that future offerings should serve. One who undertakes product planning should acknowledge product development and product management as two important, interlinked processes within an overarching process called product planning.

Product Planning Roles

Product planning serves various key roles in the company. One of these roles is resource allocation. Product planning analyzes each product or service, whether current or new, to determine the resources that it will need to be successful and prioritize the impact that it has for the company. The company's finite resources are then proportioned out to those products that deserve to receive these resources. Assuming most, if not all, products are deserving of resources, product planning forces the company to optimize the partitioning of company resources across products.

Related to the role of resource allocation is that of product mix coordination. Here the objective is to balance the various products that the company offers to ensure that a particular type of product is not overwhelming the company's offerings or diluting customer interest. The role of product mix coordination is to provide a product mix that distinguishes products where some or all are complementary products and provides the strongest market presence possible for each respective product.

Another role is marketing program support. Product planning can provide market information based on the current performance of existing products. Product planning also can enlighten the marketing function to customer comments regarding current products and customer needs. As a result, new marketing programs can be better focused to meet the intended target markets, and current marketing programs can be refined.

A fourth role is the appraisal of company offerings. Product planning evaluates the performance of current products (and services) to reveal their impact on the business. In many instances, this impact is measured in terms of cash flow, where products are classified as generating a profit or losing money for the company. If the product is profitable, product planners might consider how to increase the profit being generated; if the product is losing money, product planners would consider actions needed to turn the product around.

If the product continues to lose money, then one action that can be taken is the termination of the product. This is another role of product planning called product deletion. The product planner would identify products that should be deleted and chart a course of action for proper termination of the product. This course might include programs to transition customers to alternative products and plans to maintain a spare parts inventory for the product being deleted in order to avoid alienating customers of the product.

Product, Service, or Both

In the above paragraphs, varying terminology has been used to describe a company offering as a product, service, or even an idea. While historically and traditionally products and services have been distinct, they have become innately intertwined in today's marketplaces. For example, when buying a car, the product components of the car include chassis, engine, tires, and windows, among other things. But customers also receive warranties on various components of the car, may receive special financing, are given a customer service telephone number for complaints, and may participate in a special car servicing program (e.g., free oil changes, tire rotation). Together these items constitute the total package of what is considered "buying a car." Truly distinguishing products and services can be purposeless or even misleading.

Aside from slight nuances associated with their inherent characteristics, issues and the processes related to the development and management of products and services should be considered equivalent. Henceforth, the term "product" is used in this book, but the term "service" could be easily substituted, if preferred.

What Is a Product?

Having clarified the issue of product versus service, there is a need to define what is meant by "product." Basically, a product is a particular offering that a company provides to customers. This does not mean that the product is in a form that would be recognized by the final consumer market because the product may be a raw material for the buyer's product planning process. For example, integrated circuit chip manufacturers like Intel and AMD sell to computer manufacturers like Dell, Hewlett-Packard, and Lenovo, who, in turn, produce desktop computer systems to be sold to business and final consumers. Just because product in the business-to-business market differs from product in a final consumer market does not mean, however, that it is not a product. Per the given definition, it is just as much a product and requires just as much systematic product planning.

Still, there is a need to clarify what product means across different contexts. This is because product can mean different things to different people based on the context. Three particular contexts are considered: the nature of innovation, the nature of market demand, and the nature of the company's internal perspective.

Defining Product by the Nature of Innovation

One way to define product is by the nature of innovation underlying the respective product. Specifically, the terms "invention," "innovation," and "imitation" can be associated with product.

Inventions are not products. They are technical devices, which contain features, are packaged into some form, and provide a function. The distinction of inventions is that these features, form, or function may or may not satisfy a need, want, or desire in the marketplace. Crawford (1987, 23) defines inventions as "taking pre-existing knowledge and combining it in such a way as to develop something that never existed before."

Innovations are basically inventions around which a marketing program has been built to clearly offer a benefit to customers, which in turn satisfies the market need, want, or desire. Innovations are considered products because customers clearly understand how they satisfy the need, want, or desire. In other words, innovations represent a total package of features, form, and function concentrating on delivering the benefit to customers.

Innovations can be classified as continuous and discontinuous innovations. Continuous innovations are slight product changes or products that customers can readily understand and use. Such innovations can be the result of the normal upgrading of products and in most cases do not

6

require a change in customer behavior. New flavors or brands of potato chips would be characteristic of continuous innovations. Discontinuous innovations revolutionize the market infrastructure, make other technologies obsolete, and in many cases change the lifestyles of consumers. A technology like fusion-powered vehicles would be characteristic of discontinuous innovations.

At this point, it should be recognized that many new products do *not* succeed because they really were not products, but rather inventions. Even famous products have auspicious beginnings. One example is the photocopier described below.

Plagued by the need for copies of patent drawings and specifications, Chester Carlson investigated ways of automatic text and illustration reproduction, working out of his apartment. While others sought chemical or photographic solutions to "instant copying" problems, Carlson turned to electrostatics, and in 1938, succeeded in obtaining his first "dry-copy" and the first of many patents two years later. However, he was initially unsuccessful at convincing companies that the technology would be preferable to carbon paper. In fact, it was only after calling on twenty companies that the Batelle Development Corporation agreed to invest in his concept in 1944. Batelle's investment provided the necessary resources to "commercialize" the technology, and in 1947, the Haloid Corporation acquired a license to Carlson's basic xerographic patents from Batelle. In 1948, Haloid and Batelle announced the development of "xerography" and a year later, the first xerographic printer, the Model A, was introduced. Of course, today the photocopy machine is an invaluable business tool. (Xerox 2010)

So why over six years did twenty companies pass on the idea? In short, Carlson's patent was an invention. As previously stated, inventions lack clear benefits and are not in a recognizable form. Batelle's vision and resources took the invention and transformed it into an innovation, which Haloid then realized it could use. As defined, an innovation is a product because the marketing component clarifies the benefits and helps prospective customers understand the offering. Customers do not buy inventions; they buy innovations. This corresponds to the general marketing tenet that customers buy benefits, not features.

Various versions of the photocopy machine have emerged since the 1950s. Some of these were branded by different companies and were more or less imitations of photocopiers on the market. Yet imitations are products too. Imitations are copies of innovations, which may or may not have enhanced features, enhanced form, and/or enhanced function. Successful products can be and in many cases have been imitations or "me-too" products. Such success might derive from a lower price or an enhanced product feature even though the product is essentially the same as the original innovation.

Defining Product by the Nature of Market Demand

Product also can be defined from a market perspective. This perspective is based on the premise that all products derive from a core benefit and that products can be represented as building upon the core benefit. Product therefore can be portrayed as a group of concentric circles building upon the issues of the inner circles, as shown in Exhibit 1.1.

As shown in Exhibit 1.1, the essential component of any product is the core benefit. The core benefit represents the fundamental service or benefit that the consumer is really buying, derived from the consumer's need or want. Consumers cannot buy just a benefit, though. The benefit must be put into some form or given some features through which the benefit can be delivered. Based on this framework, decisions regarding products (or services) must begin with what the core benefit is (or should be).

The second level of a product is the generic product. The generic product is the basic version of the product and typically a less developed product. "Less developed" means that the product does not have features or forms that generally distinguish the given product or services. The features and/ or forms given to the product or service allow the consumers to receive the benefit that they want.

The third level is the expected product. The expected product includes a set of attributes and conditions that buyers normally expect and agree to when they purchase this product.

The fourth level is the augmented product. The augmented product includes additional services and benefits that distinguish the company's offering from competitors' offerings. At this level, the product is complemented by services, and vice versa. Note that most national brands compete at the augmented product level.

At the fifth and top level is the potential product. The potential product is all the augmentations and transformations that the product might undergo in the future. The potential product represents a product that attempts to satisfy all consumers' needs and wants related to the product, thereby creating "customer delight."

Consider the example of a hotel. Essentially the core benefit of staying at a hotel is shelter. But because one cannot buy the concept of shelter by itself, a hotel provides features and services that allow a consumer to obtain, and satisfy the need for, shelter. The generic level might comprise hostels and YMCAs, which provide a bed and a roof over your head. Tents or a similar option might be considered generic too, yet tents are not really a solution in the hotel consideration set because "hotel" characteristically suggests someone else providing you shelter—not you providing your own shelter. Of course,

Exhibit 1.1 **Product as Defined From a Market Perspective**

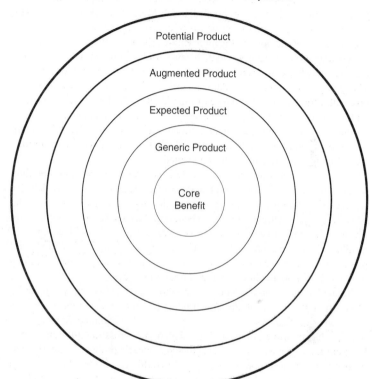

if a service provided you a tent for shelter, then that would be considered a valid generic option.

Simple hotels like Motel 6 or Super 8 would be characteristic of the expected level. These products provide features that consumers would expect for a hotel room—for example, a private room, a television, a telephone, and a private bathroom (which characteristically is a hotel expectation in the United States).

The augmented level would be represented by hotels like Hilton, Hyatt, Marriott, Omni, and Westin, which provide multiple services in association with the providing of shelter. These include room service, a newspaper at your door every morning, a concierge, a business support center, a fitness center, and in-room computerized checkout.

Arguably, the potential level would be hotels that attempt to delight hotel guests. These would be resort hotels like JW Marriott and Four Seasons Hotels. Another hotel chain that prides itself on exceptional service and may be characteristic of the potential level is Ritz-Carlton.

A simple product example would be macaroni and cheese. The core benefit associated with macaroni and cheese is to satisfy hunger and provide nutrition. The generic level would be a plain, generic version of the product—a simple box with little use of color. The expected level would be a branded product with more use of color. The augmented level would be a nationally branded product with a consumer complaint phone line and a kids' club. The potential product might be a delivery service, which would provide you gourmet macaroni and cheese whenever you wanted.

As you move toward the outer circles, the product becomes a premium product, be it a Ritz-Carlton Hotel or a gourmet macaroni and cheese delivery service. As you move toward the outer circles, the customer would pay (and be willing to pay) a higher price for a better product and service. As you move inward, the product becomes less expensive and more basic. The model of Exhibit 1.1 can therefore be used to devise a strategic product portfolio comprising products based on a margin strategy (at the outer levels) and simplified products based on a volume strategy (at the inner levels).

Related to the point of a product portfolio is the fact that many companies offer different versions of the same product category. Each of these versions varies on price, features, and associated services. For example, Marriott Corporation has multiple hotel offerings, which fall across the different levels: Fairfield Inn arguably could be considered a generic product in the Marriott portfolio; Courtyard by Marriott arguably could be considered an expected product; Marriott Hotels could be considered augmented products; and JW Marriott and Ritz-Carlton (which is owned by Marriott Corporation) could be considered potential products (see Exhibit 1.2).

Another issue inherent in the product model of Exhibit 1.1 is the affirmation of the statement that all products must have a core benefit. As shown in this Exhibit, the core benefit serves as the focal point of the product, not features or form (styling). Customers cannot buy a benefit directly and so the benefit is encapsulated within features and form to make the respective product understandable and compatible with the customer's environment.

One final point needs to be made about the effect of customer learning. The services and features that enhance a product at the augmented product level can over time become expected services. Thus, one can view the given product model like an onion, which develops multiple levels all cascading down to the center. This means that a company cannot be satisfied with existing offerings because customers can be trained to expect certain features or add-on

Exhibit 1.2 **Marriott International, Inc.**

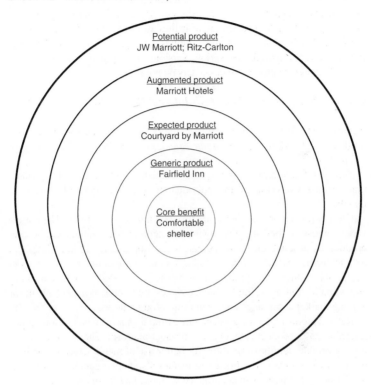

Marriott International, Inc. (NYSE: MAR) is a leading lodging company with more than 3,000 lodging properties in the United States and sixty-seven other countries and territories. The Marriott Corporation website describes the above hotel offerings as follows:

- Fairfield Inn & Suites: Provides business and leisure travelers with everything they need at an exceptional value.
- Courtyard by Marriott: Offers travelers the choices and options that let them make the most of their time on the road.
- Marriott Hotels & Resorts: Flagship brand of quality-tier, full-service hotels and resorts that provide consistent, dependable, and genuinely caring experiences to guests on their terms.
- JW Marriott: Most elegant and luxurious Marriott brand that provides business and leisure travelers a deluxe level of comfort and personal service on their terms.
- Ritz-Carlton: Worldwide symbol for the finest in accommodations, dining, and service.

Source: Marriott International, www.marriott.com.

11

services because of continued augmentation of the product by the company and/ or augmentation activities by competitors. One approach for managing this situation is to provide multiple offerings, as in the case of the Marriott Hotel descriptions shown in Exhibit 1.2. Another option is not to provide a potential product immediately, but instead offer various versions of the product over time, each time enhancing the product so customers do not expect everything at once.

Defining Product by the Company's Internal Perspective

A third way to define product is from an internal company perspective, where product is defined in terms of *product item, product line, product family,* or *product mix.*

A *product item* represents a specific model, brand, or size of a product that a company offers and is the individual product that a particular customer may buy.

Closely related product items are grouped into a *product line.* There are a variety of reasons for distinguishing product items by product lines. Organizing products by product lines may indicate a new opportunity. Product lines can help to spread resources across products so as to use company resources in an optimal fashion. And product lines can serve as a signal to the consumer about quality and/or desirable characteristics, plus serve as a mechanism for gaining market acceptance and promoting product items.

Related product lines are grouped into a *product family,* which is sometimes referred to as a product category or a product platform. The basis for determining product families can allow for better use of manufacturing capabilities or other company resources. Companies also may organize their overall organizational structures in accordance with product families.

At the highest level of aggregation is the *product mix.* Product mix consists of all the different product families, product lines, and product items a firm offers. Three characteristics used to describe the product mix are width, depth, and consistency. Width represents the number of different product lines. A wide product mix suggests many product lines, while a narrow product mix suggests fewer product lines. Depth represents the number of product items within each line. A deep product mix suggests many product items per each product line; a shallow product line suggests fewer product items per line. And consistency is the degree of commonality among lines with respect to end-use, distribution outlets, consumer groups, and/or price range. A consistent product mix would suggest similar product lines; an inconsistent product mix would suggest a diverse mix of product lines.

The characteristics of width, depth, and consistency can be illustrated with the product mixes of Pillsbury and Verizon. As shown in Exhibit 1.3,

Exhibit 1.3 **Pillsbury**

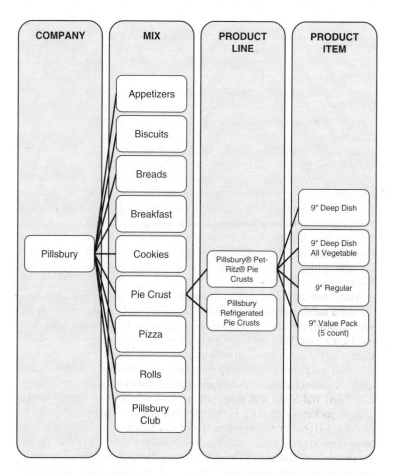

COMPANY	MIX	PRODUCT LINE	PRODUCT ITEM
	Appetizers		
	Biscuits		
	Breads		9" Deep Dish
	Breakfast		9" Deep Dish All Vegetable
Pillsbury	Cookies	Pillsbury® Pet-Ritz® Pie Crusts	
	Pie Crust	Pillsbury Refrigerated Pie Crusts	9" Regular
	Pizza		9" Value Pack (5 count)
	Rolls		
	Pillsbury Club		

About Pillsbury: Families have trusted Pillsbury to make mealtimes special for well over a century. Whether it's breakfast, lunch, or dinner, consumers can plan meals in minutes with products that have endured since 1869. Pillsbury is owned by General Mills, Inc.

Source: General Mills, www.generalmills.com.

Pillsbury has a wide and deep product mix, which comprises a number of product families: appetizers, biscuits, breads, breakfast, cookies, pie crust, pizza, rolls, and Pillsbury Club. Within each of these families can be multiple product lines. As shown, for example, the pie crust family of products has Pillsbury® Pet-Ritz® Pie Crusts and Pillsbury® Refrigerated Pie Crusts. Within each of these lines are often multiple product items. The Pillsbury® Pet-Ritz® Pie Crusts include nine-inch deep dish pie crust, nine-inch deep dish all vegetable pie crust, nine-inch regular, and nine-inch value pack (five count). In comparison, Verizon, as shown in Exhibit 1.4, has a relatively narrower but deep product mix. Verizon has the three business units of domestic wireless, wireline telecom, and wireline business, with each reflecting a distinct family of product offerings. The wireline telecom business unit has voice, Internet, and television families. Each of these families of services has different lines of service plans, and within each plan are specific items of offerings. As shown, there are three plans in the voice family: Freedom Unlimited Calling Plans, Local and Long Distance Calling Plans, and International Calling Plans. The specific line of Local and Long Distance Calling Plans includes Flat Rate Service, Sensible Service, Exchange Only Service, Message Rate Service, and Economy Message Service. Note that the Verizon example illustrates that while family, line, and item are predominant levels for aggregation, companies may have (and often do employ) additional levels for aggregation.

Visualizing the product mix as a hierarchy of products helps product planners address a number of issues. One issue is product proliferation, which occurs when a company faces severe resource constraints as the width and depth of the mix increase and becomes overwhelmed with the number of products offered. Even with the use of common product platforms across the mix, product proliferation makes product planning more difficult. In the final consumer market especially, manufacturers typically must provide multiple mass merchants (e.g., Target and Wal-Mart) with their own universal product code (UPC—the bar code on packages), resulting in the individual product item becoming a set of products and contributing to product proliferation. For example, one television being shipped to three mass merchandisers would be three products (1 product item × 3 unique customer UPCs = 3 separate product items to be managed). This obviously gets more complicated if there are three different television models going to three different mass merchandisers; a total of nine products would need to be managed (3 television models × 3 unique customer UPCs).

Related to product proliferation is the issue of cannibalization. Cannibalization occurs when a product takes sales from another product offering. Typically, companies want to avoid new product introductions that cannibalize their own product offerings. However, there is a saying that "if you are go-

Exhibit 1.4   **Verizon**

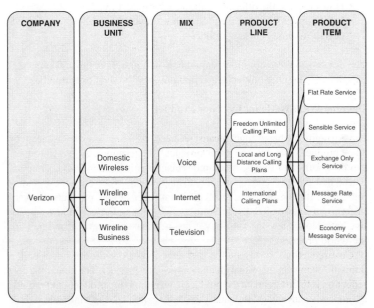

COMPANY	BUSINESS UNIT	MIX	PRODUCT LINE	PRODUCT ITEM
				Flat Rate Service
			Freedom Unlimited Calling Plan	Sensible Service
	Domestic Wireless	Voice	Local and Long Distance Calling Plans	Exchange Only Service
Verizon	Wireline Telecom	Internet	International Calling Plans	Message Rate Service
	Wireline Business	Television		Economy Message Service

About Verizon: Verizon Communications, Inc., headquartered in New York, is a leader in delivering broadband and other wireline and wireless communication innovations to mass market, business, government, and wholesale customers.

Source: Verizon, www.verizon.com.

ing to have to deal with cannibals, you may as well keep the cannibals in the family." In other words, companies would rather cannibalize their own sales than have a competitor cannibalize sales. Sometimes companies introduce new products without considering the potential cannibalization of existing product sales. Companies need to ensure that products are positioned correctly to minimize cannibalization. Reducing cannibalization effects also minimizes the duplication of resources and the lack of efficiency in the product planning effort. For instance, computer chip manufacturers must carefully plan the launch of new chips in order to stay ahead of competitors plus maximize revenue of current chips because once launched, sales of older chips will be cannibalized by newer chips. The introduction of new product technology represents a way to establish clear competitive advantage, but it requires careful planning. Product planners should ask three general questions in the course of evaluating the company's product mix:

15

- What product lines does the company offer?
- How deep are the offerings within each product line?
- What gaps exist within the product line that could be filled by new products or modified current products?

The answers to these questions should help to highlight company competencies, identify lagging products, and pinpoint new product opportunities.

Defining What Is Meant by "New Product"

Having defined what product means, we need to distinguish what is meant by "new product." Just like the term "product," the terminology "new product" can mean different things. A common misnomer is the general presumption that all new products correspond only to major changes and major new product initiatives. Rather, there are seven different types of new products that vary in terms of "newness." These are cost reductions, product improvements, line extensions, new markets, new uses, new category entries, and new-to-the-world products.

Cost reductions correspond to a change in price and do not represent a dramatic change in the visual characteristics of a product. The aim of the cost reduction is to differentiate the product from competing products and provide a competitive advantage. In January 2009, for example, Apple introduced three new pricing tiers for iTunes tracks—$0.69 for older tracks, $0.99 for recent tracks, and $1.29 for new hits. The cost reduction attracted media attention and potentially increased customer purchases. The inverse of a cost reduction, a price increase, also may be possible and has the potential to change the perceived image of a product. Like a cost reduction, a price increase differentiates the product from competitors on price and does not represent a dramatic change in the visual characteristics of product. During the 1990s, Rolling Rock beer increased its price in the course of national advertising and promotion to position what had been a regional brand toward a national brand; significant growth was achieved and heralded by industry observers (Khermouch 1994).

Product improvements are product enhancements that improve the product's form or function. Examples of a product improvement are those products labeled as "new and improved" or "better flavor." A product improvement serves as a replacement for the original product, which is thus no longer available to consumers. A new and improved Tide laundry detergent that is now "even better than before" is characteristic of a product improvement. Product improvements also include packaging changes, assuming the core product that the customer is buying does not change. In January 2009, Kellogg's announced plans to test market a new cereal package. The packaging contained the same amount of food, but the shorter, fatter package was designed to fit more easily into customer pantries; save shelf space in grocery stores, allowing retailers to offer a wider variety of products; and decrease packaging materials by 8 percent, providing "green" benefits (York 2009).

Line extensions are new versions of an existing product but with unique features that the original product (or set of products) does not have. For example, adding to the original Colgate toothpaste product line such items as Colgate Toothpaste Gel, Colgate Tartar Control Toothpaste, and Colgate Whitening Toothpaste deepens the Colgate toothpaste product line and are indicative of line extensions. The key distinction between a product improvement and a line extension is that when the line extension is introduced, the original product still can be acquired by the consumer. A product improvement always serves as the replacement for the original product.

New markets are original products taken to new markets with very minimal changes to the product. For example, in 2005 global pharmaceutical and health product manufacturer Bristol-Myers Squibb Co. announced the launch of its hepatitis B drug in China. The drug had already debuted and proven effective in the United States. The drug did not change, though the package language had to be translated into Chinese and provide the necessary information to meet Chinese government regulations.

New uses are original products positioned in new markets without any (minimal) changes to the product. A classic example of a new use product is Arm and Hammer Baking Soda. Originally positioned as a baking product, the yellow box of Arm and Hammer Baking Soda was positioned as a deodorizer for refrigerators and sinks and as a mouthwash used with hydrogen peroxide. Arm and Hammer later introduced new lines of products like toothpaste and laundry detergents—products that were in a new form, had new packaging, and provided different functions.

New category entries are products that are new to the company, but not new to the consumer as a category. For example, the entry of Kodak into the battery market represents a new category market. Batteries represented a new market and a new set of customers for Kodak because the batteries sold were not exclusively intended for the camera equipment of current customers. McDonald's foray into clothing with McKids clothing and Lenovo's entry into the ultraportable laptop market for business computing in 2010 are additional examples of a new category entry.

New-to-the-world products are technological innovations that create a completely new market that previously did not exist. These innovations would be characterized as discontinuous innovations because the new product introduces a product technology previously not available to the marketplace.

The introduction of the first commercial cellular telephone or launching the first-ever AIDS vaccine would indicate a new-to-the-world product. Takeda Pharmaceutical Company's drug Uloric® (febuxostat), launched in 2009 for the management of hyperuricemia in patients with gout, was recognized as the first new treatment in forty years (www.tpna.com) and is therefore considered a new-to-the-world product.

It is important to recognize that companies do not just deal with one type of new product. Rather, companies normally have multiple types of new products permeate the product planning process. For example, Coca-Cola may redesign a fountain dispenser to reduce material costs, indicating a cost reduction; redesign an existing soda can to be more colorful, indicating a product improvement; offer a new package size, indicating a line extension; enter a new untapped market; and begin to offer Coca-Cola clothing, representing a new category entry.

The Growing Emphasis on Product Planning

The number of new products being launched into the marketplace continues to increase. A study by Marketing Intelligence Service found that between 1998 and 2004, there was a 34 percent increase in the annual number of new products launched and subsequently tracked by its new products database called Productscan Online. This apparently growing number of new products being launched by companies places greater pressure on the product planning process to ensure success when developing, launching, and managing new products.

Such pressure exists because research has found that more than 86 percent of product concepts fail during the product development process (Barczak, Griffin, and Kahn 2009). After launch, research indicates that 59 percent of commercialized new products succeed, with 54 percent of commercialized new products considered successful from a profit perspective (Barczak, Griffin, and Kahn 2009). This begs the question of what is meant by new product success and new product failure because what may be considered a failure by one company may be a success from the perspective of another company. For instance, a new technological innovation may be a commercial failure, but the fact that the technology functions properly makes it a technological success.

Incorporating the work of Griffin and Page (1996), new product success measures can be classified into four general categories: customer-based measures, competitive-based measures, financial measures, and technical performance measures. Customer-based success can be based on customer satisfaction, customer acceptance, number of original customers, unit volume,

Exhibit 1.5

A Sample of Product Success Measures

Customer-based	Competitive-based	Financial	Technical performance
• Customer satisfaction	• Market share	• Revenue	• Performance specifications
• Customer acceptance	• Competitive benchmarks	• Profit	• Speed-to-market
• Number of original customers	• Competitive advantage	• Margin	• Development cost
• Unit volume		• Rate of return	• Quality
• Number of repeat customers		• Payback period	• On-time launch
			• Innovativeness

and number of repeat customers. Competitive-based measures can include market share, meeting competitive benchmarking, and establishing a competitive advantage. Financial measures can be revenue, profit, margin, rate of return, and payback. Technical performance measures can include performance specifications, speed-to-market, development cost, quality specifications, on-time launch, and innovativeness. The use of a particular success measure will obviously depend on the departments involved and the point that the product has reached in the development process (see Exhibit 1.5).

So Why Is Product Planning Difficult?

Product planning is difficult because of the uncertainty surrounding the proper functioning of new technology and the market acceptance of this technology. Because product planning is a multifunctional process, the process becomes complicated. Factors related to organizational culture, organizational politics, and individual personalities are involved as well, further complicating the process.

While there is no silver bullet to ensure success, there are certain steps that can be taken to improve the chances in developing, launching, and managing products. These include learning about previous experiences in order to understand what does and does not work. Understanding a systematic approach to product planning also is necessary in order to organize the process. Assembling a toolbox of ideas and heuristics will aid in managing the product planning process.

The overriding intent of this book is to impress upon the reader a broad, integrated product planning perspective. To do this, the book is organized along the lines of the eight elements of the given definition for product planning. To reiterate, product planning is defined as the process of envisioning, conceptualizing, developing, producing, testing, commercializing, sustaining, and disposing of organizational offerings to satisfy consumer needs and wants and achieve organizational objectives.

This chapter has introduced the product planning topic, provided key definitions, and identified issues inherent in product planning. Chapters 2, 3, and 4 address the *envisioning* step, with Chapter 2 discussing strategic planning, product strategy, the product planning process, and product development charters; Chapter 3 discussing product planning teams; and Chapter 4 discussing opportunity identification. Chapters 5 and 6 address the *conceptualizing* step, with Chapter 5 presenting concept generation techniques and Chapter 6 presenting concept evaluation techniques. Chapters 7 and 8 cover the *developing* and *producing* steps, and aspects of the *testing* step, with Chapter 7 addressing technical development considerations and Chapter 8 discussing the topic of design. Chapters 9 and 10 cover other aspects of *developing* and *testing,* as well as the *commercializing* step of product planning. Chapter 9 overviews market planning and market testing, while Chapter 10 overviews launch management. Chapter 11 covers the steps of *sustaining* and *disposing* of products and services by way of the topics of life cycle management, product families, and brand management. Chapters 12 and 13 present special topics related to product planning endeavor, with Chapter 13 focusing on legal considerations. Chapter 14 closes the book with observations from noteworthy studies to list product planning best practices.

Obviously, covering the breadth of these topics is a daunting, though necessary, task so that readers can be attuned to and have an understanding of the complex product planning process. Being attuned to and having an understanding of these topics will ensure a greater likelihood of success as a product planner. It is hoped that after going through this book, you will agree and realize the need for the broad view of product planning.

Prior to learning about these topics, some degree of preparation is necessary. First, shake off any particular functional viewpoint that you may have. Product planning is characteristically cross-functional. Second, be prepared to be inquisitively analytical. Product planners cannot afford to base all decisions on gut feel alone; they need to examine product data and determine what is truly going on in order to make an informed decision. Third, be creative and not critical of creative ideas. Creative product planning often leads to success. Fourth, be tolerant of failure and examine why failure occurred. Not all products succeed, and product planners make it a point to learn from mistakes in order to avoid repeating them in the future. Failure is very much a part of the process for ensuring success in the product planning process.

Discussion Questions

1. What is a product?
2. What is the difference between invention and innovation?
3. What are the seven different types of new products?
4. What are a product item, product line, and product mix?
5. What is product planning?
6. What is new product success?

References

Barczak, Gloria, Abbie Griffin, and Kenneth B. Kahn. 2009. "Trends and Drivers of Success in NPD Practices: Results of the 2003 PDMA Best Practices Study." *Journal of Product Innovation Management*, 25 (1) (January), 3–23.

Crawford, C. Merle. 1987. *New Products Management*, 2nd ed. Homewood, IL: Irwin.

General Mills. 2010. www.generalmills.com.

Griffin, Abbie, and Albert L. Page. 1996. "PDMA Success Measurement Project: Recommended Measures for Product Development Success and Failure." *Journal of Product Innovation Management*, 13 (6) (November), 478–496.

Khermouch, Gerry. 1994. "Rolling Rock's Message in a Bottle." *Brandweek*, June 20, p. 22.

Marriott International. 2010. www.marriott.com.

Pillsbury. 2010. www.pillsbury.com.

Takeda Pharmaceuticals North America. 2009. "FDA Approves ULORIC® (febuxostat) for the Chronic Management of Hyperuricemia in Patients with Gout." Press Release, February 13. www.tpna.com/newsroom/press_release_detail. aspx?year=2009&articleid=162.

Verizon. 2010. www.verizon.com.

Xerox. 2010. www.xerox.com.

York, Emily Bryson. 2009. "Kellogg Tests Shorter, Fatter Cereal Boxes: New Design Holds Same Amount of Food but Saves Space, Materials." *Advertising Age*, January 26. http://adage.com/article?article_id=134114.

2 Strategy and Process

Strategy is an important part of the product planning process. Indeed, a 2010 research study indicates that practitioners consider it the most important dimension for product development (Kahn et al. 2010) and thereby highlights strategic planning as a primary step in the product planning process. It is through thoughtful strategic planning that company objectives can be implemented by way of product planning programs and corresponding activities. Such strategic planning will mandate that the company have clearly defined goals, seek to fulfill future customer needs, build organizations dedicated to accomplishing focused goals, and partner with customers in the development process. This chapter discusses the important link between strategic planning and product planning.

The Strategic Planning Process

One way to illustrate the strategic planning process is to portray it as a pyramid, with company *mission* at the top of the pyramid, company *objectives* at the next level, and company *goals*, *strategies*, and *programs* at the lowest level (see Exhibit 2.1).

Mission defines the company's central purpose, direction, and scope. *Objectives* derive from the mission and represent specific elements to be achieved by the company (objectives are often prefaced by the phrase "to be"). *Goals* are time-specific metrics by which to measure successful attainment of a particular objective. *Strategies* characterize the way in which the objectives are to be realized. *Programs* are a way to execute individual strategies.

For example, a company mission may reflect a desire for innovation. In turn, a company objective such as "to be the recognized leader in technological innovation in our industry" may lead to a next-generation new product strategy, implemented through the company's product development program. The goal of "50 percent of company revenues will come from new product introduced in the past three years" would be one way to measure whether the given objective is being met.

22

Exhibit 2.1 **Strategic Planning Pyramid**

New Product Strategy

As mentioned in Chapter 1, a misnomer for product planning is the general presumption that all new products represent major changes and major new product initiatives. New product strategy is much broader when taking into account the different types of new products possible across the dimensions of type of market to be served (current or new market) and type of technology (current or new technology). *Current market* does not necessarily mean immediate customers, but represents customers currently within or associated with the target market or market segment, including existing customers, competitor customers, and noncustomers (a potential customer that has not made a purchase yet). *New market* pertains to a market that has not been previously served by the company. *Current technology* means the company has the technology, while *new technology* indicates that the respective technology needs to be created or acquired from somewhere else.

Overlaying these two dimensions, a new product strategy schematic called the "product-market matrix" or the Ansoff matrix (named after Igor Ansoff and based on his 1957 article) suggests four general strategies for product planning. These include *market penetration, product development, market development*, and *diversification* (see Exhibit 2.2).

A *market penetration* strategy corresponds to an objective that aims to increase market share and/or increase product usage. The current customer

Exhibit 2.2   **Product-Market Matrix**

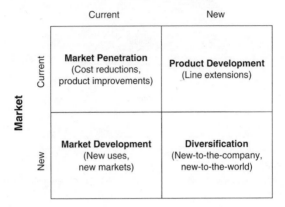

Product Technology

	Current	New
Market / Current	**Market Penetration** (Cost reductions, product improvements)	**Product Development** (Line extensions)
Market / New	**Market Development** (New uses, new markets)	**Diversification** (New-to-the-company, new-to-the-world)

base is pursued with no major changes to the existing product technology. Cost reductions and product improvements are characteristic of a market penetration strategy. Naturally, these two types of new products attempt to attract customers through a lower price, more features, and/or improved features.

A *product development* strategy derives from an objective to capitalize on existing product technology and offer more options to the customer base. In this way, the company with a more diverse product line can fend off competitors. Line extensions are characteristically associated with a product development strategy.

A *market development* strategy stems from a desire to expand sales volume of existing products through new markets. This would include geographic expansions, including international markets, as well as targeting new segments. There is disinterest in pursuing any product technology changes; the predominant interest is to take the product "as is" and find new viable markets. Finding new markets and new uses for a product are characteristic of a market development strategy.

Diversification is pursued when the company wishes to expand its business into related business and unrelated businesses. Thus, the company will undertake new customer markets and new product technologies. New category entries and new-to-the-world products are pursued in the course of a diversification strategy.

While a simple representation of product planning, the product-market matrix implies that product planning becomes more complex and riskier along the diagonal of the matrix from the upper left corner to the lower right corner. Plotting the different types of new products, the riskier projects of new category entries and new-to-the-world products are in the riskiest cell—the cell representing the diversification strategy. Diversification is the riskiest because new category entries and new-to-the-world products are the most unfamiliar and untested for the company. The least risky initiatives are cost improvements and product improvements because of company knowledge of the market and technology. These would offer a more comfortable business situation for the company than diversification.

The Product Development Process

Strategy is implemented through programs. In the case of new product development, a strategy corresponding to new products is typically coordinated through the product development process, which has historically been haphazard and unstructured. Companies have found, however, that a systematic process for product development offers a great propensity for new product success. Research shows an increasing use of a systematic, structured new product development process, with two out of three companies now using a formal product development process (Barczak, Griffin, and Kahn 2009).

Yet there is a debate over how the product development process should begin. Some product planners contend that the product development process begins with a company objective or strategy, which, in turn, orients the product development endeavor. Others argue that an idea (spurred by inspiration) is first needed to stimulate the process and that such an idea should not be constrained by strategic planning.

Both are valid ways to initiate the product development process. Strategy-driven product development represents a systematic approach to product development. The company first determines the objectives and goals that it wants to achieve and then charts a course of product development that would indeed achieve these objectives and goals. Idea-directed product development can be systematic or unstructured at times. A systematic approach would be to investigate a promising idea that has been proposed and, if it is found to have potential, pursue it. An unstructured approach would be to quickly pursue an idea without an investigation phase and rush it to market. Either approach can be successful, but more often than not, a systematic approach has a better chance of success.

Another view of product development is market-pull versus technology-push. Market-pull product development is focused on satisfying customer needs and closely parallels the strategy-directed approach to product development. The process begins with an analysis of the marketplace to determine

25

customers' needs and their views of the competition. These needs and views are then used to develop a consideration set for company objectives and goals. Continued analysis of the customer base occurs throughout the process.

Technology-push product development closely parallels the idea-directed approach to product development. A new technology (either incremental or discontinuous in nature) is developed with or without an investigation into its potential. In many cases, a technology-push process ends with a feasible product looking for a suitable market, which requires substantial postdevelopment work focused on selling the product.

This does not mean that a technology-push approach is inappropriate. Many radical innovations have come by way of a technology-push product development process. In fact, customers can have trouble articulating innovative or next-generation products so a technology-push approach can help customers envision what is possible. Technology-push product development, however, is a very risky endeavor when the customer is overlooked. When compared, market-pull product development—where customer needs drive product decisions—is generally more successful than technology-push product development—where advanced technology drive product decisions.

A merging of the philosophies underlying market-pull and technology-push product development processes would seem reasonable. However, a true merging of the two philosophies is rarely accomplished because the typical product development endeavor is biased toward one of these two philosophies. Bias stems from companies assigning responsibility to (and thereby favoring) a particular department during product development—be it the marketing department for a market-pull approach or the engineering department for a technology-push approach.

Common to any type of product development process is the organization of product development activities into multiple phases or stages. A review point or gate is placed between phases so that a particular new product concept cannot enter a subsequent development phase until a given set of company criteria is met. This product process is called a stage-gate™ or phase-review product development process. Another parallel form of the product development process is called PACE process, which was designed by the PRTM consulting group (McGrath 1996). This process parallels the typical stage-gate process, but focuses on product development speed to expedite time-to-market. The Product Development Institute offers an additional process model for product development called the fourth-generation product development process. The distinction of the fourth-generation product development process is adding a discovery stage at the front end of the product development process in order to generate breakthrough product ideas, harness fundamental research effectively, and improve project selection through effective go/kill decision points and project synergy.

26

Interestingly, product development processes are very similar across companies and industries regardless of the underlying philosophical principles that created the process. Most product development processes aim to achieve the following:

- Transfer technology to a commercial application
- Mate technical characteristics and market needs
- Perform multifunctional operations
- Implement company strategy via the development of a new product
- Provide managerial control but not be overwhelmingly intrusive

Also, most product development processes reflect similar, if not the same, types of stages: opportunity identification, concept generation, pretechnical evaluation, technical development, and launch (see Exhibit 2.3). A common shortcoming is the omission of a sixth product development stage of life cycle management, which should be considered and which some companies do include as part of their continuous product development process. Those companies that do not include a life cycle management stage favor the philosophy that the product development process ends at launch.

Opportunity identification represents the first stage of the product development process. The purpose of this stage is to delineate a direction for the product development initiative. At the conclusion of the opportunity identification stage comes the first gate. In many cases, an outline of the opportunities is generated and approved. A more formal approach is to develop a product development charter, also referred to as a product innovation charter, which would then be approved before moving on to the next stage.

Concept generation represents the second stage of the product development process. The purpose of this stage is to put together a set of potential new product ideas. Typically, the more ideas and concepts generated, the better. A variety of concept generation techniques exists to facilitate the concept generation effort. The gate after the concept generation stage is the affirmation of a pool of interesting concepts that meet a given preliminary set of criteria.

As mentioned, some companies prefer to conduct the concept generation stage prior to the opportunity identification stage. The rationale is that concept generation should not be biased by any preconceived notions of what should be developed. Instead, these companies prefer to begin the process with a clean slate in order to provide an environment for greater innovation.

Other companies prefer to conduct an opportunity identification stage first to provide boundaries for their product development process. The rationale is that concept generation can get off-track and present ideas that go beyond

Exhibit 2.3 **Schematic of a Product Development Process**

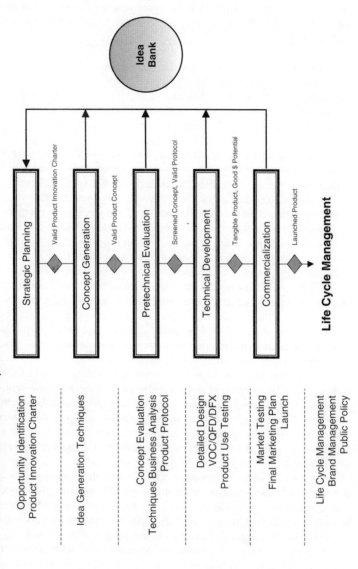

Idea
Bank

Strategic Planning

Valid Product Innovation Charter

Concept Generation

Valid Product Concept

Pretechnical Evaluation

Screened Concept, Valid Protocol

Technical Development

Tangible Product, Good $ Potential

Commercialization

Launched Product

Life Cycle Management

Opportunity Identification
Product Innovation Charter

Idea Generation Techniques

Concept Evaluation
Techniques Business Analysis
Product Protocol

Detailed Design
VOC/QFD/DFX
Product Use Testing

Market Testing
Final Marketing Plan
Launch

Life Cycle Management
Brand Management
Public Policy

28

what the company would want to offer. The opportunity identification stage has management delineate what it will accept as a new product opportunity and thereby provide a greater focus in the concept generation stage.

Pretechnical evaluation is the third stage in the product development process. Here product concepts are evaluated and prioritized. An important element in the pretechnical evaluation stage is a business analysis conducted on the product concept. Those concepts showing the greatest potential to meet company objectives and goals are further defined via product protocols. The gate at the end of the pretechnical evaluation stage is selection of a final set of concepts to continue in the product development process and approval of their respective product protocols.

The fourth stage in the product development process is technical development. In this stage, the technology behind the product concept is realized and tested to ensure that it meets the specifications in the product protocol. A viable business or marketing plan is constructed. The gate at the conclusion of this stage assesses whether a tangible product has been developed and functions as desired. The financial viability and marketability (profit potential) of the product also is gauged in order to determine whether to continue work on the product.

The fifth stage of the product development process is the launch. This stage comprises activities related to solidifying the market acceptance of the new product, including market testing, prelaunch preparation, launch, and postlaunch control. The gate at the conclusion of the launch stage is the successful launch of the product and favorable sales levels.

The sixth stage of the product development process is life cycle management. This stage represents continuous monitoring, the possible refinement of the launched product, and the possible augmentation of the product to create a product line should one not already exist. Such refinements are necessary to keep up with changing consumer needs and wants, competitor actions, government regulations, and/or new technologies. The latter part of this stage focuses on the eventual disposal of the product and substitution by the next-generation product.

While the process as described is a sequential process, it is actually a concurrent process and at times, steps will overlap. The process also is inherently multifunctional. That is, multiple company departments are involved in the process to cover the variety of activities necessary to develop, launch, and manage the product successfully.

There also is the fuzzy front end (FFE). Depending upon the company, the FFE precedes the opportunity identification stage. The FFE is the amassing of new technologies and is characteristic of a research and development function. The big issue in the FFE is determining which technologies should be pursued.

The given generic product development process somewhat simplifies what truly happens in practice. The process does not necessarily follow a path as described. For example, sometimes the process needs to be expedited so fuzzy gates are used. "Fuzzy gates" is a term used to describe the fact that a new product concept will go through a gate without resistance in order to allow the project to continue. The goal is to ensure that the process continues with the expectation that a more stringent gate will be used later in the product development process. Fuzzy gates are commonly used when "first-to-market" is critical to success and when a gate review meeting cannot be scheduled because key members of the review team are unavailable.

All the steps of a product development process also are not necessarily delineated in the given schematic of the product development process. Many times, bottlenecks due to technology problems or market changes force a change in the expected course of action.

Many companies, nonetheless, provide a schematic of their product development process to frame expectations for their product development initiatives. In this way, company personnel understand the general steps and criteria necessary to get products to the marketplace. The following are criteria that any good product development process should have:

- The process should provide some structure of checkpoints along the way.
- The process should allow the product development team and its support group substantial degrees of freedom.
- The new product development process must be flexible to accommodate changing conditions.
- The new product development process must deal with especially critical points in development.
- The new product development process should integrate the team with the rest of the firm and the world.
- The new product development process should permit a smooth launch.
- The new product development process should provide for organization learning.

Note that even if a product development process exists, companies can abuse how the process is used. These abuses include the following:

- Too much faith in the product being developed
- Lack of concern for the customer
- Faulty research (skewed findings)
- Meeting technical needs and certain customer needs, but not all customer needs

Special attention needs to be taken to ensure that these abuses do not emerge, or else the respective product development process will not reach its potential for success.

Implementing a Product Development Process

While many companies have a structured product development process, other companies do not have a process. There also are situations where a current product development process should be revised to be more effective. To do this, O'Connor (1994) lays out a five-step process:

1. *Lay the foundation:* Gather information; establish the need for a product development process; analyze current practices and benchmark with best practices; identify and attempt to understand hurdles for implementation.
2. *Gain initial commitment:* Sell senior management on the need for a product development process; note and address management concerns; detail the activities per stage and criteria per gate; compose an implementation plan; obtain a budget to implement the process.
3. *Effect change:* Train management and participating players; sustain active participation in the process; develop tools to support the process; put new projects into the process.
4. *Work the transition:* Seek continual feedback; analyze feedback and take appropriate action; continue training; improve tools.
5. *Monitor and improve:* Benchmark process with best practices; seek improvements in tools and product development activities; refresh product development process, if needed.

O'Connor also indicates a variety of challenges to implementing a product development process. These also apply to the ongoing use of an existing product development process:

- *Process optimization and validation:* A preoccupation with achieving an optimal process may be infeasible; a workable process may be just as, if not more, efficient and effective.
- *Gaining top management commitment and involvement:* Without top management support, the process will not be sustained.
- *Structured decision-making:* Clarifying who makes which decisions will avoid confusion and/or conflict.

31

- *Developing new product development leaders and high-performance teams:* Cross-functional communication and collaboration are necessary to effect product development activities.
- *Training critical skills and knowledge* to support the process.
- *Portfolio optimization:* The company needs to develop a portfolio management process that decides which projects to pursue and which to shelve.
- *Linking and positioning the process:* The product development process must fit with other company processes.

Evaluating the Product Development Process

There are various ways to evaluate the effectiveness and efficiency of the product development process. One technique is statistical in nature and can be readily applied to assess the risk, cost, and time characteristics inherent in the product development process. Results can indicate the riskiest, costliest, and most time-consuming product development stages.

To apply this technique, the risk, cost, and time associated with each product development stage must be determined. Risk should be given in terms of the percent of product concepts that successfully make it through the stage (i.e., successfully pass the respective stage's gate review). Cost should be given as the standard cost for one product concept to progress through the given stage. Time should be given as the standard time for one product concept to progress through the given stage.

Consider the example presented in Exhibit 2.4. A new product development comprises the five stages of opportunity identification, concept generation, pretechnical review, technical development, and launch. Note that the life cycle management stage is not considered in the analysis because it is an ongoing stage after launch. Assume that 90 percent of the proposed product concepts (ideas) successfully go through the opportunity identification stage, 60 percent of product concepts successfully go through the concept generation stage, 40 percent of product concepts successfully go through the pretechnical evaluation stage, 50 percent of product concepts successfully go through the technical development stage, and 80 percent of product concepts successfully launch.

Using these percentages, the overall probability of success for one product concept at the beginning of the product development process is an 8.64 percent chance of success. In other words, less than nine concepts out of a hundred original product concepts will ever be officially launched. To ensure that the company can launch successfully one product, 12 likely product concepts will be needed at the beginning of the product development process. This is calculated by taking the reciprocal of 8.64 percent or 11.57 product concepts; 11.57 is rounded up to 12 because .57 product concepts is unrealistic.

Exhibit 2.4

Evaluating the Product Development Process

Stage	Risk	Cost	Time (in person-weeks)	Number of concepts needed	Cost to complete stage	Time to complete stage (in person-weeks)
Opportunity identification	90%	$2,000	2	11.57	$23,140	23.14
Concept generation	60%	$10,000	6	10.41	$104,100	62.46
Pretechnical evaluation	40%	$30,000	6	6.25	$187,500	37.50
Technical development	50%	$200,000	12	2.50	$500,000	30.00
Launch	80%	$125,000	4	1.25	$156,250	5.00
Totals					$970,990	158.10

Probability of success for a given product concept $.9 \times .6 \times .4 \times .5 \times .8 = .0864$ or 8.64%

Number of product concepts needed for one success $1/.0864 = 11.57$ product concepts

33

If the company wants to launch two new products in a given year, then 24 (2 launched products × 11.57 concepts necessary for each launch = 23.15 rounded up to 24) product concepts will be needed at the beginning of the product development process.

This methodology can be used to show how many product concepts will enter each stage. For example, assume that one launched product is the goal. If 11.57 entered the process, 10.41 (11.57 × .9) concepts would enter the concept generation stage; 6.25 (10.4 × .6) concepts would enter the pretechnical evaluation stage; 2.50 (6.25 × .4) concepts would enter the technical development stage; 1.25 (2.50 × .5) concepts would enter the launch stage; and 1 (1.25 × .8) concept would be launched as a product. These values are shown in Exhibit 2.4.

Using these values, one can construct a decay curve as shown in Exhibit 2.5. A decay curve is a representation of the funneling effect that the product development process has. In other words, the decay curve shows how stringent the product development process is in reducing the total sample of product concepts to eventually launch one product.

The decay curve can be used as a benchmark to compare with industry decay curves. The Product Development Management Association (PDMA) periodically surveys its members and publishes data for constructing a standard decay curve. These data help companies compare their process to an industry standard to see if their process is too stringent or too lax. Exhibit 2.5 compares the data of the previous example to PDMA standard decay curve data (see Barczak, Griffin, and Kahn 2009).

The decay curve can be used as an evaluative tool for individual product development project teams too. In particular, the decay curve suggests two regions. Above the curve is indicative of a "slow decay" or a situation where product concepts are not necessarily being eliminated as they should be. A product development project team staying above the curve might be allowing too many product concepts through the process and may have too many product concepts at the end of the process. Below the curve is indicative of a "fast decay" or a situation where many product concepts are being eliminated. Here a product development project team staying below the curve might not have enough product concepts to sustain the product development process and will not have a product to launch. A product development project team staying near the company's decay curve would closely approximate the expected product development process for the company.

The number of product concepts needed per stage also can be used to calculate cost and time estimates for each of the product development stages. Assume the cost and time necessary to have one product concept complete each of the product development stages are as follows: opportunity identification—$2,000 in 2 person-weeks; concept generation—$10,000 in 6

Exhibit 2.5   **The Decay Curve**

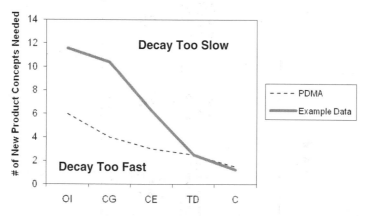

person-weeks; pretechnical evaluation—$30,000 in 6 person-weeks; technical development—$200,000 in 12 person-weeks; and launch—$125,000 in 4 person-weeks. The cost and time necessary across each product development stage to ensure one launched product are determined by multiplying the number of product concepts in each stage by the cost and time figures. Hence, in the example presented in Exhibit 2.4, to ensure one launched product, Opportunity identification will cost $23,140 (11.57 × $2,000) and consume 23.14 (11.57 × 2) person-weeks; concept generation will cost $104,100 (10.41 × $10,000) and consume 62.46 (10.41 × 6) person-weeks; pretechnical evaluation will cost $187,500 (6.25 × $30,000) and consume 37.50 (6.25 × 6) person-weeks; technical development will cost $500,000 (2.50 × $200,000) and consume 30.00 (2.50 × 12) person-weeks; and launch will cost $156,250 (1.25 × $125,000) and consume 5.00 (1.25 × 4) person-weeks (see Exhibit 2.4).

These calculations provide insightful information into the product development process. Added information can be gained by calculating the relative and cumulative percentages for cost and time across each product development stage, as shown in Exhibit 2.6. The costliest product development stage is technical development, which accounts for more than half of the total project cost to develop one product. The most time-consuming stage is concept generation, which accounts for more than half of the total project time to develop one product. The cumulative percentages indicate that only one-third of costs are expensed before technical development. However, almost 80 percent of the time to complete the product development project occurs before technical development. A company could reflect on whether this would seem appropriate.

Exhibit 2.6

Evaluating Cost and Time per Product Development Stage

Stage	Cost to complete stage	Relative percent of total cost	Cumulative percent of total cost	Time to complete stage (in person-weeks)	Relative percent of total cost	Cumulative percent of total cost
Opportunity identification	$23,140	2	2	23.14	15	15
Concept generation	$104,100	11	13	62.46	39	54
Pretechnical evaluation	$187,500	19	32	37.50	24	78
Technical development	$500,000	52	84	30.00	19	97
Launch	$156,250	16	100	5.00	3	100
Totals	$970,990	100		158.10	100	

36

Additional information can be gained by constructing a cost-expenditure curve. This curve portrays the cumulative percentage of cost versus the cumulative percentage of time (see Exhibit 2.7). By developing an expenditures curve, product planners can benchmark company product development projects to determine if costs are running too high versus time. A project falling above the curve would suggest that the budget is being spent too quickly (overbudget). Being below the curve could suggest that not enough money is being expensed on the project or that the budget is not being expensed properly; both of these situations could signal problems with the likely success of the project.

Initiatives to Reduce Cost or Time

Performing an assessment of a company's product development process can identify particular product development stages that would appear to be too costly or time-consuming. Such criteria would be based on company expectations or data comparing product development stages to each other. Various initiatives can be undertaken to reduce costs and time consumed in the product development process. A sample of these initiatives is described below:

- *Get slack out of the system:* Avoid unnecessary steps; reduce the number of activities pursued in a particular product development stage.
- *Use technology to shorten steps:* Computer-aided design, computer-aided manufacturing, and rapid prototyping may be useful in shortening product development cycle time.
- *Get early customer input to prevent redesign:* Early customer involvement can help to focus the product development effort on key issues or attributes.
- *Inventory up-front marketing and engineering projects:* Consider using off-the-shelf ideas so that projects do not necessarily have to go through a full product development process.
- *Use flexible manufacturing:* A flexible manufacturing process offers a wide variety of options for product development.
- *Join alliances:* Alliances can sometimes reduce the time and resources necessary to achieve a product development objective because of shared resources.
- *Skip a step in the process:* While not preferable, sometimes it is necessary to skip a product development activity in order to get a product to the market quickly; this should only be employed when first-to-market is critical (even when skipping a step, it is necessary to make sure that everything is good to go before launching the new product).

Exhibit 2.7 **The Terminology Cost-Expenditure Curve**

Cost vs Time

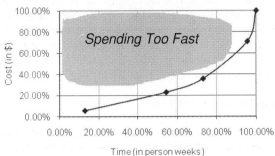

Time (in person weeks)

Discussion Questions

1. How do company mission, objectives, strategies, and goals influence the product development process?
2. What are the four general strategies for product planning?
3. What is the difference between market-pull and technology-push product development?
4. What is a stage-gate product development process?
5. What are the common characteristics of a product development process?

References

Ansoff, Igor. 1957. "Strategies for Diversification." *Harvard Business Review*, 35 (5) (September–October), 113–124.

Barczak, Gloria, Abbie Griffin, and Kenneth B. Kahn. 2009. "Trends and Drivers of Success in NPD Practices: Results of the 2003 PDMA Best Practices Study." *Journal of Product Innovation Management*, 25 (1) (January), 3–23.

Kahn, Kenneth B., Gloria Barczak, John Nicholas, Ann Ledwith, and Helen Perks. 2010. "An Examination of New Product Development Best Practice." *Journal of Product Innovation Management*, in press.

McGrath, Michael E. 1996. *Setting the PACE® in Product Development: A Guide to Product and Cycle-time Excellence*. Burlington, MA: Butterworth-Heinemann.

O'Connor, Paul. 1994. "Implementing a Stage-Gate Process: A Multi-Company Perspective." *Journal of Product Innovation Management*, 11 (3) (June), 183–200.

Product Development Institute. www.prod-dev.com/index.php.

3 ✕ Organizing People

Product planning activities are affected by how people are organized to carry out these activities. Several important issues to understand are traditional department responsibilities, general organization structure, team structure, and team roles.

Department Responsibilities

Within the company organization, product planning activities can be the responsibility of various departments (note that the term "departments" is used instead of "functions" because departments can serve multiple functions). Preference for which department oversees product development and product management activities depends on company history, tradition, culture, and the objectives of the company's product planning activities.

Product development may be under the auspices of the technical or marketing side of the organization. The technical side of the organization would include research, development, and engineering departments; the marketing side of the organization would include marketing and/or sales departments. Product management can fall under the auspices of the marketing or operations sides of the organization; marketing, distribution, logistics, manufacturing, and/or operations are the corresponding departments. Some companies have made product development and product management separate departments within the company, though normally product development and product management represent traditional responsibilities for one of the previously mentioned departments.

The technical side of the organization generally serves a product techno-scientific role for the company. That is, the role is focused on discovery of new product technology and the refinement of the discovery into a feasible product technology. The research and development (R&D) department serves a research function by being responsible for finding new promising technology inventions and a development function by being responsible for building upon the benefits offered by such technology to provide innovations. Some companies separate R&D functions into two departments, while other

39

companies combine the two functions into an R&D department. Other companies assign technoscientific responsibilities to an engineering department, whose purpose is akin to that of a development department and not one of fundamental research. The decision to have product development under the auspices of the technical organization would be based on the objectives "to be technically driven" and "to be a technology leader."

The marketing side of the organization serves a demand management role for the company. Such a role includes the identifying, understanding, stimulating, and servicing of market demand, which would encompass demand of current, potential, and competitor customers. Various departments can constitute the marketing side of the organization, including marketing, advertising, promotion, sales, market research, and distribution. Marketing and sales are commonly separated, with marketing serving a general market interface role and sales a specific customer interface role. The decision to have product development and/or product management under the auspices of the marketing organization would be based on the objective "to be market-driven."

The operations side of the organization serves a production technoeconomic role for the organization. Such a role is focused on development of new production processes, techniques, and capabilities to improve company effectiveness and efficiencies in offering products. Manufacturing, operations, and production departments are responsible for composing the actual product so that it can be offered to the market (service companies typically have an operations department). Logistics is responsible for the proper delivery of the product to the marketplace. The decision to have product management under the auspices of the operations organization would be based on the objectives "to achieve operational efficiency" and possibly "to be price-competitive or a low price provider."

Interdepartmental Integration

One of the emerging themes for successful product planning is the integration of departments. However, a common definition for interdepartmental integration is not apparent. Various literature has stressed the need for communication or interaction, where "meetings" and "documented information exchange" predicate the relationships between departments (e.g., Fisher, Maltz, and Jaworski 1997; Griffin and Hauser 1993; Lim and Reid 1992; Moenaert et al. 1994; Ruekert and Walker 1987). This characterization would favor the use of more meetings, greater written documentation, and increased information flows to promote interdepartmental unity.

Other literature has used the terminology of collaboration, where "teamwork" and "resource-sharing" typify interfunctional relationships (e.g., Clark and Fujimoto 1991; Lawrence and Lorsch 1986; Schrage 1990; Souder 1987).

In this vein, efforts that instill collective goals, mutual respect, and teamwork between departments would be favored.

Other literature suggests that integration via information-sharing and involvement typifies marketing's relationships with other functions (Gupta, Raj, and Wilemon 1986; Kahn 1996; Kahn and Mentzer 1998; Song and Parry 1993). This "composite view" implies that interaction and collaboration are both important elements of relationships among departments and that interdepartmental integration depends on the balancing of interaction and collaboration.

Empirical work by various researchers (e.g., Fisher, Maltz, and Jaworski 1997; Kahn 1996; Kahn and Mentzer 1998; Maltz and Kohli 1996) finds that collaboration appears to be most important for product development and product management performance. This does not necessarily mean that communication or interaction is not important. Rather, it is generally concluded that communication should be viewed as a necessary, but not sufficient factor for improved performance; collaboration appears to be the distinguishing factor for improved performance.

Given the various characterizations of interdepartmental integration, how might a company successfully "integrate" departments? The work of Griffin and Hauser (1996) suggests six general approaches for integrating departments: co-location; personnel movement; formal product planning processes; informal social systems; incentives, rewards, and recognitions; and organizational structure:

- Co-location represents the relocation of departmental personnel to the same location to reduce the distance between these colleagues. The underlying premise of co-location is that close proximity of personnel will provide a higher level of information transfer and opportunities to collaborate.
- Personnel movement is the rotation of personnel between departments so that individuals are cross-trained and appreciate the contributions of each department to the product planning process. The underlying premise is that job rotation increases department familiarity and sensitivity. This, in turn, would facilitate interchanges between departments. Because of the difficulty in truly comprehending multiple skill sets characteristic of different departments, it is recommended that such personnel movements be temporary.
- Formal processes are akin to the stage-gate process and other processes that specify activities in the product planning endeavor. The underlying premise for formal processes is to structure the decision-making process across departments, organize the process, indicate information requirements and information flows, and establish process responsibilities.

- Informal social systems indicate that informal mechanisms need to be utilized in addition to traditional formal mechanisms such as scheduled meetings. Informal meetings like impromptu hall meetings, impromptu lunches, and impromptu outings will build familiarity and a willingness to communicate and collaborate.

- Incentives and rewards correspond to performance evaluations and compensation to motivate department personnel to accomplish their department objectives, interdepartmental objectives, and corporate objectives. The use of such incentives, rewards, and recognitions encourages interdepartmental participation and task completion.

- Organizational structure represents the design of the company's hierarchy to facilitate interdepartmental integration. Various types of organization structures are possible, including a change in the entire organizational structure or the implementation of project teams. Because of the prevalent use of organizational structure solutions for interdepartmental integration, especially with respect to the use of teams, organization and team structure is further discussed in the next sections.

Note that each of these approaches can manifest integration in the product planning process. However, each approach consumes resources, requires a carefully thought-out plan of implementation, and, alone, may not provide an immediate level of commitment on the part of company colleagues to work together. The latter point emphasizes that multiple approaches may be necessary over a longer time horizon.

Organization Structure

Organization structure represents a prevalent approach that pervades and affects product planning efforts. Decisions on how to structure an organization and capitalize on department strengths and company core competencies vary. Yet the drivers of those decisions are commonly industry forces, company tradition, and management preferences. In the simplest forms, there are three general ways to structure the organization for conducting product development and product management activities.

The most popular structure is the functional approach (Exhibit 3.1). This approach represents the use of departments specializing in a core set of activities. A vice president heads each department with the responsibility of coordinating the department's activities. The advantage of this approach is simple administration of activities. The disadvantage is that specialization divides the organization and often leads to conflict over resource needs and organizational status.

Exhibit 3.1 **Functional Organization**

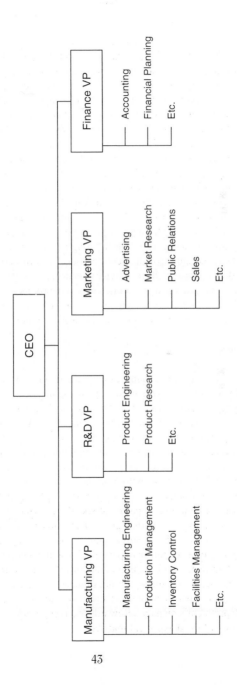

43

The second type of organizational structure is the matrix management approach (Exhibit 3.2). In this approach, the functional organization is retained, but a project management department is created. The project management department assigns project managers or team leaders to product planning projects and coordinates these projects. The individual project managers (team leaders) form project teams by selecting key representatives from the other departments. The premise of the matrix management approach is that responsibility for functional performance is vertical and the responsibility for getting projects done is horizontal. The advantage of this approach is the merging of department capabilities to create a cross-functional perspective and thus capitalize on department abilities. The disadvantage is that this approach can become very complicated, especially with regard to authority, responsibility, and reward issues.

A third general approach is the project program approach (Exhibit 3.3). This approach is only valid when a given project is so large that personnel work full-time on the project over the long term, such as in designing and building the space shuttle or an aircraft carrier. The project manager heads the project and serves essentially as the vice president for the project, coordinating traditional department responsibilities within the project. The advantages of this approach are strong focus and control of the project; the disadvantages are high resource requirements due to the need to duplicate activities.

Team Types

Regardless of the type of organization structure, most, if not all, companies will employ teams to manage product planning activities. Teams represent a temporary organization structure that focuses on the achievement of a specific objective. While the organization structure biases the types of teams that a particular company might use, there are generally five types of teams: functional, multifunctional, balanced matrix, cross-functional, and venture teams. The characteristics of each of these types of teams are shown in Exhibit 3.4.

A functional team works within an individual department with minimal to no contact with other department personnel. Activities best served by a functional team would be department-specific activities that are narrow in scope and have a specific, distinct goal. An example would be electrical engineering personnel working to solve a power glitch in a new amplifier system. The addition of other department personnel would not necessarily benefit the project and, in fact, could inhibit engineering's ability to resolve the matter in a cost-effective and timely fashion. Functional teams have a team leader from the given department and are under the auspices of that department and that department's manager. Rewards and recognition are 100 percent the responsibility of the department manager.

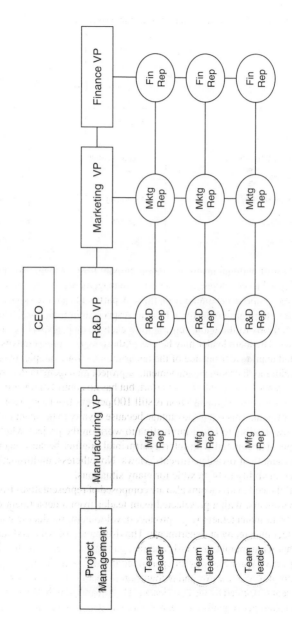

Exhibit 3.2 **Matrix Organization**

45

Exhibit 3.3 **Project Management Organization**

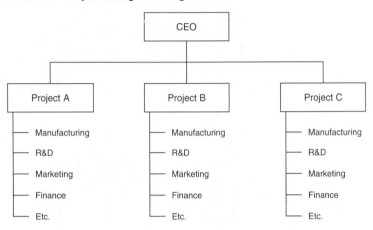

Multifunctional teams are a predominant form of team and employed for both product development and product management purposes. Multifunctional teams comprise personnel from those departments having skills necessary to achieve the team's objectives. In some respects, multifunctional team members are liaisons to the team, representing each of their respective department's views. The team leader may be one of these team representatives or a preselected team leader outside of the departments—for example, from a product development, product management, or project management department. This team leader directs the project effort, but has no control of rewards and recognitions because compensation is still 100 percent from each representative's department. This is a disadvantage because loyalty to the team initiative may be low, leading to lower motivation to work on the project. Multifunctional teams also contend with interdepartmental conflict because team members represent their own departments' views. Nonetheless, multifunctional teams offer an ability to be flexible for many situations.

Balanced matrix teams also are composed of representatives from different departments, with a preselected team leader from a department responsible for team management (e.g., product development, product management, or project management department). The distinction of balanced matrix teams is that team member rewards and recognitions are split equally between the respective team member's department and the team. That is, 50 percent of an employee's rewards and recognition is decided by the department and 50 percent is decided by the team leader. The advantage of balanced matrix teams is an attempt to equalize the team effort with department efforts. Unfortunately,

Exhibit 3.4

Team Characteristics

	Functional team	Multifunctional team	Balanced matrix	Cross-functional team	Venture team
Department representation	Single department	Multiple departments	Multiple departments	Multiple departments	Multiple departments
Accountability	100 percent department	Mostly department	50 percent department, 50 percent team	Mostly team	100 percent team
Appropriate product development projects	Cost improvements, simple product improvements	All types of product development projects	All types of product development projects	All types of product development projects	New category entries, new-to-the-world products
Issues	Focused on single, specific product issue	Addresses issues affecting multiple departments, but conflict can arise due to team members' loyalties to their own department	Team member confusion can arise due to uncertainty over equally splitting time between department and team	Team members work on team issues predominantly, although there are departmental responsibilities as well	Personnel removed from organization to address key corporate objective(s); department managers may resist losing their best people

47

it becomes very difficult to equalize team and department efforts, leading to team members' confusion over compensation and conflicts between department managers and team leaders over team members' responsibilities. Balanced matrix teams are not very common due to the complexity surrounding rewards and recognition to team members.

Cross-functional teams, also called project matrix teams, are composed of representatives from different departments with a preselected team leader from a department responsible for team management. The distinction of cross-functional teams is that team member rewards and recognitions are mostly the responsibility of the team leader. This means that team members are mostly dedicated to the project. While there still can be conflict between department and team priorities and responsibilities, cross-functional teams emphasize a greater focus by team members on attaining project objectives.

Venture teams are created when team members are pulled out of their departments to serve on a self-contained team and their time is 100 percent dedicated to the project. Department managers may resist venture teams if the best people in their department are pulled out of the department to serve on the venture team. The company also needs to provide adequate resources to support a stand-alone team. However, venture teams offer the advantage of being completely focused on the given task. Because of these issues, venture teams are typically reserved for new-to-the-world product development projects. This purpose leads to another, more subtle reason for the use of venture teams in that there is the possibility of creating a new division around the venture team should the product being developed succeed. Even more subtly, the separating of the venture team allows the opportunity for the company to more easily sell off the new division (venture team) should company management decide that the developed product is outside of corporate objectives.

Two types of venture teams are possible. An in-house venture team uses the company infrastructure and facilities. A spin-out venture team meets at a different location and creates its own quasi organization, if not an entirely new organization. The latter type of venture team obviously is more expensive to support, given the duplication of resources.

Distinguishing the Core Team, Ad Hoc Team, and Extended Team

For each of the above types of teams, there is an implicit team structure. This structure encompasses a core team, an ad hoc team, and an extended team, as shown in Exhibit 3.5. The core team consists of the original, permanent team members who represent the key skill sets necessary for achieving the team's given objective. The ad hoc team includes team members who are added when

Exhibit 3.5 **Team Structure**

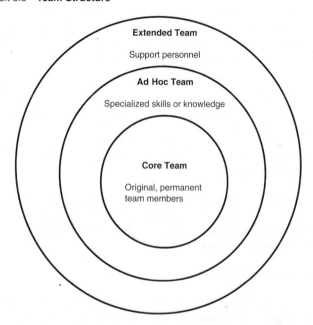

specialized skill or knowledge outside of the core team's skill and knowledge set is needed. For example, purchasing may be added to a product development team if discussions of how to acquire a new material persist. Ad hoc team members remain on the team only as long as they are needed. The extended team represents support personnel who help the core team accomplish its given objective. Administrative staff is characteristically part of the extended team.

Team Roles

Another consideration for team structure is team member roles. There are multiple roles prevalent in teams. The following are a sample of the major roles played:

- *Team leader* (also known as the project manager): The team leader is deemed responsible for organizing, directing, monitoring, and motivating team members to achieve the given team objective.
- *Inventor:* The inventor is the original source for the product concept or idea on which the team is working; the inventor educates team members on basic knowledge underlying the concept or idea.

- *Champion:* The champion promotes the team project, substantiates its importance to the company, and works to surpass roadblocks. In some cases, the team leader is the product champion. In other cases, the champion is not an official member of the team, but rather an upper-level company manager who is intimately knowledgeable about the team project.
- *Sponsor:* A sponsor is an upper-level company manager who is supportive of the team project and assists in providing necessary resources. The sponsor is not a team member and is typically a higher level manager than the champion.
- *Rationalist:* The rationalist attempts to ground the team with a sense of reality by questioning team decisions. The rationalist's role is to ensure that team decisions are sound.

The importance of recognizing these multiple roles is that teams require multiple skill sets in order to function properly. Thus, team leaders need to find team members and upper managers who can play critical roles to help the team achieve its objective.

Factors for Team Effectiveness

Holahan and Markham (2005) present three sets of factors that underlie effective teams. These factors include the structure of the product development process, organizational support for teams, and general team management issues.

Two issues inherent in the structure of the product development process are the ability of the product structure to link departmental activities and to provide opportunities for interdepartmental activities to exist. These two issues highlight to employees how important teams are to the organization. Failure of the existing product development process to account for either of these two considerations precludes a need to use teams (aside from functional teams).

Organizational support for teams concerns issues related to performance appraisal, career development, pay and promotion, and organizational culture. Each of these issues correlates to the motivation of individual team members and their willingness to work toward the given team objective.

General team management deals with issues related to team size, team leader selection, team member selection, team training, and team decision-making and conflict resolution. Some specific recommendations are that teams remain small (eight to twelve members generally); employ team leaders who have interpersonal, technical, and political skills; and consist of members who have team player and technical skills. Overall, general team management recognizes the need for team functioning and the ability to perform as a cohesive unit.

Discussion Questions

1. What have been traditional department responsibilities in product planning?
2. What is interdepartmental integration?
3. What are the five general types of teams?
4. What are some key roles to be played in teams?
5. How might a team be made effective?

References

Clark, Kim B., and Takahiro Fujimoto. 1991. *Product Development Performance: Strategy, Organization, and Management in the World Auto Industry*. Boston: Harvard Business School.

Fisher, Robert J., Elliot Maltz, and Bernard J. Jaworski. 1997. "Enhancing Communication Between Marketing and Engineering: The Moderating Role of Relative Functional Identification." *Journal of Marketing*, 61 (July), 54–70.

Griffin, Abbie, and John R. Hauser. 1993. "The Voice of the Customer." *Marketing Science*, 12 (1) (Winter), 1–27.

———. 1996. "Integrating R&D and Marketing: A Review and Analysis of the Literature." *Journal of Product Innovation Management*, 13 (May), 191–215.

Gupta, Ashok K., S.P. Raj, and David Wilemon. 1986. "A Model for Studying R&D–Marketing Interface in the Product Innovation Process." *Journal of Marketing*, 50 (April), 7–17.

Holahan, Patricia J., and Stephan K. Markham. 2005. "Factors Affecting Multifunctional Team Effectiveness." In *The PDMA Handbook of New Product Development*, 2nd ed., ed. Kenneth B. Kahn, 144–157. New York: John Wiley.

Kahn, Kenneth B. 1996. "Interdepartmental Integration: A Definition with Implications for Product Development Performance." *Journal of Product Innovation Management*, 13 (March), 137–151.

Kahn, Kenneth B., and John T. Mentzer. 1998. "Marketing's Integration With Other Departments." *Journal of Business Research*, 42 (May), 53–62.

Lawrence, Paul R., and Jay W. Lorsch. 1986. *Organization and Environment: Managing Differentiation and Integration*. Boston: Harvard Business School Press.

Lim, Jeen-Su, and David A. Reid. 1992. "Vital Cross-Functional Linkages with Marketing." *Industrial Marketing Management*, 21, 159–165.

Maltz, Elliot, and Ajay K. Kohli. 1996. "Market Intelligence Dissemination Across Functional Boundaries." *Journal of Marketing Research*, 15 (February), 47–61.

Moenaert, Rudy K., William E. Souder, Arnoud DeMeyer, and Dirk Deschoolmeester. 1994. "R&D–Marketing Integration Mechanisms, Communication Flows, and Innovation Success." *Journal of Product Innovation Management*, 11 (January), 31–45.

Ruekert, Robert W., and Orville C. Walker Jr. 1987. "Marketing's Interaction with Other Functional Units: A Conceptual Framework and Empirical Evidence." *Journal of Marketing,* 51 (January), 1–19.

Schrage, Michael. 1990. *Shared Minds: The New Technologies of Collaboration.* New York: Random House.

Song, X. Michael, and Mark E. Parry. 1993. "R&D–Marketing Integration in Japanese High-Technology Firms: Hypotheses and Empirical Evidence." *Journal of the Academy of Marketing Science,* 21 (Spring), 125–133.

Souder, William E. 1987. *Managing New Product Innovations.* Lexington, MA: Lexington Books.

4 ✕ Opportunity Identification

Although not all companies begin the product development process with a formal strategic planning stage, many companies engage in some sort of opportunity identification stage at the start of the product development process. Opportunity identification represents an assessment of what potential opportunities present themselves to the company, and of these, which opportunities are the best ones for the company to pursue.

Sources of Opportunity

Opportunities can come about because of underutilized resources, new resources, external mandates, and internal mandates. Underutilized resources such as excess production capacity can offer a new product opportunity. An ability of the production system to handle a greater variety of product types and volume allows the company to pursue business associated with line extensions, new product uses, and/or new markets.

New resources can emerge from the development of new skills or technologies, as in the case of high-technology companies. Intel through its research and development (R&D) efforts continues to revolutionize integrated circuit chip and computer technology. New resources also can come about as a result of a corporate acquisition. FedEx's acquisition of Kinko's in 1995 helped FedEx enter the retail business services market; that company is now called FedEx Office.

External mandates can come from multiple sources, stimulating the product development endeavor. New government regulations, self-imposed industry standards, changes in customer attitudes, and competitors' actions all can lead to new product opportunities. For example, the U.S. government's mandate for the elimination of chlorofluorocarbons in air conditioning and refrigeration equipment forced manufacturers to develop new types of refrigerant, equipment, and systems. Another example is the strong emphasis on gas efficiency by almost all major car manufacturers due to a strong emerging consumer preference for this feature in automobiles.

Upper management mandates by a new company president also can stimulate the company and lead to new product opportunities. Steve Jobs upon his return to Apple Computer Company as CEO in 1996 proclaimed that Apple needed to develop a web-friendly machine. His vision and emphasis led to the development and launch of the iPod in 1998.

It is important to realize that an opportunity is not usually a concrete product concept. An opportunity can be an insight, a raw technology, a new customer, or something that needs further study. The essential purpose of opportunity identification is to delineate a valid arena for product development considerations.

Segmentation of the Market and Technology

One way to identify opportunities is to divide a market or technology into distinct segments through a methodology called market segmentation or technology segmentation, respectively. Once distinct segments are established, each segment would be examined to discern what opportunities exist within it. Market segmentation can be performed using breakdown structures (also called breakdown analysis). Breakdown structures attempt to provide an underlying structure that organizes and identifies possible, unforeseen opportunities.

Market Segmentation

Compared to technology segmentation, market segmentation is a more common and prevalent activity in the early stages of product development. To conduct a market segmentation via a breakdown structure requires an understanding of the definitions of "market," "market segment," and "target market." A market represents all current and potential buyers sharing a particular need or want who might be willing and able to engage in exchange to satisfy that need or want. A market segment is a subset of customers that behave in the same way, reflect similar characteristics, and/or have similar needs. A target market is the particular group of customers the company proposes to serve or whose needs the company proposes to satisfy with a particular marketing program.

The theoretical rationale for segmentation is the presumption that market demand can come in one of three basic forms: diffused demand, clustered demand, and homogeneous demand. Diffused demand characterizes a market situation where there is no one universal factor for explaining or describing marketplace customer behavior; that is, customers in a diffused demand market situation have different reasons for purchasing the same product. Clustered demand characterizes a situation where subsets of customers within the given marketplace reflect distinct preferences and behaviors; that is, customers in a clustered demand market situation will distinguish themselves as different customer groups reflecting unique attitudes, traits, behaviors, and so on. Homogeneous demand characterizes a situation where all customers are relatively similar in terms of their preferences, traits, and behaviors. Customers in a homogeneous demand situation essentially represent one market segment in the overall market.

In response to each of the market demand situations are three general marketing strategy approaches: an undifferentiated approach, a differentiated approach, and a concentrated approach. An undifferentiated approach to the marketplace, which is also referred to as mass marketing, means that the company will use a broad-based, general marketing campaign for all customers in the marketplace. Because demand is scattered in a diffused demand situation, a general campaign indicative of an undifferentiated approach is recommended. A differentiated approach to the marketplace recognizes and simultaneously attempts to address multiple subsets of customers by catering marketing and business initiatives to individual demand characteristics reflected by the specific market segments being pursued. Serving multiple market segments characteristic of a clustered demand situation can be accomplished through a differentiated approach. A concentrated approach to the marketplace, which also can be called niche marketing, is a special case of the differentiated approach where the company focuses its efforts exclusively toward just one market segment. A concentrated approach can be employed when the market reflects clustered demand or homogeneous demand; in the case of clustered demand, only one segment will be targeted among all the segments available.

Most markets reflect clustered demand situations and so identification of subsets or clusters via a process of segmentation is a natural course to pursue. Five predominant ways to conduct market segmentation are demographic segmentation, geographic segmentation, psychographic segmentation, benefit segmentation, and behavior or usage segmentation. Demographic segmentation divides the market by objective, quantifiable characteristics that can be used to describe customers. Consumer demographics include characteristics such as gender, marital status, location, age, and education, while business-to-business demographics include characteristics such as company age, type of product manufactured as indicated by the company's North American Industry Classification System (NAICS) code, and employment size. Geographic segmentation is a special case of demographic segmentation, where the distinguishing characteristic among segments is geography—for example, the Northeast, Southeast, Midwest, West Coast, international markets. Psychographic segmentation divides the market by subjective characteristics like lifestyle, personality, and culture in the case of consumer psychographics and organizational culture and customer orientation in the case of business-to-business psychographics. Benefit segmentation distinguishes segments according to the benefit desired or benefit received by the respective customer base. For example, two segments based on benefit segmentation for a diet soft drink might be a taste segment ("I buy the product because I like the taste") and a weight loss segment ("I buy the product because it helps me lose weight"). Behavior or usage segmentation distinguishes segments according to the way the customer behaves when using the product or how the customer uses the given product. For example, two possible segments for boxed chocolates based on usage segmentation are a gift-giving segment ("I purchase the product to give as a gift") and a self-consumption segment ("I purchase the product to eat at home"). Note that while there are five general ways to conduct market segmentation, a more effective approach is to combine the five ways to discern better segments.

The different ways to conduct market segmentation are illustrated in the market breakdown structure shown in Exhibit 4.1. This illustration presents a simple business-to-business example of the corrugated box market (corrugated box industry) and attempts to identify possible opportunities by hierarchically segmenting (breaking down) the overall market. As shown, the corrugated box market can be broken down by demographics in terms of perishable versus nonperishable products offered by customers. Geographic segmentation is used to break down the perishable products side, while psychographics are employed to break down the nonperishable side. Benefit segmentation is used to break the West Coast perishable products into two possible opportunities identified as (1) corrugated boxes for perishable products on the West Coast that keep water out, and (2) corrugated boxes for perishable products on the West Coast that are easy to handle. Usage segmentation is used to break innovative firms providing nonperishable products and identify these two possible opportunities: (1) corrugated boxes for nonperishable products of innovative firms for use in work-in-process storage, and (2) corrugated boxes for nonperishable products of innovative firms for use in finished goods storage. At the bottom of the breakdown structure, four possible market opportunities are identified.

After identifying segments, the validity of each segment should be assessed. The following criteria can clarify the validity of a given market segment:

- *Sizable:* The market segment or target market should be of sufficient size in terms of potential sales revenue and potential profit to make it worth pursuing.

Exhibit 4.1 **Market Segmentation Breakdown Structure for a Corrugated Box Market**

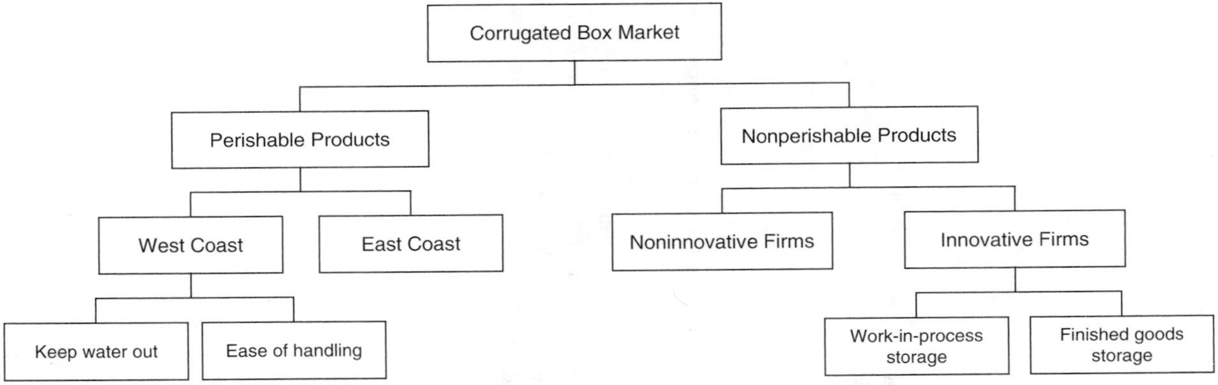

A tree diagram showing the market segmentation breakdown structure:

- **Corrugated Box Market**
  - **Perishable Products**
    - **West Coast**
      - Keep water out
      - Ease of handling
    - **East Coast**
  - **Nonperishable Products**
    - **Noninnovative Firms**
    - **Innovative Firms**
      - Work-in-process storage
      - Finished goods storage

- *Identifiable:* The market segment or target market should be able to be recognized and described.
- *Reachable:* The market segment or target market should be able to be feasibly contacted in an efficient manner.
- *Able to respond differently:* Each of the market segments should respond uniquely to different product attributes and promotion programs; otherwise, market segments should be combined.
- *Coherent:* Members of the same market segment or target market should be basically homogeneous in the way they behave and/or have the same preferences.
- *Stable:* Customer patterns and preferences in the market segment or target market should not drastically change in the near future.

Empirical Methods for Market Segmentation: Similarity and Dissimilarity Analyses

The market breakdown structure previously discussed is one approach for segmenting the market. There are other approaches as well, ranging from judgmental techniques to sophisticated statistical analyses. Two approaches somewhere in the middle of this range are similarity and dissimilarity analyses, which represent analyses that classify and group customers (or other items under examination) in accordance with a set of given characteristics. These two approaches are relatively easy to apply, can provide meaningful insight, and can be employed to validate a market breakdown structure.

Similarity analysis uses a similarity index to reflect the degree of similarity between characteristics (customer characteristics). While there are different ways in which to calculate a similarity index, the use of "yes/no" questions regarding whether a customer reflects a given characteristic or does not reflect that characteristic is rather straightforward. After all customers are evaluated on the same set of characteristics, the percentage of similar responses between pairs of customers is calculated (number of common characteristics divided by the total number of characteristics considered) to determine a similarity index. In other words, each customer is compared with the other customers to reveal the number of matched characteristics; the similarity index is the ratio of matched characteristics to total number of characteristics. A matrix containing all indices is generated to summarize the analyses. The matrix data are examined to identify and group customers, with each group conceivably a market segment or, if specific enough, a target market.

An example in presented in Exhibit 4.2. Assume seven business copier customers are evaluated on the four characteristics of (1) downtown location, (2) high copier usage, (3) interested in service plan, and (4) single division.

Yes or no answers to whether a customer reflects the given characteristics provide a raw data matrix as shown in Exhibit 4.2. Similarity indices between each of the customers are calculated using the formula of number of matched characteristics divided by the total number of characteristics (refer to the similarity matrix in Exhibit 4.2). Each similarity index between two customers would indicate the percentage of "same" characteristics between the two customers. For example, Customers A and B reflect the exact same characteristics and thus reflect a similarity index of 1. Customers A and C only have two out of four characteristics in common and thus reflect a similarity index of .5.

The next step is to group similar customers into segments, with each segment potentially representing distinct target markets. Decisions concerning how to group customers can be made based on a simple heuristic (e.g., group two customers if they are greater than 50 percent similar) or by use of cluster analysis (a sophisticated statistical analysis technique). Using the simple heuristic approach, three distinct segments or potential target markets can be identified: [A, B]; [D, F]; and [C, E, G]. Note that use of a different heuristic can lead to a different set of segments. The judgmental nature of the simple heuristic approach not only applies to the identification of segments, but also to what the segments represent. In the current example, it is speculated that [A, B] represent customers interested in a service plan; [D, F] represent customers not interested in a service plan; and [C, E, G] represent customers who are multidivision enterprises interested in a service plan. The benefit of segmentation is to give insight into how to tailor a marketing plan to best serve the needs of customers. These results suggest three separate plans: a plan targeted at satisfying single-division firms interested in a service plan, a plan targeted at satisfying single-division firms *not* interested in a service plan, and a plan targeted at satisfying multiple-division firms interested in a service plan.

Dissimilarity analysis focuses on the differences between customer characteristics. A simple approach is to assess dissimilarity based on a set of quantitative characteristics reflected by customers; such characteristics would likely be key demographic information. The data is first standardized and then Euclidean distances (Euclidean distance = $\sqrt{(x_1 - x_2)^2 + (y_1 - y_2)^2}$) are calculated to show the distance or dissimilarity between customers, where a larger distance signifies greater dissimilarity. A matrix containing dissimilarity indices is constructed to identify and group like customers.

For example, assume four business copier customers are evaluated on the three demographic characteristics of (1) number of years in business,

Exhibit 4.2

Market Segmentation Using Similarity Analysis

Data

Customer	Downtown location	High copier usage	Interested in service plan	Single division
A	Yes	No	Yes	Yes
B	Yes	No	Yes	Yes
C	No	No	Yes	No
D	Yes	No	No	Yes
E	Yes	No	Yes	No
F	Yes	No	No	Yes
G	Yes	No	Yes	No

Similarity Matrix

	A	B	C	D	E	F
A	—	—	—	—	—	—
B	1	—	—	—	—	—
C	0.5	0.5	—	—	—	—
D	0.75	0.75	0.25	—	—	—
E	0.75	0.75	0.75	0.5	—	—
F	0.75	0.75	0.25	1	0.5	—
G	0.75	0.75	0.75	0.5	1	0.5

Similarity Groupings

Customer Segment #1: A, B
Customer Segment #2: D, F
Customer Segment #3: C, E, G

---

(2) distance from downtown, (3) number of copiers used in business. The raw data is presented in Exhibit 4.3 along with the subsequent dissimilarity indices based on standardized data and Euclidean distance. To illustrate, the dissimilarity index between customer A and customer B is 6.38 equals

$$\text{sqrt} \ (-0.87 - 0.87)^2 + (-0.21 - 1.47)^2 + (0.78 - 1.31)^2.$$

The next step is to group like customers into segments by amassing those customers reflecting low dissimilarity ratings into the same groups. The results of this analysis would suggest possible distinct target markets. Akin to similarity analysis, decisions concerning how to group customers can be made based on a simple heuristic (e.g., group two customers if they have less than a dissimilarity index of 2) or by use of cluster analysis. Using the simple heuristic approach, three distinct segments or potential target markets are identified: [A, D], [B], and [C]. A and D appear to represent companies

Exhibit 4.3

Market Segmentation Using Dissimilarity Analysis

Original Data

Customer	Age of business (in years)	Distance (miles) from downtown	Number of copiers used in business
A	20	1	5
B	21	5	3
C	21	0	4
D	20	0	5
Average	20.5	1.5	4.25
Standard deviation	0.577	2.380	0.957

Standardized Data

Customer	Age of business (in years)	Distance from downtown (in miles)	Number of copiers used in business
A	−0.87	−0.21	0.78
B	0.87	1.47	−1.31
C	0.87	−0.63	−0.26
D	−0.87	−0.63	0.78

Dissimilarity Matrix Based on Standardized Data

	A	B	C
A	—	—	—
B	3.19	—	—
C	2.07	2.35	—
D	0.42	3.43	2.02

Groupings

Customer Segment #1: A, D
Customer Segment #2: B
Customer Segment #3: CM

in business for twenty years that have five copiers. B represents companies away from downtown; and C represents downtown companies in business for twenty-one years that have four copiers. The use of a different heuristic could lead to a different classification of customers.

Other more statistically sophisticated approaches are available and can be employed for market segmentation. One prominent methodology is cluster analysis, which is an advanced statistical technique for generating item classes or groups among data. Refer to Hair et al. (2005) and Lilien, Rangaswamy, and De Bruyn (2007) for more detailed discussion of cluster analysis.

Technology Segmentation

Technology segmentation using a breakdown structure parallels the approach of a market breakdown structure. Subtechnologies, subcomponents, product attributes, or product functions would hierarchically break down from a given technology or product. Exhibit 4.4 presents a breakdown structure applied to a stapler. As shown, a breakdown by functions, attributes, and subcomponents offers four possible opportunities: (1) a light-duty stapler with plastic staples, (2) a light-duty stapler with metal staples, (3) a heavy-duty stapler that is waterproof, and (4) a heavy-duty stapler that is nonconductive. Further definition of these opportunities naturally can be undertaken. Market-related information like potential market and customers also could be incorporated into the technology breakdown structure. The merging of market and technology structures may be able to bring about the best-defined opportunities. Criteria to evaluate the validity of the technology segment include market potential, technical feasibility, and financial attractiveness; each of these criteria would help determine which opportunities pertaining to technology should be pursued.

The Product Innovation Charter

Once a set of potential opportunities is identified, product planners need to describe what is the opportunity. One approach is to provide a mission statement for the opportunity via a product innovation charter (Bart 2002; diBenedetto and Crawford 1998). A product innovation charter (PIC) is essentially a documented statement that identifies and describes the rationale for the product development or product planning initiative to be undertaken, the objectives or goals to be achieved, and the guiding principles that the initiative should heed.

As suggested in Exhibit 4.5, product innovation charters can be employed at the strategic business unit level, product platform level, and project level. In all cases, the charter is an extension of the company's overall corporate strategy and strategic planning process.

The product innovation charter is most often expressed in paragraph form and comprises four particular sections—although not necessarily equating to four paragraphs. The four sections, which often are combined for legibility, are background, arena, objectives and goals, and special guidelines.

Background provides the rationale for the product development initiative. As part of the background statement, the intended market and/or industry in which the initiative will be focused should be identified.

Exhibit 4.4 **Breakdown Structure for a Stapler Product Opportunity**

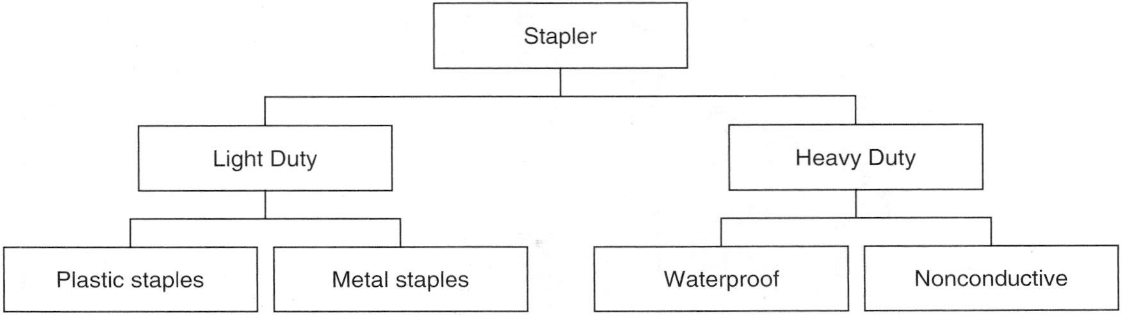

Exhibit 4.5 **The Product Development Charter and Corporate Strategy**

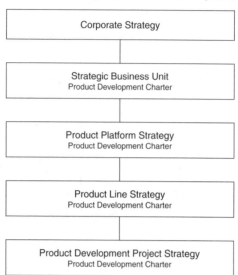

Arena identifies the core competencies of the company and identifies those competencies to be emphasized in the product development initiative. Such competencies could correspond to marketing strength, financial strength, production strength, R&D strength, or a combination of any of these or some other key company function.

Objectives and goals outline the ultimate benchmark by which the product development initiative will be measured. Objectives are broader statements than goals, but either can be used. Profit, growth, market status, competitiveness, and so on may be recognized.

Special guidelines are a catch-all category that provides any extra information that should be remembered during the product development initiative. These could include special features that must be included in the new product or specific elements of the marketing plan. Special guidelines also can attune the company to the key success factors of the initiative, such as being first-to-market with state-of-the-art, breakthrough technology or being second-but-better.

Together these four elements provide a comprehensive statement about the opportunity. One methodology for constructing a PIC is to list information separately in the four categories of background, arena, goals and objectives, and special guidelines. Then the information is combined in narrative form to delineate the potential opportunity. For example, consider the opportunity of the light-duty stapler with plastic staples. The following, brief information is listed per category:

Background	Arena	Goals and objectives	Special guidelines
• Children can injure themselves with regular household staples	• Company has a core competency in stapler manufacturing	• Want a 20 percent return on investment within two years	• Staples should be made of recyclable plastic materials
• Plastic staples are less expensive			

While very brief (normally, more detailed information would be listed), the following PIC can be composed based on this information:

> Children can very easily injure themselves using typical household staplers with metal staples. It is proposed that a new stapler using plastic staples, which are potentially less expensive, be developed. To accomplish this new product, we want to rely on our core competency as a leader in stapler manufacturing.
>
> A 20 percent return on investment is expected within two years after launch of the product. Particular attention should be paid to plastic staples made of recyclable plastics.

Obviously, the more information, the longer the PIC. The length is not necessarily the issue, however. The overall intent of a PIC is to give enough information to provide an appropriate characterization of the opportunity so that management can decide whether it truly is a valid opportunity to be pursued; the PIC can then be used as a guide throughout the entire product development effort.

Screening the PIC

Management must decide which product innovation charters are most valid and deserving of resources for further development. Decisions concerning selection of PICs to pursue should be based on market-related and technology-related criteria. A manager or team of managers would use these criteria to grade each PIC.

Various criteria can be used to evaluate each PIC. Twenty sample criteria are offered below, partitioned into the two categories of market-related criteria and technology-related criteria. Each question can be assessed on various scales. For example, a 1–5 scale, where 1 = "poor," 2 = "fair," 3 = "good," 4 = "very good," and 5 = "excellent," would work well with the criteria below.

Sample Market-Related Criteria

- Market demand for the product
- Market need for the product
- Uniqueness of the product relative to competitors
- Competitive advantage
- Ability to explain the product to customers
- Ability to demonstrate the product to customers
- Trade channel for the product
- Company's understanding of the product market
- Customer acceptance of the product
- Synergy of the new product with current products offered by the company

Sample Technology-Related Criteria

- Uniqueness of the technology
- Potential length of life cycle for the technology
- Ability to develop the technology
- Ability to patent the technology
- Ability to keep development costs under control
- Ability to keep development time short
- Ability to manufacture the technology
- Applicability of technology to future products
- Synergy of technology with company's current technology base
- Ability to keep potential risks associated with the technology to a minimum

Each company would need to develop its own set of criteria and determine an appropriate scoring methodology in order to best address its business situation. Those PICs with high (favorable) scores on the given criteria would be deemed acceptable for further consideration in the product development (entire product planning) process. PICs with lower scores would not necessarily be discarded, but may be reserved for future consideration or undergo a revision process to further clarify the opportunity.

Discussion Questions

1. What are some sources of opportunity?
2. What are the differences between a market, market segment, and target market?
3. What criteria can help clarify the validity of a market segment?
4. What is a product innovation charter?
5. What are some criteria for evaluating a product innovation charter?

References

Bart, Christopher K. 2002. "Product Innovation Charters: Mission Statements for New Products." *R&D Management*, 32 (1), 23–34.

diBenedetto, C. Anthony, and Merle Crawford. 1998. *New Products Management*. 6th ed. Boston: Irwin.

Hair, Joseph, William Black, Barry Babin, Rolph Anderson, and Ronald Tatham. 2005. *Multivariate Data Analysis*. 6th ed. Upper Saddle River, NJ: Prentice-Hall.

Lilien, Gary L., Arvind Rangaswamy, and Arnaud De Bruyn. 2007. *Principles of Marketing Engineering*. State College, PA: Trafford.

5 ✕ Concept Generation

Concept generation represents ideation activities that a team or company undertakes to amass a valid set of product concepts. Ideation, by definition, is the conceiving, imagining, and forming of ideas. As a distinct stage in the product development process, concept generation serves to generate as many concepts as possible, screen these concepts, and determine the most valid concepts for further development. Depending on the nature of the product development process and company strategy, concepts may be very broad (and unrelated) in nature or very narrow in scope.

A variety of concept generation techniques can be employed to spur ideation. The techniques to be discussed in the present chapter are needs assessment, scenario analysis, group creativity, attribute analysis, relationship analysis, and lateral search. Discussion begins with the product concept statement in order to illustrate the importance of understanding what constitutes a good product concept statement when applying each of these techniques. Because creativity plays a key role during concept generation, the topic of creativity is discussed after the presentation of the concept generation techniques.

The Product Concept Statement

Like the product innovation charter, a product concept serves as a foundation upon which to further the product development effort. Whereas the product innovation charter presents the overall opportunity and provides the product development team with a mission statement, the product concept statement defines what the product is to be. This purpose mandates that each generated concept should have a corresponding product concept statement. At the end of the concept generation stage, the application of one or more concept generation techniques will result in a set of product concepts and a corresponding set of product concept statements. There is always the possibility of a common thread emerging across these product concept statements, which will afford a general product concept statement.

A meaningful product concept statement should include the three important elements of form, technology, and benefits. Of these three, benefits are the most important element because, as previously discussed, customers buy benefits and not necessarily features or form. Each product concept statement therefore should explicitly highlight the key benefits to be offered by the product, where benefit is defined as the innate need that has to be satisfied or the underlying desire for the product.

Form and technology are the attributes of the given product concept. Form is the view or physical thing created or, in the case of a service, the sequence of steps by which the service is created. Technology represents the functionality of the product (how the product will work) or the source by which the product is made (manufacturing and research and development processes).

A beverage example is used to illustrate the important roles that each of these three product concept elements plays in formulating a complete product concept. A proposed product concept statement mentioning just one element in isolation would be rather limiting and probably lacking in marketplace appeal:

- a cola drink that has a great taste (benefit only)
- a cola drink that has a dark, rich color (form only)
- a cola made by a totally new sweetening process (technology only)

Each of these statements alone does not sound appealing and would not necessarily encourage consumers to buy the new cola drink. Combining these statements provides the following complete product concept statement:

> A new sweetening process creates a cola beverage with a dark, rich color and great taste.

This statement is much more appealing and robust than the three statements presented individually, showing the importance of developing product concept statements that include all three elements of form, technology, and benefits. Recognizing that each of these three elements should be incorporated into the product concept statement ensures that the product retains and reflects form, technology, and benefits elements as it enters subsequent stages of the product development process and is eventually launched.

Concept Generation Techniques

There are many available techniques for concept generation. Six general types of concept generation techniques are specifically discussed to illustrate the variety of techniques available. These techniques are needs assessment, scenario analysis, group creativity, attribute analysis, relationship analysis, and lateral search.

Needs Assessment

Needs assessment focuses on understanding current and future needs of the marketplace. This may include identifying current and potential problems in the marketplace. Matching these problems with appropriate solutions that the company can offer through its products will generate a set of product concepts.

Needs assessment can be accomplished through routine market contacts transpiring from sales visits and customer service calls, focus groups with customers as part of ongoing market research, customer suggestion boxes, customer complaints, and general customer comments. Even observation of customers can lead to insights into problems and customer preferences. Customers and noncustomers, including competitors' customers, should be considered valid points of contact.

When interacting with customers, it is important to listen to what they are saying about what they need, instead of trying to sell them on a particular product or product concept. Multiple departments from the company also should be represented during customer interactions so that all departments can learn from the customer as well as afford multiple interpretations of the "customer voice." McQuarrie (1993) offers the following methodology for conducting "customer visits":

1. *Set objectives:* Indicate the kind of information the company wants to collect.
2. *Select a sample:* Describe the types of customers to be visited; estimate the required number of customers.
3. *Compose the visit team:* Identify the individuals from different functional areas who should participate in the visits.
4. *Develop the discussion guide:* Generate the topics and questions to be covered in each visit, organize the topics into a sequence, and set priorities.
5. *Conduct the interviews:* Specify roles for team members; seek a loosely structured interaction.
6. *Debrief after each interview:* Assess whether any changes need to be made to the interviews; begin process of analysis.
7. *Analyze, report, and store visit data:* Heed limitations of qualitative research; disseminate reports to interested parties; archive reports in a customer database.

Another approach for needs assessment is to employ a panel of experts representing individual consultants or members of an advisory board. Such experts can help to identify future needs and provide market intelligence on market direction, possibly more so than customers themselves. Household or industrial panels are akin to expert customers. Typically, market research companies maintain their own panels, using them to better understand a particular market with which these panels are familiar.

One specific technique that relies on experts is lead user analysis as proposed by von Hippel (1988). As apparent in its name, the technique attempts to analyze the needs and wants of lead users, which represent market experts. The underlying premise of lead user analysis is that lead users will reflect needs of the main market early on, so if a company can tap into lead users and identify their needs, it can develop products that satisfy the main market expeditiously with forethought. The tenets of lead user analysis are as follows (von Hippel 1988, 107):

1. Lead users face needs that will be general in the marketplace, but they face them months or years before the bulk of that marketplace encounters them.
2. Lead users are positioned to benefit significantly by obtaining a solution to those needs.

The lead user methodology is as follows:

1. Specify product market segment.
2. Identify trends.
3. Identify lead users.
4. Develop new product specifications with lead users.
5. Test lead user product concept with routine users.

Lead user analysis is not necessarily easy to apply. In fact, many companies have found it difficult to identify proper lead users. Assuming one can identify lead users, Geoffrey Moore points out in his book *Crossing the Chasm* (1991) that lead users sometimes do not reflect the same concerns as the main market and can be misleading in terms of what a market will truly accept. Lead user analysis is a potential technique that has been employed effectively (see Herstatt and von Hippel 1992), but careful application is recommended.

Along with direct contact with customers, published sources can underlie a needs assessment. Key trade and popular press periodicals are sources for new concepts and suggest contemporary market problems. These periodicals also can highlight competitor activities through product announcements. Editorials in these periodicals can serve as and closely align to expert opinion.

Employees are a good source of concepts too. In fact, various companies provide employees with monetary rewards for promising ideas. Employees also can role-play the customer in an effort to identify problems and needs by putting themselves in the shoes of the customers, frame what problems they have, and indicate what solutions they would need.

Scenario Analysis

Scenario analysis aims to paint futuristic scenarios, frame potential problems emerging from these scenarios, and envision new product concepts to solve these problems. Akin to technology forecasting (e.g., see Levary and Han 1995), scenario analysis can be conducted using the "extend" approach or the "leap" approach (see Exhibit 5.1).

The distinction between the extend approach and the leap approach is the starting point. The extend version of scenario analysis starts out in the present; gathers all current trends and facts, called "seed trends"; moves out to the future; and speculates about future events and happenings. For example, an extend approach to assess new product concepts for cellular telephones would consider the current trends of free domestic long-distance, small telephones, and long-life batteries and then extend those trends into the future. For example, one possible future consideration based on the trend of free long-distance would be free international calling using a cellular telephone.

In contrast to the extend approach, the leap begins in the future by some given number of years and paints a scenario of what is going on. Future products associated with this scenario are then speculated. Two variations of the leap approach are a static leap and a dynamic leap. The static leap jumps into the future and stays out in the future to paint a futuristic scenario. The dynamic leap jumps into the future and then works back from the future to the present, attempting to connect today's products with future products. For example, assume we are interested in transportation products. Jumping out fifty years into the future, we might envision the use of hydrogen cars, "mag-lev" trains, and battery-powered cars. If we stop here, the leap is static. However, working back to the present to plot a course of action that links today's technology to these future products is characteristic of a dynamic leap. So we might consider how today's technology might be utilized to move toward the proliferation of hydrogen car use fifty years from now.

Group Creativity

Group creativity represents those techniques that stimulate groups to think of new ideas. The most common technique associated with group creativity is brainstorming.

Brainstorming is an approach that aims to develop as many ideas as pos-

Exhibit 5.1   **Scenario Analysis**

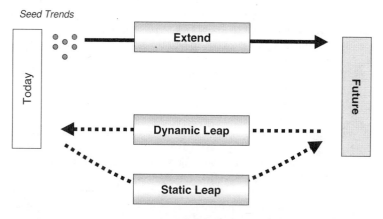

sible from a group, based on two general guidelines. First, all judgment must be deferred so that all ideas are welcomed; any initial criticism of original ideas is inappropriate. Second, quantity breeds quality, meaning that the more ideas, the better. To undertake a brainstorming session, the following guidelines should be followed:

1. Brainstorming works best in a small group of four to ten people.
2. There needs to be a target. That is, there must be a single, defined question or item on which to focus that everybody understands.
3. All suggested ideas are publicly recorded; none are edited out.
4. All group members must have equal opportunity to express themselves.
5. All possible answers should be encouraged and actively sought out, including impractical, wild, or even bizarre ideas.

Adhering to these guidelines, brainstorming can proceed according to the following steps:

1. Review the rules for brainstorming, stressing the need to avoid criticism.
2. State the single question or topic to be brainstormed, and make sure everybody understands it. The more specific the question or topic, the better.
3. Give everyone a turn in sequence, going around in clockwise order, to state one idea or to pass on that round. This ensures that quiet

members of the group are heard and that dominant individuals do not get all the airtime.

4. Keep going around the circle until all ideas are collected and recorded on a flip chart or blackboard. Sometimes a time limit like ten minutes creates energy to beat the clock, and if the team agrees, the time can be extended in five-minute increments.

5. Allow an incubation time, such as overnight. If you choose, make copies of the ideas and provide to all team members. Or at least leave the ideas up on the paper or board so individuals can go back and review them.

6. After the initial brainstorming sessions have generated an exhaustive list of product ideas, you need to combine, refine, and improve the list of generated ideas, whittling it down to a shorter, stronger list of ideas. Robert Eberle (1996) offers the SCAMPER technique, which is an acronym for seven questions to aid in refining brainstormed ideas:

   S What could you substitute? Is there something else that might be better put in this idea's place?

   C What could you combine? Can any of the ideas be combined?

   A What could you adapt? Can any of these ideas be adapted together?

   M What could you magnify, minify, multiply? Can an idea be broadened or shortened in scope?

   P What could you put to other uses?

   E What else? Who else? Where else?

   R What could you rearrange or reverse?

7. Poll team members to vote for ideas they prefer (they do not vote against ideas).

8. If a group of ten ideas is left, give team members a certain number of ranked votes that they provide for each of the remaining ideas. This prioritizes the "final" or desirable ideas.

Attribute Analysis

Attribute analysis is a category of techniques that employs product characteristics (attributes) to generate new product ideas. Two approaches within this category are determinant gap analysis and perceptual gap analysis.

Determinant Gap Analysis

Determinant gap analysis starts with key attributes of the potential product idea being listed or given. The fact that attributes are known from the beginning distinguishes determinant gap analysis from perceptual gap analysis. Next, the most important attributes or drivers of the marketplace (from either the company's or consumer's perspective) are selected. A judgmental approach can then be undertaken to map existing product offerings or potential offerings on the given attributes or dimensions. If a more quantitative approach is desired, scales for each attribute or dimension can be determined. Existing products or potential ideas would then be mapped based on their respective scores for each attribute. The outcome of both approaches is a multidimensional map of the marketplace. Typically only the top two or three drivers are used to produce an intelligible map of the marketplace.

Areas on the constructed map where there is a noticeable gap serve as potentially new ideas. However, just because a gap exists does not necessarily mean that it is a viable new product idea. Judgment is necessary to identify the most appropriate and meaningful gaps.

Determinant gap analysis is referred to as the attribute rating (AR) method because distinct attributes are given and rated. An example of an AR map illustrating various tire product offerings is provided in Exhibit 5.2. These offerings are organized by a price dimension (high versus low price) and expected mileage dimension (high versus low mileage expected). As shown, there are noticeable gaps for a lower price, lower mileage tire; lower price, higher mileage tire; and a higher price, lower mileage tire. Obviously, among these three gaps, the lower price options represent the most feasible options and the most likely new product concepts.

Should a large set of characteristics describe a particular marketplace or product offering, then some form of grouping of these characteristics may be appropriate. One technique used in conjunction with determinant gap analysis (AR maps) is factor analysis. Factor analysis is an advanced statistical technique that can be applied to large sample sizes of respondents or customers who would evaluate each product offering on the given set of characteristics. Factor analysis will group multiple characteristics into broad underlying categories of characteristics and establish underlying dimensions prevalent within a marketplace. See Hair et al. (1998) and Lilien et al. (2007) for a more detailed discussion of factor analysis.

Perceptual Gap Analysis

Perceptual gap analysis is employed when attributes are not known or not easily identified. The methodology for a perceptual gap analysis is to pair all existing products and then make an evaluation of the similarity between the two paired product offerings. After all pairs have been evaluated, a map

Exhibit 5.2 **AR Product Positioning Map**

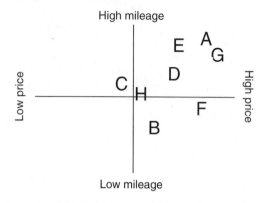

is constructed in an attempt to illustrate the relationships among all existing products—that is, all existing products are plotted on this map to show their relationships to every other product. If a large sample of respondents or customers is available to evaluate the pairings, then multidimensional scaling (MDS) can be used to aggregate all paired comparisons and construct a map. Again, one must realize that areas on the map where there is a noticeable gap represent potential concepts, but they do not necessarily represent a viable new product idea. Identifying the most appropriate and meaningful gaps requires judgment on the part of the product planner.

Perceptual gap analysis is referred to as the overall similarity (OS) method because evaluations are made based on OS between product offerings or potential product offerings. An example of an OS map is provided in Exhibit 5.3, now illustrating the various tire product offerings based on their similarities. Take special note that the axes of the map are not labeled. In this map, there is a noticeable gap in the lower left-hand quadrant. There also appears to be a gap in the center of the map because only product C is the competition in this area. To ascertain what these gaps represent, an assessment of the product offerings is made to identify the common characteristics associated with the group offerings; that is, the common characteristics shared by A, B, and H in the upper left-hand quadrant; E and G in the upper right-hand quadrant; and D and F in the lower right-hand quadrant. Identifying common characteristics is not necessarily an easy task, but if achieved, may present very meaningful new product concepts.

MDS is an advanced analytical technique that provides a visual representation of proximities among a set of objects, thereby resulting in an OS map. For a more detailed discussion of MDS, refer to Wickelmaier (2003).

Exhibit 5.3 **OS Product Positioning Map**

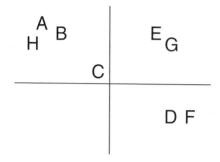

Relationship Analysis

Relationship analysis is a category of techniques that force relationships between seemingly unrelated issues in order to discover new product ideas. Like the ideas produced by gap analysis, sometimes these ideas are not feasible, but sometimes they can be potentially viable. The three relationship analysis techniques to be discussed are two-dimensional matrix, morphological analysis, and conjoint analysis.

Two-Dimensional Matrix

The two-dimensional matrix approach requires identifying two key elements or dimensions and listing items that specifically correlate to each of the dimensions. Matching items across the two dimensions results in a set of product concepts. For example, a web marketing company might be interested in developing new services. Two key dimensions for these services could be "type of customer" and "web function." Four types of customers are listed: sole proprietorship, limited liability corporation, C-corporation, and nonprofit organization, whereas three types of web functions are listed: website development, website promotion, and website analytics. Matching the four types of customers with the three types of web functions represents potentially twelve (4 × 3) product ideas (see Exhibit 5.4). Some of these ideas might already be offered by the company, and some ideas may be infeasible. Nonetheless, assessing the relationship between customer type and website function may identify a product concept the company has not yet considered. Listing more types of customers and more types of website functions naturally increases the number of possible product concepts.

Exhibit 5.4

Two-Dimensional Matrix Example

Website services	Customer types			
	Sole proprietorship (individual)	Limited liability corporation (small business)	C-corporation (large business)	Nonprofit organization
Website development	1	2	3	4
Website promotion	5	6	7	8
Website analytics	9	10	11	12

Twelve Possible Product Concepts

Website development for individuals
Website development for small business
Website development for large business
Website development for nonprofit
Website promotion for individuals
Website promotion for small business
Website promotion for large business
Website promotion for nonprofit
Website analytics for individuals
Website analytics for small business
Website analytics for large business
Website analytics for nonprofit

Morphological Analysis

Morphological analysis is a technique that identifies different attributes (or dimensions) for a potential product and subsequently lists multiple levels or characteristics that correspond to each attribute. For example, price could be an attribute and the types of price such as low, moderate, and high would be the different levels that correspond to price. After listing each attribute and its respective levels, each level per individual attribute is combined with a level from every other attribute to generate a set of possible product attribute combinations. For example, consider an iced tea product that has the following four given dimensions: flavor, size, packaging, and caffeine content. Flavor has the three levels of regular, fruit, and mint; size has the four levels of eight-ounce, twelve-ounce, sixteen-ounce, and twenty-ounce; packaging has the two levels of bottle and can; and caffeine content has the two levels of caffeinated and decaffeinated.

Applying morphological analysis as shown in Exhibit 5.5, a total of forty-eight new product concepts ($3 \times 4 \times 2 \times 2$) are generated. One possible product concept from the combination of attribute levels is a regular flavor,

Exhibit 5.5

Morphological Analysis Example

Flavor	Size	Packaging	Caffeine content
Regular	Eight-ounce	Bottle	Caffeinated
Fruit	Twelve-ounce	Can	Decaffeinated
Mint	Sixteen-ounce		
	Twenty-ounce		

Total Number of Possible Ice Tea Concepts = $3 \times 4 \times 2 \times 2 = 48$

Possible Ice Tea Concepts

- Regular, Caffeinated Iced Tea in an Eight-Ounce Bottle
- Regular, Decaffeinated Iced Tea in an Eight-Ounce Bottle
- Regular, Caffeinated Iced Tea in an Eight-Ounce Can
- Regular, Decaffeinated Iced Tea in an Eight-Ounce Can
- Regular, Caffeinated Iced Tea in a Twelve-Ounce Bottle
- Regular, Decaffeinated Iced Tea in a Twelve-Ounce Bottle
- Regular, Caffeinated Iced Tea in a Twelve-Ounce Can
- Regular, Decaffeinated Iced Tea in a Twelve-Ounce Can
- Regular, Caffeinated Iced Tea in a Sixteen-Ounce Bottle
- Regular, Decaffeinated Iced Tea in a Sixteen-Ounce Bottle
- Regular, Caffeinated Iced Tea in a Sixteen-Ounce Can
- Regular, Decaffeinated Iced Tea in a Sixteen-Ounce Can
- Regular, Caffeinated Iced Tea in a Twenty-Ounce Bottle
- Regular, Decaffeinated Iced Tea in a Twenty-Ounce Bottle
- Regular, Caffeinated Iced Tea in a Twenty-Ounce Can
- Regular, Decaffeinated Iced Tea in a Twenty-Ounce Can
- Fruit, Caffeinated Iced Tea in an Eight-Ounce Bottle
- Fruit, Decaffeinated Iced Tea in an Eight-Ounce Bottle
- Fruit, Caffeinated Iced Tea in an Eight-Ounce Can
- Fruit, Decaffeinated Iced Tea in an Eight-Ounce Can
- Fruit, Caffeinated Iced Tea in a Twelve-Ounce Bottle
- Fruit, Decaffeinated Iced Tea in a Twelve-Ounce Bottle
- Fruit, Caffeinated Iced Tea in a Twelve-Ounce Can
- Fruit, Decaffeinated Iced Tea in a Twelve-Ounce Can
- Fruit, Caffeinated Iced Tea in a Sixteen-Ounce Bottle
- Fruit, Decaffeinated Iced Tea in a Sixteen-Ounce Bottle
- Fruit, Caffeinated Iced Tea in a Sixteen-Ounce Can
- Fruit, Decaffeinated Iced Tea in a Sixteen-Ounce Can
- Fruit, Caffeinated Iced Tea in a Twenty-Ounce Bottle
- Fruit, Decaffeinated Iced Tea in a Twenty-Ounce Bottle
- Fruit, Caffeinated Iced Tea in a Twenty-Ounce Can
- Fruit, Decaffeinated Iced Tea in a Twenty-Ounce Can
- Mint, Caffeinated Iced Tea in an Eight-Ounce Bottle
- Mint, Decaffeinated Iced Tea in an Eight-Ounce Bottle
- Mint, Caffeinated Iced Tea in an Eight-Ounce Can
- Mint, Decaffeinated Iced Tea in an Eight-Ounce Can
- Mint, Caffeinated Iced Tea in a Twelve-Ounce Bottle
- Mint, Decaffeinated Iced Tea in a Twelve-Ounce Bottle
- Mint, Caffeinated Iced Tea in a Twelve-Ounce Can
- Mint, Decaffeinated Iced Tea in a Twelve-Ounce Can
- Mint, Caffeinated Iced Tea in a Sixteen-Ounce Bottle
- Mint, Decaffeinated Iced Tea in a Sixteen-Ounce Bottle
- Mint, Caffeinated Iced Tea in a Sixteen-Ounce Can
- Mint, Decaffeinated Iced Tea in a Sixteen-Ounce Can
- Mint, Caffeinated Iced Tea in a Twenty-Ounce Bottle
- Mint, Decaffeinated Iced Tea in a Twenty-Ounce Bottle
- Mint, Caffeinated Iced Tea in a Twenty-Ounce Can
- Mint, Decaffeinated Iced Tea in a Twenty-Ounce Can

caffeinated iced tea in an eight-ounce bottle. Another combination is fruit flavor, decaffeinated iced tea in a twelve-ounce can. As in the case of the two-dimensional matrix, not all product combinations may be feasible. The overall intent of morphological analysis is to force relationships between more than two dimensions to see if a valid idea exists.

Note that the number of product concepts in a morphological analysis can grow exponentially if there are a lot of dimensions and many levels per dimension. For example, the iteration of four types of attributes and three levels per attribute provides 81 ($3 \times 3 \times 3 \times 3$ or 3^4) potential product concepts. Adding just one more level to one of the attributes increases the number of potential product concepts to 108 ($3 \times 3 \times 3 \times 4$), and adding one more attribute with three levels to the mix increases the number of potential product concepts to 243 ($3 \times 3 \times 3 \times 3 \times 3$ or 3^5)!

Conjoint Analysis (Trade-Off Analysis)

One of the challenges in morphological analysis is to discern which attributes and which levels are more preferred by customers. One way to quantify customer preferences within the guise of a quasi-morphological analysis is by way of trade-off analysis, also referred to as conjoint analysis.

Conjoint analysis is a quantitative technique for calculating the desirability of a particular product's attributes. This can lead to the aggregation of an optimal set of attributes that provides the greatest desirability. Conjoint analysis involves the iteration of all possible combinations of levels across the given product attributes and then having a customer rank the desirability of each product attribute combination. A metric of desirability for each level on a given product attribute can then be calculated to suggest the utility afforded by that specific level. This metric is called a part-worth. Totaling the part-worths for all levels in a product attribute combination provides a total desirability score for that combination. Because some levels will be less desirable and others more desirable, resulting in different total desirability scores, customers have the ability to make trade-offs when comparing the levels available on each of the given attributes. This is why the analysis is called trade-off analysis. Normally, a group of customers will be assessed, versus just one customer, to determine overall desirability and preferences for a given set of attributes.

Like morphological analysis, trade-off analysis can become cumbersome when numerous attributes and multiple options per attribute are considered. For instance, three attributes and two levels per attribute lead to eight product attribute combinations. The addition of one more attribute comprising two levels increases the number of product attribute combinations to sixteen (doubling the number that a customer will need to rank). Still, trade-off analysis when applied correctly can serve as a valuable technique for identifying the most important attributes for a new product concept.

Conjoint analysis begins by establishing the attributes and levels for the product. For example, zoom, screen size, and water resistance represent a set of attributes or dimensions for a compact camera. Each dimension is broken into distinct options or levels. Zoom includes the three levels of 2X, 5X, or 10X; screen size includes the two levels of two inches or three inches; and water resistance includes the two levels of waterproof or water resistant. Individual levels across the three dimensions are combined procedurally to list twelve distinct product offerings (3 levels × 2 levels × 2 levels = 12 possible product offering combinations).

Customers would be asked to evaluate each of the twelve product offerings; the resulting data would be collected for analysis. One simple evaluation methodology is to ask customers to rank the product combinations from 1 (most preferred combination) to 12 (least preferred combination). The rankings data are then converted to a "desirability" score by flipping around the rankings in order that the most preferred combination reflects that highest desirability score (in other words, higher scores mean higher desirability). With twelve combinations, each ranking is converted to a desirability score by subtracting the ranking from thirteen (12 + 1). The reason for collecting ranking evaluations from customers, instead of desirability scores, is because ranking is usually more intuitive for customers to understand and a more commonplace procedure for customers to perform.

With desirability scores now calculated, an average desirability score for each level is calculated by averaging the desirability scores of all combinations containing the respective level. Consider Customer One's data provided in Exhibit 5.6. Customer One rankings are first converted to desirability scores. Average desirability scores are calculated for each individual level on each dimension by averaging the desirability scores for combinations including that particular level. For example, the average desirability for 2X zoom is 4.5, which is the average of all product combinations that contain the 2X level [(1 + 2 + 7 + 8)/4 = 4.5]; the average desirability for the 5X zoom is 6.5, which is the average of all product combinations containing the 5X level [(3 + 4 + 9 + 10)/4 = 6.5]; and the average desirability for 10X zoom is 8.5, which is the average of all product combinations containing the 10X level [(5 + 6 + 11 + 12)/4 = 8.5]. Based on these calculations, this customer finds 10X more desirable than 5X and much more desirable than 2X; the results could be interpreted as suggesting that 10X is almost two times more desirable than 2X. Similar calculations can be made to determine the average desirability for the remaining levels: two-inch screen size with an average desirability of

81

Exhibit 5.6

Conjoint Analysis

Zoom	Screen size	Water resistance	Rankings	Desirability	Total summed desirability
2X	2 inches	WR	12	1	14.0
25	2 inches	WR	10	3	16.0
10X	2 inches	WR	8	5	18.0
2X	2 inches	WR	11	2	15.0
5X	2 inches	WR	9	4	17.0
10X	2 inches	WR	7	6	19.0
2X	3 inches	WR	6	7	20.0
5X	3 inches	WR	4	9	22.0
10X	3 inches	WR	2	11	24.0
2X	3 inches	WR	5	8	21.0
5X	3 inches	WR	3	10	23.0
10X	3 inches	WR	1	12	25.0

Midpoint = 19.5 Neutral Point

Average Desirabilities

Zoom:

2X	4.5
5X	6.5
10X	8.5

Screen Size:

2 inches	3.5
3 inches	9.5

Water Resistance:

Waterproof	7
Water Resistant	6

Relative Importances

Zoom	4.0	36%
Screen Size	6.0	55%
Water Resistance	1.0	9%
Total	11.0	

3.5 versus three-inch screen size with an average desirability of 9.5, and water resistant with an average desirability of 6 versus waterproof with an average desirability of 7. Note that when there are only two levels, the desirabilities will add up to the number of combinations plus one (in the given example, the two levels should add up to thirteen).

Two types of analyses can now proceed after the average desirabilities have been calculated. One analysis compares the summed or total desirability scores across all possible attribute-level combinations. That is, the average desirability scores for each level associated with a given combination are added together to provide a summed desirability score. For example, the summed desirability for the 5X, three-inch, and water resistance combination is 22 (6.5 + 9.5 + 6 = 22). These summed desirability scores can be used to compare combinations and determine which ones are close in summed desirability. This is beneficial when there is a need to substitute one combination for another because of the inability to deliver a particular attribute level. Summed combinations also are useful in distinguishing those combinations that provide positive versus negative desirability. Positive versus negative desirability is determined by observing whether specific levels are above or below the midpoint value. Those levels above the midpoint value represent positive desirability, and those below the midpoint value represent negative desirability (a desirability value equivalent to the midpoint value would signify neutrality or indifference). For the given example, the midpoint value is 6.5 on each dimension. Those levels above 6.5 indicate positive desirability, so those levels reflecting much higher values than 6.5 are considered more desirable. The levels of 10X, three-inch, and waterproof provide positive desirability in the eyes of Customer One; the combination of these levels would represent the highest level of desirability (8.5 + 9.5 + 7 = 25). Providing these three levels might not always be feasible, though, so other feasible combinations need to be identified. Those items above the summed midpoint would suggest desirable combinations—combinations that the customer would find still desirable. The summed midpoint is calculated by multiplying the midpoint value by the number of dimensions. In the given example, 6.5 times three dimensions calculates a summed midpoint of 19.5. Those combinations with summed desirability scores above 19.5 would be considered desirable and feasible combinations (trade-offs). As shown in Exhibit 5.6, six combinations reflect positive desirability.

A second popular analysis involves calculating the relative importance of each dimension. This analysis begins by calculating the range of average desirability scores per each dimension. For example, the zoom dimension reflects a range of 4, which is the difference between the high and low average desirability scores (8.5 − 4.5 = 4). The screen size dimension has a range of 6 (9.5 − 3.5 = 6), and the water resistance dimension has a range of 1 (7 − 6 = 1). The relative importance of each dimension is calculated by totaling these ranges and determining the proportion of the total that each dimension provides. As shown in Exhibit 5.6, the total of the range values equals 11 (6 + 4 + 1 = 11). The relative importance of the zoom dimension is calculated by dividing 4 by 11 or 36 percent. This percentage is interpreted as the zoom dimension accounting for 36 percent of the variability associated with Customer One's desire for the compact camera product. The screen size dimension accounts for 55 percent (6 divided by 11) of this variability, and the water resistance dimension accounts for 9 percent (1 divided by 11) of the variability. The conclusion from the relative importance analysis is that screen size accounts for over half of the desire that Customer One has in the compact camera product. Zoom accounts for one-third of the desire in the digital camera product. Therefore, most product development attention should emphasize screen size. A loose interpretation is that screen size has the potential to drive 55 percent of the demand and decision-making behind purchases for the compact camera product.

Conjoint analysis can obviously become cumbersome when numerous attributes and multiple options per attribute are considered. The addition of one more level to the screen size dimension would increase the number of combinations to eighteen ($3 \times 3 \times 2$) combinations. The addition of a fourth dimension with two levels to the original set of data would result in the need to consider twenty-four ($3 \times 2 \times 2 \times 2$) combinations, doubling the number of combinations that the customer would need to consider and likely leading to customer fatigue during the ranking exercise. It is recommended that only those attributes and levels considered critical should be evaluated. If the number of attributes and levels results in a set of combinations greater than, say, twelve combinations, advanced analytical approaches are available to quickly eliminate undesired product attributes (IntelliQuest 2000). These advanced approaches are statistically sophisticated in nature, although various software packages and consulting agencies are available to assist in performing conjoint analysis studies (e.g., Sawtooth Software at www.sawtoothsoftware.com).

A final comment is that this example analyzed data from only one customer whereas typical conjoint analyses involve multiple customers. Various methodologies for merging multiple customer data exist, with the simplest approach being the averaging of results across individual customers' rank data. For further reading on conjoint analysis, see Dolan (1993), Hair et al. (1998), and IntelliQuest (2000).

Lateral Search

Lateral search is a catch-all category of concept generation techniques that do not fit the previously given categories. The overall theme underlying lateral search techniques is to force thinking away from the current product offering or attributes of the current product offering in order to conceive new product ideas. In doing so, these techniques attempt to encourage "out-of-the-box" thinking.

While there are numerous techniques available (refer to Crawford 1997), four techniques are discussed for illustrative purposes: competitor review, avoidance technique, big winner technique, and creative stimuli technique.

As the name suggests, a competitor review is a review of what competitors are doing relative to the proposed product offering. In this manner, product attributes, product offerings, and other initiatives that make competitor products popular can be identified and possibly incorporated into a new product concept. A competitor review also can attune thinking to how the respective company can establish a competitive advantage given current competitor activities.

84

The avoidance technique constantly challenges team members to consider why they think a certain way. In this manner, the team can better understand why certain team preferences exist and how such preferences can be best served. To perform the technique, discussion begins on a particular topic and then the question why or why not is posed. This continues until the team is satisfied with the preferences and corresponding ideas generated.

The big winner technique attempts to iterate the reason underlying the success of products, people, things, and so on. The technique begins by listing "things" that are successful to focus discussion, and then reasons why this product, person, or thing, is successful are iterated (brainstormed). For example, the National Football League team that won the most recent Super Bowl could serve as the discussion's focal point. The team's success might be attributed to rigorous practice, drive, a good quarterback, and teamwork—as examples. These reasons are discussed to see how such characteristics can be incorporated into a new product concept. For instance, how might an industrial equipment manufacturer make use of the "practice" theme to develop a new industrial equipment concept? One answer may be a lot of testing. A cellular telephone manufacturer may stretch the idea of "drive" to suggest designing a telephone explicitly for car driving use only. Anything deemed "successful" is acceptable; the overall intent of the big winner technique is to stimulate different ways of bringing elements of success into a new product concept.

The creative stimuli technique brainstorms ideas based on a given adjective or noun. Akin to the big winner technique, the creative stimuli technique attempts to connect different ways of making a product by reflecting certain elements of a listed word. The key difference in the case of the creative stimuli technique is that a word, not a success characteristic, is listed and that disconnected words bring about the greatest creativity. For example, if the word "wild" was given in the case of a cellular telephone, thinking would focus on how to make a new product concept "wild." Based on this word, the cellular telephone manufacturer might generate new product concepts with "wild" shapes, "wild" colors, and/or "wild" names. Note that the creative stimuli technique is especially useful for ideating on new marketing program ideas. A sample of words for use with the creative stimuli technique is provided in Exhibit 5.7.

Creativity

Abraham Maslow defined creativity as being correlated with the ability to withstand a lack of structure, lack of future, lack of predictability, and lack of

Exhibit 5.7

A Sample of Thirty-four Words That Can Be Used With the Creative Stimuli Technique

Amazing	Outer Space
Charity	Participation
Curiosity	Personal
Decorative	Romance
Direct	Security
Education	Showmanship
Efficiency	Sophisticated
Family	Spectacular
Glamorize	Style
Guarantee	Symbolism
Habit	Testimonials
Holiday	Timeliness
Legal	Transportation
Legend	Truth
Magic	Weather
Music	Wild
Mysterious	World

Note: This list is just a sample. Any adjective or noun can be used as a focal point for stimulating new product concept generation.

control, plus a tolerance for ambiguity and planlessness. In the end, he stressed that creativity takes considerable courage and trust. Creativity plays a role in all concept generation techniques and a particularly important role in the categories of brainstorming and lateral success. Creativity affords a broad range of thinking and encourages making connections that otherwise would be overlooked, leading to better product concepts. Creativity also could involve taking existing objects and combining them differently for new purposes or playing with the way in which they are interrelated. Without creativity, the concept generation process becomes more focused, narrowed in scope, and refined in output. This does not mean that creativity is always required for concept generation; sometimes the concept generation objective is very specific and should not be expanded. A related question is whether the form of creativity is structured or unstructured. Unstructured creativity is personal creativity that is not directly purposeful or task-oriented, whereas structured creativity provides the tools and techniques to help convert problems to solutions (Miller 2000).

Creative thinking and the creative process are supported by the following abilities, which can be considered applicable to both individuals and organizations:

- *Fluency:* the ability to generate a volume of thoughts, ideas, concepts, or answers to a question or problem.

- *Flexibility:* the ability to handle and produce different kinds of information.
- *Originality:* the ability to generate new, different, novel, or unique thoughts or concepts; the ability to provide an unusual response when compared to the norm.
- *Elaboration:* the ability to embellish or build on a thought or concept by adding detail or depth.
- *Sensitivity:* the ability to have a level of analytical and intuitive awareness to find problems and see to the heart of the problem.
- *Freedom:* the ability to be free from internal biases and external constraints, not fearful of consequences or reprisals, and not bound by habit, tradition, expectation, or emotion.

Some company environments are more conducive to creativity than others. To spur creativity, it is important for a company climate to embrace these characteristics, allowing people to feel safe, trusted, accepted, and willing to share feelings and take risks (Miller 2000). Accordingly, a productive climate for creativity should reflect the following: support for ideas, challenge, dynamism and liveliness, playfulness and humor, debates, dialogue, risk-taking, trust and openness, freedom, time, and absence of conflicts.

Some companies have implemented organization-wide programs that allow and enable opportunities for employees to be creative. Companies like 3M, Motorola, and Sony have incorporated at least one of the below program elements to stimulate creativity among their workforce:

- *Free time:* Allow employees time to explore and pursue new product ideas during the workweek.
- *Flextime:* Allow employees to make their own schedules in order to capitalize on the periods when they feel most productive—some employees work better in the morning hours and others work better in the late afternoon.
- *Special rewards:* Offer rewards for innovative thinking and risk-taking.
- *Killer phrases removal:* Create a company culture that does not say such things as "cannot be done," "done that before," and "that is too different for our company." Such phrases suggests attitudes that stymie creativity.
- *Bureaucracy reduction:* Create a company environment that minimizes paperwork and approval processes on top of every product planning function. Provide some degree of individual decision-making.
- *Cross-functional teams:* Use cross-functional teams to enlighten personnel to multiple perspectives, as well as cross-fertilize ideas.

To summarize how to frame and spur creativity within the organization, especially during concept generation, Innovation Focus, a company specializing in concept generation, suggests applying the following rules (Miller 2000; www.innovationfocus.com):

1. Ideas are infinite. There is always more than one right answer.
2. Only those who attempt the absurd achieve the impossible. There are limits to logic and irrelevance has real uses.
3. Intuition is your friend.
4. All things are connected. Use metaphors and create the meaning later. Mine the power of diversity of resources.
5. Pain plus time equals humor. Never underestimate the power of humor in creativity. Humor opens the door to creativity. Play has the power to spark creativity as well.
6. Risk-taking and resistance produce a pro-survival balance. It takes ten risk-takers to balance one well-meaning voice of reason.
7. Make time and space for creativity. It is sloppy and inefficient.
8. Creativity takes practice and an intense desire to be good at it.

Discussion Questions

1. What are the three components of a good product concept statement?
2. What are the six general types of concept generation techniques?
3. What is the main difference between an AR map and an OS map?
4. Why is conjoint analysis referred to as trade-off analysis?
5. How might a company create a climate that spurs creativity?

References

Crawford, C. Merle. 1997. *New Products Management*. 5th ed. Boston: Irwin.

Dolan, Robert J. 1993. *Managing the New Product Development Process: Cases and Notes*. Reading, MA: Addison-Wesley.

Eberle, Robert. 1996. *SCAMPER: Games for Imaginative Development*. Waco, TX: Frufrock Press.

Hair, Joseph F., Jr., Rolph E. Anderson, Ronald L. Tatham, and William C. Black. 1998. *Multivariate Data Analysis*. 4th ed. New York: Macmillan.

Herstatt, Cornelius, and Eric von Hippel. 1992. "From Experience: Developing New Product Concepts Via the Lead User Method: A Case Study in a Low Tech Field." *Journal of Product Innovation Management*, 9 (3), 213–221.

IntelliQuest. 2000. *Preference Structure Measurement: Conjoint Analysis and Related Techniques*. 2nd ed. Austin: American Marketing Association.

Levary, Reuven R., and Dongchui Han. 1995. "Choosing a Technological Forecasting Method." *Industrial Management*. 37 (1), 14–18.

Lilien, Gary L., Arvind Rangaswamy, and Arnaud De Bruyn. 2007. *Principles of Marketing Engineering*. State College, PA: Trafford Publishing.

McQuarrie, Edward F. 1993. *Customer Visits: Tools to Build Market Focus*. Thousand Oaks, CA: Sage.

Miller, Christopher W. 2000. *The Creative U: A Workbook for Creativity*. Lancaster, PA: Innovation Focus.

Moore, Geoffrey. 1991. *Crossing the Chasm*. New York: Harper Collins.

von Hippel, Eric. 1988. *The Sources of Innovation*. New York: Oxford University Press

Wickelmaier, Florian. 2003. *An Introduction to MDS*. Sound Quality Research Unit Report. May 4. Aalborg University, Aalborg, Denmark.

6 Concept Evaluation

Once a set of product concepts has been generated, an evaluation of each concept is conducted. The purpose of concept evaluation is to refine the set of concepts to only those concepts that should continue in the product development process. Naturally, the decision regarding how many concepts can remain in the product development process will depend on the resources available.

Five general approaches can be used to evaluate concepts. In most cases, these approaches are used together to achieve a broad perspective of which concepts should be continued. These approaches, discussed in the current chapter, are the product development charter review, concept testing, scoring models, snake plots, and financial analysis.

Product Development Charter Review

The product development charter review is basically the evaluation by the management team or project team of the respective product concept against the criteria established in the product innovation charter (PIC). A product concept that appears to meet the expectations established in the PIC is allowed to proceed into the next product development stage, technical development. Ultimately, the decision of "go/no-go" using the PIC review approach is based on managerial intuition and judgment.

Concept Testing

Concept testing is a process by which the customer—be it a current customer, potential customer, or a general consumer—evaluates a new product concept and gives an opinion on whether the concept is something that the customer may have interest in and would likely buy. Other questions to be asked during a concept test include why the concept is (or is not) appealing, what are the main strengths of the product concept, what are the key weaknesses of the product concept, and what improvements can be suggested (Cooper 1993).

The aim of concept testing is to incorporate customer opinion into the evaluation process. Common data collection methods employed during concept testing include focus groups, in-person interviews, telephone interviews, mail surveys, and online surveys (Peng and Finn 2008).

There are four general types or approaches for conducting a concept test: the narrative concept test, the pictorial concept test, the prototype concept test, and the virtual concept test.

The narrative concept test involves a text description of the concept being presented to consumers for their opinions. Two styles in which the text description or concept statement can be written are noncommercialized and commercialized. A noncommercialized concept statement, also called a stripped description, is a simple factual statement about a proposed product concept that contains a minimum of attributes; a commercialized concept statement, also called an embellished description, is a persuasive statement about a product concept written in such a way as to promote the product and its attributes, similar to how a product would be promoted at launch. Exhibit 6.1 shows examples of a noncommercialized concept statement and a commercialized concept statement for a battery-powered bicycle motor that were used as part of a concept test for this product. Rather than using either of the two types of concept statements, a noncommercialized concept statement might be first introduced to gauge customers' general opinion and understanding of the concept. Then a commercialized concept statement can be presented to gauge the influence of commercial elements in the concept statement on customers' opinions and attitude. Based on published research, comparing the two types of concept statements during a concept test may find marginal differences in customers' attitude and purchase intention responses (Lees and Wright 2004).

The second type of test is a pictorial or sketch concept test. In this test, a black-and-white or color drawing is presented to consumers for their opinions. In choosing between a narrative concept test and a pictorial concept test, product planners should consider whether to show consumers what the product looks like or to have consumers attempt to visualize what the product would or should look like before being presented with a picture of the concept. Exhibit 6.2 shows a picture used in conjunction with the narrative description of the motorized bicycle.

The third type of test is a prototype concept test. Here the consumer is shown and possibly can handle a facsimile of the product and/or see a working prototype of the product. The consumer therefore witnesses the product firsthand. In the case of the motorized bicycle, customers were given a chance to ride a bicycle fitted with a motor, thus experiencing the concept directly.

The fourth type of test is a virtual reality concept test. In this test, the

---

Exhibit 6.1

Noncommercialized and Commercialized Concept Statements for a Motorized Bicycle Concept

Noncommercialized Concept Statement

This lightweight, durable, environmentally safe product will power your bicycle so you don't have to pedal. The product has a long-life rechargeable battery to travel significant distances. It can be easily attached to any standard bicycle. The price for the motor, battery, carrying case, and installation kit is $250.

Commercialized Concept Statement

Acme Bike Company, the recognized leader in bicycle manufacturing, has just developed a lightweight, durable, environmentally safe product that will power your bicycle so you don't have to pedal. The unique and revolutionary product has a long-life rechargeable battery to travel significant distances. It can be easily attached to any standard bicycle, so no worries. The price for the motor, battery, carrying case, and installation kit is a reasonable $250.

---

consumer views a computer image of the product and possibly interacts with the virtual prototype.

While there are four types of concept tests, product concepts are typically evaluated through a combination of these concept tests. For example, a concept test can be staged to observe consumers' evolving opinions as a result of being exposed first to a narrative text statement (narrative concept test), then to a picture (pictorial concept test), and finally to a working prototype (prototype concept test). Each subsequent test provides additional information that the consumer can process and respond to. As already mentioned, when choosing between a narrative concept test and a pictorial concept test, product planners will consider whether the concept test objective is to show customers how the product looks so that they can register an opinion or whether it would be beneficial to have customers attempt to visualize what the product would or should look like. The latter may be useful in designing an idealized version of the product according to consumer opinion.

Scoring Models

Scoring models comprise lists of criteria and associated rating scales that are generated by the team or established by the company. Each individual product concept is evaluated on the given criteria by using the given scale per criterion. Scores across the list of criteria are then summed to provide a total score per concept. Those concepts with higher scores are given priority over other concepts having lower scores.

Exhibit 6.2 **Pictorial Concept Test: Motorized Bicycle Concept**

A set of thirteen points of evaluative criteria is suggested by the Industrial Research Institute. The criteria include the following:

- cost to do
- likelihood of technical success
- profitability
- size of potential market
- development time
- fit with overall corporate objectives and strategies
- the firm's capability to market the product
- market trends and growth
- the firm's capability to manufacture the product
- market share expected
- patent status
- potential product liability
- capital investment required

Employing the simple five-point scale of "very weak on this criterion," "weak on this criterion," "meets this criterion," "strong on this criterion," and "very strong on this criterion," a set of new product concepts can be evaluated and compared using these criteria. Such an evaluation can be performed by a product development team or group of managers. Given the subjective nature of scoring product concepts, the use of multiple persons to evaluate concepts leads to a consensus approach for selecting promising new product concepts.

Exhibit 6.3 illustrates a scoring model applied to three new product concepts. As shown, concept A has the highest score (48) and would have priority over concepts B and C. Should enough funding be available to pursue two product development projects, concept C (with a score of 46) would be chosen over concept B (which has a score of 42).

If desired, the criteria in a scoring model can be weighted to emphasize issues critical to new product success. For example, assume that time-to-market and market potential are critical to new product success. Weighting these two criteria higher relative to the other criteria changes the previous scoring model's outcome. As shown in Exhibit 6.3, concept B has a weighted score of 3.57 and would be favored over the other two product concepts. Concept A with a weighted score of 3.51 would be favored over concept C, which has a weighted score of 3.20.

Various approaches can be used to determine criteria weights. One approach for determining a criterion's weight is managerial judgment; that is, managers decide which criteria will be given greater importance over other criteria. The derived weights in this case are very subjective in nature. A statistical approach is another way to calculate appropriate weights. Correlations or regression (e.g., multiple linear regression or logit regression) can be used to determine coefficients (weights) for each of the criteria by analyzing historical data of the scoring model scores and the project outcome (i.e., project success or project failure). Through the use of logit regression with project success and project failure as the dependent variable, the criteria important to success and failure would be identified. Assuming that a satisfactory regression model can be constructed, criteria weights would be derived from the standardized coefficients.

Snake Plots

Snake plots are an extension of the scoring model approach. For each product concept, the unweighted score per criterion is plotted. Plotting the scoring profiles of multiple product concepts allows a comparison regarding which profile is most reasonable or appealing. Typically, a favorable profile would be one that reflects higher scores uniformly across all the given criteria. A favorable profile also could be where a product concept reflects a higher score on certain desirable criteria. For example, Exhibit 6.4 shows a snake plot of

Exhibit 6.3

Scoring Model Example

Criteria	Concept A	Concept B	Concept C
Cost to do	4	2	4
Likelihood of technical success	4	3	3
Profitability	3	3	3
Size of potential market	3	3	2
Development time	3	5	2
Fit with overall corporate objectives and strategies	3	3	4
The firm's capability to market the product	4	5	5
Market trends and growth	4	3	4
The firm's capability to manufacture the product	4	3	3
Market share expected	5	3	5
Patent status	5	3	2
Potential product liability	3	3	4
Capital investment required	3	3	5
	48	42	46

| | If weighted criteria used . . . | | | | Weighted scores | | |
| | | Unweighted | | | Weighted | | |
Criteria	Weight (in percent)	Concept A	Concept B	Concept C	Concept A	Concept B	Concept C
Cost to do	5	4	2	4	0.200	0.100	0.200
Likelihood of technical success	5	4	3	3	0.200	0.150	0.150
Profitability	9	3	3	3	0.270	0.270	0.270
Size of potential market	15	3	3	2	0.450	0.450	0.300
Development time	22	3	5	2	0.660	1.100	0.440
Fit with overall corporate objectives and strategies	4	3	3	4	0.120	0.120	0.160
The firm's capability to market the product	9	4	5	5	0.360	0.450	0.450
Market trends and growth	5	4	3	4	0.200	0.150	0.200
The firm's capability to manufacture the product	5	4	3	3	0.200	0.150	0.150
Market share expected	7	5	3	5	0.350	0.210	0.350
Patent status	4	5	3	2	0.200	0.120	0.080
Potential product liability	5	3	3	4	0.150	0.150	0.200
Capital investment required	5	3	3	5	0.150	0.150	0.250
		48	42	46	3.51	3.57	3.20

Exhibit 6.4 **Snake Plot Example**

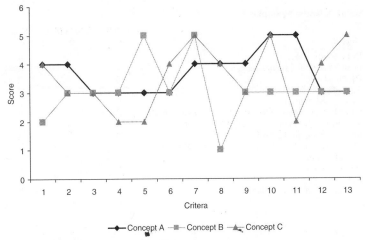

Source: Based on data in Exhibit 6.3.

the scoring data in Exhibit 6.3. As shown, concept A's profile is 3 or higher across all the given criteria, while concept B's profile only falls below a score of 3 once. If it was desired to at least meet all the given criteria and because a score of 3 represents "meets the given criterion," these snake plots indicate that concept A should be given the highest priority, followed by concept B.

Financial Analysis

Although early in the product development process, most upper managers will desire a financial analysis of a particular product concept to determine whether it will be a profitable venture. There are multiple ways to calculate financial impact. Two ways discussed below are the ATAR model and the ECV approach.

ATAR Model

A simple approach commonly used in the consumer packaged goods industry is the ATAR model. ATAR stands for awareness, trial, availability, and repeat purchase (Crawford and Di Benedetto 2003: Kahn 2006). As presented in Exhibit 6.5, the ATAR model begins with the potential target market size and uses the ATAR components to break down the target market size proportionally—this is why the ATAR model can be referred to as a breakdown model

Exhibit 6.5 **The ATAR Model**

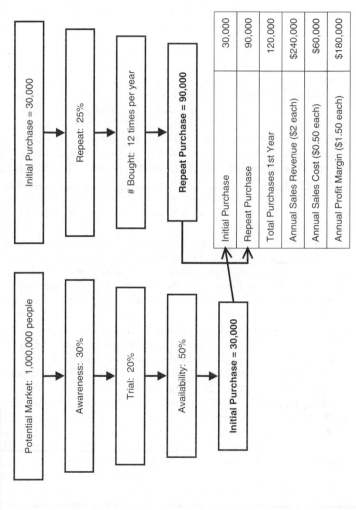

Potential Market: 1,000,000 people	
Awareness: 30%	
Trial: 20%	
Availability: 50%	
Initial Purchase = 30,000	

Initial Purchase = 30,000	
Repeat: 25%	
# Bought: 12 times per year	
Repeat Purchase = 90,000	

Initial Purchase	30,000
Repeat Purchase	90,000
Total Purchases 1st Year	120,000
Annual Sales Revenue ($2 each)	$240,000
Annual Sales Cost ($0.50 each)	$60,000
Annual Profit Margin ($1.50 each)	$180,000

approach. The awareness factor breaks down the potential target market size to suggest the magnitude of those who are aware of the new product. Those that are aware are then proportioned down to those who are aware and willing to try the new product. Those that are aware and willing to try the new product are proportioned down to those who are aware, willing to try, and able to get availability of the new product. At this point, potential target market × awareness × trial × availability provides an initial trial market size, assuming that customers buy only one trial. In other words, a model based on just potential target market × awareness × trial × availability provides an estimate of the likely sales jump due to customers becoming aware, deciding to try, and actively going out to buy the new product for the first time. Exhibit 6.5 illustrates a forecast for a new adult daily vitamin targeted to a city with an adult population of 1 million (total market size = 1,000,000). The proposed advertising and promotion plan will contact 30 percent of this population (awareness = 30 percent); market research suggests that approximately 20 percent of the aware adults will try the product (trial = 20 percent); and approximately half of the retailers in the city will provide shelf space for the new product (availability = 50 percent). Given these figures, the initial trial market size is 30,000 (1,000,000 × 30 percent awareness × 20 percent trial × 50 percent availability).

Adding the components of repeat and number bought per period estimates the expected repeat sales rate. The repeat purchase rate would represent the percent of those who are aware, willing to try, are able to get availability, who wish to buy again, and how much they would buy in a given period (e.g., month, quarter, year). This calculation is the total new product volume resulting from repeat purchases. Returning to the adult daily vitamin example in Exhibit 6.5, market research suggests that one out of four adults will continue to buy the vitamin (repeat purchase = 25 percent) and that a thirty-tablet bottle would be purchased monthly (# bottles bought per year = 12). The ATAR model calculates that an annual repeat rate of 90,000 (1,000,000 × 30 percent × 20 percent × 50 percent × 25 percent × 12).

Adding together the resulting figure from the initial trial market size model and the figure from the repeat rate market size model generates a total volume estimate for a new product during the given period (typically annually). For the adult daily vitamin example, first year unit sales would be 120,000 bottles, consisting of 30,000 bottles from trial sales and 90,000 bottles from repeat sales. Multiplying this unit sales number by the product price, cost, and/or profit margin converts this number to a financial figure. A per bottle price of $2 would result in annual sales revenue of $240,000; a per bottle cost of $0.50 would result in an annual sales cost of $60,000; and a profit margin of $1.50 per bottle would result in a profit of $180,000 (see Exhibit 6.5).

ATAR does not account for competition or R&D

Because the ATAR model does not factor in competition explicitly, the output of the ATAR model should be viewed as a total market potential estimate. One way to address competition is to add a proportional value to the ATAR model that estimates the company's market penetration rate (or market share). Including a market share or penetration rate reflects the fact that rarely does 100 percent of the market immediately buy a new product. For example, a market penetration rate of 20 percent in the case of the adult daily vitamin would suggest an annual sales level of 24,000 bottles sold per year. Multiplying this by the profit margin suggests a profit of $36,000 per year.

The ATAR model also does not account for research and development costs and/or other costs incurred in getting the product concept to market. To provide a more comprehensive financial analysis, the total cost of the project should be estimated by including such costs as development cost (e.g., hours, capital); prototype and pilot costs; manufacturing costs (tooling and scale-up), in addition to ongoing manufacturing cost; marketing costs (e.g., advertising, packaging, promotion); pricing; anticipated sales; and payback measures (e.g., return on investment, profit contribution, anticipated margin). Using the ATAR model to estimate revenue minus the estimated total cost of the project will estimate the profitability of the product concept. If the product development project should exceed a one-year time horizon, a net present value methodology should be used to estimate the profitability of the product concept.

Applying the ATAR Model to Other Business Contexts

The ATAR model is indicative of a breakdown or chain model approach because an aggregate market size number is broken down by interconnected proportions. It represents a class of models called assumptions-based models (see Kahn 2006) because each individual variable in the model derives from an assumption (an educated or even calculated estimate) about that individual variable, respectively. Assumption-based models are flexible frameworks that can be fashioned to serve varying market situations and industries besides consumer packaged goods.

For example, if the new product does not lend itself to frequent period repeat purchases, as in the case of automobiles, major home appliances, and industrial equipment, the repeat purchase rate and number bought components can be removed. The ATAR model also can be modified to meet specific characteristics of a given market—be it a final consumer market or a business-to-business market. Consider the example of a car theft deterrent device targeted to rental car agencies in a small metropolitan area. The following assumptions are made: there are 30,000 rental cars in the market

Exhibit 6.6   **ATAR Model Applied to a Business-to-Business Context**

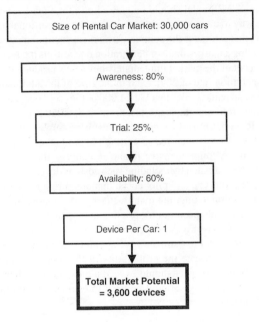

(total market size = 30,000), eight of the ten rental car companies will receive literature on the product (awareness = 80 percent), one out of four companies are expected to express an interest in trying the product (trial = 25 percent), 60 percent of those interested companies will be able to purchase equipment (availability = 60 percent), and only one device per car. Given these assumptions, the ATAR model suggests a total market potential of 3,600 units sold. If a penetration rate of 10 percent were achieved, only 360 devices would be sold on an annual basis (see Exhibit 6.6).

In accordance with the nature of any assumptions-based model, components of the ATAR model can be modified to align with key assumptions common to a particular industry. Thomas (1994) presents a variation of the ATAR model in the course of forecasting high-definition television sales. The model comprises the components of population, technology acceptance, awareness, availability, and intention-to-buy in order to estimate market potential. In the pharmaceutical industry, a common model to estimate the potential target market size is to start with the population size having a particular medical condition. This population number is multiplied by the proportion of those who get diagnosed, then multiplied by the proportion of those who receive a prescription for a given brand, then multiplied by the proportion of those who actually fulfill their prescription, and then multiplied by channel availability (see Exhibit 6.7).

Assumptions-based models are very sensitive to the percentages inputted in the model. Because of this, companies usually evaluate a range of possible percentages for a given assumption that correspond to pessimistic, likely, and optimistic cases, versus fixating on one specific percentage. Evaluating a range of input allows for a better understanding of the variability surrounding each component of the assumptions-based model and how fluctuations in each component might influence the overall market estimate. This is called sensitivity analysis. For example, a sensitivity analysis of the components in the previously discussed vitamin product could be conducted. Focusing on the awareness component, the possible range for awareness is suggested to fall between 25 percent (pessimistic case) and 35 percent (optimistic case), with the original number of 30 percent (likely or base case) within this range. Should awareness be really 25 percent, then overall sales (trial plus repeat sales) will be 100,000 bottles, versus the original number of 120,000. Should awareness be really 35 percent, overall sales would be 140,000 bottles. Exhibit 6.8 presents the data of this sensitivity analysis on awareness (the other ATAR components could be similarly examined). The consequences of going to lower and higher ranges on each of the assumptions would need to be discussed and addressed. For more information on sensitivity analysis and assumptions-based models see Kahn (2006).

Expected Commercial Value Approach

A deterministic approach akin to the ATAR model or a strict net present value approach may unfairly penalize certain types of new product concepts. The net present value approach does not specifically take into consideration various options that may arise during a product concept's development. A probabilistic approach can be employed to evaluate product concepts as part of a company's portfolio management process (Cooper, Edgett, and Kleinshmidt 1998). The specific approach to be discussed calculates the expected commercial value (ECV) of a particular product concept using a decision tree methodology. This methodology incorporates the probability of technical success and the probability of commercial success to estimate the overall expected commercial worth of a particular product concept. The formula is: $ECV = [(NPV \times P_{cs} - C) \times P_{ts} - D]$, where ECV is the expected commercial value of the product concept, NPV is the net present value of the product concept's future earnings discounted to the present, P_{cs} is the probability of commercial success (given

$$ECV = [(NPV \times P_{cs} - C) \times P_{ts} - D]$$

Exhibit 6.7   **Assumptions-Based Model Applied to the Pharmaceuticals Marketplace**

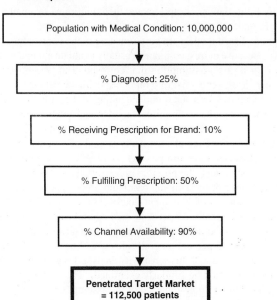

technical success), *C* is commercialization costs, P_{ts} is the probability of technical success, and *D* is development costs (remaining in the project). Exhibit 6.9 illustrates this formula via the decision tree framework. The formula can be modified to reflect more than the two given decision points (technical success and commercial success) if a more detailed analysis is desired.

Exhibit 6.10 also provides a numerical example to illustrate the ECV approach. Product concepts A, B, and C are considered. As shown, product concept C reflects the highest ECV ($7.9 million), even though it does not have the highest NPV. This illustrates how the probabilities of technical success and commercial success can impact the consideration of product concepts. In fact, product concept B, which had the highest NPV, reflected the lowest ECV.

The ECV approach is very much predicated on estimates for probabilities of technical success and commercial success; inaccurate estimates of these probabilities will lead to an erroneous ECV calculation. Cooper, Edgett, and Kleinschmidt (1998) recommend four approaches for calculating these probabilities: (1) Delphi consensus approach, (2) matrix approach, (3) scoring model, and/or (4) NewProd model. The Delphi consensus approach consists

Exhibit 6.8

Sensitivity Analysis Example

	Market size	Awareness	Trial	Availability	Repeat	# Bought		Unit sales	Sales revenue
Trial model	$1,000,000	30%	20%	50%				30,000	$60,000
Repeat model	$1,000,000	30%	20%	50%	25%	12		90,000	$180,000
							Total	120,000	$240,000
								Price	$2.00

Assumptions Range for Awareness

	Pessimistic		Likely		Optimistic
Awareness	0.25		0.3		0.35

Sensitivity Analysis on Awareness

	Pessimistic		Base		Optimistic
Awareness	100,000		120,000		140,000

Exhibit 6.9 **The ECV Decision Tree Framework**

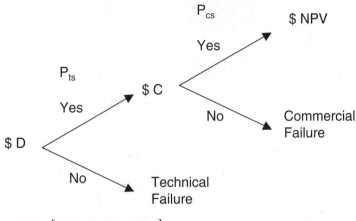

$$\$ECV = \left[(NPV \times P_{cs} - C) \times P_{ts} - D\right]$$

where $ECV = expected commercial value of the product concept
  $NPV = net present value of the product concept's future earnings
  P_{cs} = probability of commercial success
  $C = commercialization (launch) costs
  P_{ts} = probability of technical success
  $D = development costs remaining in the project

Source: Adapted from Cooper, Edgett, and Kleinschmidt (1998).

of each manager anonymously submitting probability estimates, which are then compiled and presented back to each of the managers. Discussion about the numbers usually will take place if there are significant differences across the estimates, followed by subsequent rounds of anonymously submitting probability estimates. The process ends when consensus on the numbers is reached.

The matrix approach consists of documentation in two-dimensional matrices, which specify probability of technical success across different scenarios and probability of commercial success across different scenarios. Such probabilities, which are calculated from company experience and intuition, serve as standards to be used by all product development projects in the company. Exhibit 6.11 shows an example of the matrix approach.

The scoring model approach is a more detailed version of the previous matrix approach. As previously discussed, a scoring model comprising key criteria will be given. In this case, the scores across these criteria are summed

Exhibit 6.10

An Example of the ECV Approach

Product concept	$NPV	P_{ts}	P_{cs}	$D	$C	$ECV
A	30	0.8	0.5	3	4	5.8
B	45	0.5	0.4	5	4	2
C	35	0.7	0.6	4	4	7.9

$$ECV = [(NPV \times P_{cs} - C) \times P_{ts} - D]$$

where ECV = expected commercial value of the product concept
   NPV = net present value of the product concept's future earnings
   P_{cs} = probability of commercial success
   C = commercialization (launch) costs
   P_{ts} = probability of technical success
   D = development costs remaining in the project

and compared to a given standard score to indicate the probabilities for technical success and commercial success.

The last approach, NewProd, is a proprietary model developed by Dr. Robert Cooper (1993). The model is an empirically based computer model that is customized to a company's situation. Responses from a team of company representatives answering a series of thirty questions are inputted into the NewProd computer model; these data are compared to profiles within the model, and then a prediction of success or failure is given.

When using any of the above approaches for estimating probabilities, it must be realized that any derived probability is an estimate and so inaccuracy is expected. Still, a systematic approach to estimating a probability should lead to a better estimate versus a guess. Indeed, very seldom can one assume that any new product concept has a 100 percent chance of technical success and 100 percent chance of commercial success. The use of probabilities in evaluating new product concepts is an attempt at getting a more realistic perspective and a better prioritization of new product concepts.

Summary

The goal of the concept generation stage is to select a promising set of product concepts that can be further developed. Typically, the final concepts are elaborated in what is called a product protocol—this is discussed at the beginning of the next chapter. The product protocol is used to direct the technical development stage, which is where mostly intangible concepts become tangible and ever closer to eventual launch. As for those concepts that did not successfully

Exhibit 6.11

The Use of Scoring Models for Determining Probabilities of Commercial and Technical Success

Matrix for Commercial Success Probabilities

Market type	Probability scores			
Current	0.5	0.6	0.85	0.95
New to the company	0.1	0.2	0.5	0.7
New to the world	0.05	0.05	0.1	0.2
	Low	Moderate	High	Very high
	Competitive advantage			

Definitions
Low competitive advantage = Me-too or catch-up product; minor cost reduction; benefits cannot overcome significant switching costs
Moderate competitive advantage = Benefit seen as marginally great enough to switch in absence of other factors
High competitive advantage = Benefit perceived to justify switching costs in the context of all competing demands
Very high competitive advantage = Enabling benefit that opens significant new business opportunities for the customer

Matrix for Technical Success Probabilities

Likelihood that the process will work successfully	Probability scores				
Very high	0.2	0.5	0.75	0.9	0.95
High	0.15	0.4	0.65	0.8	0.9
Moderate	0.15	0.3	0.5	0.65	0.75
Low	0.1	0.2	0.3	0.4	0.5
Very low	0.05	0.1	0.15	0.15	0.2
	Very low	Low	Moderate	High	Very high
	Likelihood that the product will work successfully				

Definitions
Very high = Solution already demonstrated; need only final engineering; repackage
High = Prototype in hand demonstrating all necessary characteristics, but need to optimize performance
Moderate = Prototype not yet in hand, but good lead within current technology; experts believe that this can be done
Low = Technology route/lead not well established; scouting work to be done; experts think this probably can be done with available technology
Very low = Probably beyond current technology or do not know how to approach; need to import new technology

Source: Adapted from Cooper, Edgett, and Kleinschmidt (1998).

traverse the concept evaluation phase, better companies typically place these concepts into the idea bank, where they can be accessed for use as background information in the future should a similar concept arise.

Discussion Questions

1. What are the four types of concept testing?
2. What is the difference between a commercialized and noncommercialized concept statement?
3. What is a scoring model?
4. What is a snake plot?
5. What are the components of the ATAR model?
6. What are the components of the ECV model?

References

Cooper, Robert G. 1993. *Winning at New Products: Accelerating the Process from Idea to Launch*. 2nd ed. Reading, MA: Addison-Wesley.

Cooper, Robert G., Scott J. Edgett, and Elko J. Kleinschmidt. 1998. *Portfolio Management for New Products*. Reading, MA: Addison-Wesley.

Crawford, C. Merle. 1997. *New Products Management*. 5th ed. Boston: Irwin.

Crawford, Merle, and Anthony Di Benedetto. 2003. *New Products Management*. 7th ed. Boston: McGraw-Hill/Irwin.

Kahn, Kenneth B. 2006. *New Product Forecasting: An Applied Approach*. Armonk, NY: M.E. Sharpe.

Lees, Gavin, and Malcolm Wright. 2004. "The Effect of Concept Formulation on Concept Test Scores." *Journal of Product Innovation Management*, 21 (6), 389–400.

Peng, Ling, and Adam Finn. 2008. "Concept Testing: The State of Contemporary Practice." *Marketing Intelligence & Planning*, 26 (6), 649–674.

Thomas, Robert J. 2004. *New Product Development: Managing and Forecasting for Strategic Success*. New York: John Wiley.

7 ✕ Technical Development

The technical development stage represents the point in the product development process at which a tangible new product emerges or where the specifics of a service to be delivered are determined. Although characterized as a single stage, multiple sets of activities and substages may be conducted within the technical development stage. This chapter highlights engineering-related tasks in the technical development stage.

The Product Protocol

In most cases, some version of a product protocol is employed to drive all activities in the technical development stage. A product protocol would be constructed for a particular product concept after it has been selected for continued development. Construction of the product protocol may occur at the end of the concept generation stage after concept evaluation or at the beginning of the technical development stage. In either case, the product protocol is an important guiding document because it specifies what should be ultimately "developed" in order to match what was initially intended to be developed.

By definition, a protocol is a signed document containing a record of the points on which agreement has been reached by negotiating parties. A product protocol identifies the points of agreement between all departments and senior management on the product specifications and deliverables (not all deliverables can be known, but critical deliverables are assumed to be known). The product protocol communicates essentials to all team members and lays out what each department will provide in order to deliver the final product to the "customer." The product protocol also establishes clear boundaries for managing development cycle time and provides definitions of product success so that proper measures or metrics can be used.

One approach to constructing a product protocol is to address twelve distinct elements in twelve distinct paragraphs or sections (Crawford 1997). The recommended twelve elements are:

1. *Target market:* who the intended purchaser is of the product.
2. *Product positioning:* how the product is to be positioned in the market relative to existing company offerings and competitor offerings.
3. *Product attributes:* what technology and form the product will have by way of specific product functions and features. Attributes are typically viewed by the development staff as product specifications: a precise description of what the product has to do. This description is typically technical in nature, comprising a metric and a target value. The metric represents a specific function or feature to be built into the product and the target value represents the boundary conditions for building that function or feature into the product. Using a laptop as an example, "weight" would be a metric and "no more than three pounds" would be the value. There are various ways to find target values: customer opinion; internal research, judgment, and experimentation; and competitive benchmarking. It also should be recognized that specifications are established at least twice. As Ulrich and Eppinger (1995) suggest, there are initial target specifications and refined target specifications. Generally, there are five ways in which to set target values for metrics:

   - *At least X:* These specifications establish targets for the lower bound on a metric, with high values being the goal. Example: the range for a new electric car (metric) must be at least fifty miles (target value).
   - *At most X:* These specifications establish targets for the upper bound on a metric, with small values being the goal. Example: the weight of a new cellular phone (metric) can be no more than eight ounces (target value).
   - *Between X and Y:* These specifications establish both upper and lower bounds for the value of the metric. Example: the page count for a new book (metric) can range from 200 to 250 pages (target value).
   - *Exactly X:* These specifications establish a target of a particular value of a metric, with any deviation degrading performance. Example: the duration of a new movie (metric) must be ninety minutes (target value).
   - *A set of discrete values:* Some metrics will have values corresponding to several discrete choices. Example: case sizes for a new beverage product (metric) can come in counts of six or twelve (target value).
4. *Competitive comparisons:* what competitors are currently doing.
5. *Augmentation dimensions:* how the product is to be differentiated; what the product's competitive advantage is.

6. *Timing:* what the product development schedule is; what dates need to be met.

7. *Marketing requirements:* any special marketing issues.

8. *Financial requirements:* any special financial issues.

9. *Production requirements:* any special production issues.

10. *Regulatory requirements:* any special regulatory or legal considerations.

11. *Corporate strategy requirements:* what core competencies are to be emphasized in developing the product.

12. *Potholes:* any foreseeable problems in developing this product.

Exhibit 7.1 shows a sample product protocol for a trash disposal and recycling system that targets home use.

Themes Underlying "Design for Excellence" Engineering

One of the prevalent themes underlying engineering-related activities during the technical development stage is "design for excellence" (DFX). DFX represents a philosophy in which careful consideration is given to cost-effective operations, distribution, installation, service, and customer use of the product. Bralla (1996, 22–23) defines DFX as "a knowledge-based approach that attempts to design products that maximize all desirable characteristics—such as high quality, reliability, serviceability, safety, user friendliness, environmental friendliness, and time-to-market—in a product design, while at the same time, minimizing lifetime costs, including manufacturing costs." DFX should therefore be recognized as a philosophy that underlies not only engineering-related activities during the technical development stage, but also all departmental activities (engineering departments plus all other departments) throughout the entire product development process.

Below are themes inherent in the DFX philosophy.

1. *Ensure that the product performs in the way it is intended.*

2. *Design the product to protect consumers and society in general from harm when the product is used.* Bralla (1996) offers the following guidelines to ensure product safety:

- Design products to be fail-safe.
- Allow for human error.
- Avoid sharp corners.
- Do not design parts with unguarded projections that can catch body members or clothing.
- Provide guards or covers over sharp blades and similar elements.

Exhibit 7.1

Example of a Product Protocol

Sample Product Protocol for a Trash Disposal and Recycling System for Home Use

1. Target Market:
   - Ultimate: Top 30 percent of income group in cities of over 100,000 with upscale lifestyle.
   - Intermediate: Stakeholders in building industry for homes over $300,000, especially developers, architects, builders, bankers, and regulators.

2. Product Positioning:
   - A convenient, mess-free method for recycling items in the home.

3. Product Attributes:
   - The system must automate trash disposal in a home environment with recycling (separating trash, compacting, placing bags outside, rebagging empty bins, and notifying user when the bag supply is running low) at a factory cost not to exceed $800.
   - The system must be clean, ventilated, and odor-free. The user will want an easy-to-use appliance. Rodents, pets, and angry neighbors could become a problem if odors exist.
   - Installation must be simple. Distributors and other installation personnel must have favorable experience in installations.
   - The system must be safe enough for operation by children of school age.
   - The entire working unit must not be larger than twice a 22-cubic-foot refrigerator.

4. Competitive Comparisons:
   - None—first of its kind.

5. Augmentation Dimensions:
   - Financing will be available.
   - Generous warranty.
   - Competent installation service, and fast, competent post-installation service.
   - Education about recycling and about the product will be essential.

6. Timing:
   - Being right overrides getting to market fast. However, window will not be open for more than two years.

7. Marketing Requirements:
   - Marketing announcement must be made at national builders' shows and environmental shows
   - A new channel structure will be needed for the intermediate target market, but it will eventually collapse into the regular channel.
   - Small, select sales force will be needed for introduction.
   - To capitalize on announcement value, fifty installations during the first four months are needed.

(continued)

Exhibit 7.1 *(continued)*

8. Financial Requirements:
   - Development and intro period losses cannot exceed $20,000,000. Break-even is expected by end of second year on the market.
   - The project must achieve a five year net present value of zero, based on a 35 percent cost of capital.

9. Production Requirements:
   - Once the product is launched, there must be no interruptions of supply.
   - Quality standards must be met without exceptions.

10. Regulatory Requirements:
    - Regulations are from many sources and vary by states and localities.
    - There are multiple stakeholders. A clear understanding of each stakeholder and their role is needed.

11. Corporate Strategy Requirements:
    - Corporate strategy is driving this project, and upper management is committed to this project.
    - The company seeks a diversification of markets, enhanced reputation for innovativeness, and sustainable margins higher than those in current markets.

12. Potholes:
    - This project has massive pothole potential because of its newness. There is concern regarding (1) regulatory approval, (2) accomplishing the $800 cost constraint, and (3) getting fast market acceptance for early installations.

Source: Crawford (1997).

- Make sure repair, service, and maintenance pose no safety hazards.
- Provide clearances between moving parts and other elements to avoid shearing or crushing points in which hands or other parts of the operator's body might be caught or injured.
- Arrange controls so that the operator does not have to stand or reach them in an unnatural, awkward position.
- Anticipate the environment in which the product will be used and provide safeguards against those environmental factors that could create safety hazards.
- Ground electrical products properly.
- Utilize electrical interlocks in circuits with potentially injurious voltage so that unless a guard is in proper position the circuit is open and no current will flow.
- Make small components bulky enough so that they cannot be accidentally swallowed by children.
- Make the product from high-impact or resilient materials so that if the product is dropped or otherwise broken, neither sharp edges, sharp points,

nor small fragments that are potentially swallowable by small children will result.

- Give special attention to the strength of all parts whose failure might result in injury to the operator.
- Do not use paints or other finishing materials with more than 6 percent content of heavy metals.
- Incorporate warning devices that become actuated if any hazardous materials in the product are released or if dangerous components are exposed.
- Make sure point-of-operation guards are convenient and do not interfere with the operator's movement or affect the output of the product.
- Check that plastic bags used in packaging are not too thin.
- Minimize, as much as possible, the use of flammable materials, including packaging material.
- Eliminate cuts from paper edges by serrating edges.
- Make markings, especially those for safety warnings, very clear, concise, and long-lasting.
- Avoid the use of hazardous materials, including those that may become a hazard when burned, recycled, or discarded.
- Develop products that do not require heavy or prolonged operation in order to avoid the kinds of user actions that can lead to cumulative trauma disorders like carpal tunnel syndrome.

3. *The product should have quality and be perceived as having quality.* This recognizes that quality is both objective and perceived. Often a product's commercial success is predicated on the customer's perception of quality. Thus, product planners should view quality as whatever it is judged to be by customers. To do this, customer surveys can be used to investigate customer satisfaction with the product and postsales service. Objective quality is predominantly an internal measure of quality and more product-focused and cost-focused. Minimizing design costs and production costs are indicative of internal company quality.

Company quality initiatives often reflect a total quality management (TQM) program. Such a program stresses that quality must be designed into the product rather than tested for at the end of the production process. TQM guidelines include:

- A strong orientation toward the customer in matters of quality.
- Emphasis on quality as a total commitment for all employees of all functions at all levels in the organization.
- A striving for error-free production.

- Use of statistical quality control data and other factual methods rather than intuition to control quality.
- Prevention of product defects rather than reaction after they occur.
- Continuous improvement.

4. *The product should be reliable.* Although related to quality, reliability is defined as "the probability that a product will perform satisfactorily for a specified period of time under a stated set of conditions" (Bralla 1996, 165). Explicit in this definition are the notions that reliability is probabilistic in nature, predicated on satisfactory performance, time-based, and bounded by specific operating conditions. It is probabilistic in nature because it is usually expressed as a fraction or percentage showing the likelihood that a product, a product component, or a product subcomponent will successfully operate over a given period of time. Determining what is successful operation corresponds to the notion of satisfactory performance. Thus, in order to assess reliability, it is necessary to establish what indicates satisfactory (successful) performance. The time factor is critical to the notion of reliability in order to assess the probability that the product (and its components and subcomponents) can last that long. Time also is typically used to translate reliability into observable measures like mean time to failure and mean time between failures. Using a time factor, reliability can be plotted to create a failure-rate curve, also referred to as the bathtub curve. This curve illustrates a higher rate of initial failures during the "debugging" stage; a lower, constant rate during the product's expected life; and an increasing rate of failures at the end of the product's life during the "wearout" stage (see Exhibit 7.2). Naturally, specific operating conditions like temperature, humidity, and vibration when a product is functioning, stored, and transported will affect what the failure-rate curve looks like, and thus, consideration to operating conditions is necessary to evaluate reliability.

5. *The product should be designed to account for manufacturing issues and to minimize manufacturing problems, manufacturing cycle time, and manufacturing costs.* To do this, various programs can be employed including design for assembly (DFA), design for manufacturability (DFM), design for manufacturability and assembly, group technology, and synchronized manufacturing.

Two themes of DFM are that (1) maximum savings occur when a part is eliminated or combined with another, rather than just being simplified; and (2) final product assembly often is a high labor cost in a typical cost structure and that assembly support is a high overhead item. These two themes pervade the following design for manufacturability recommendations:

114

Exhibit 7.2 **Failure Rate Curve**

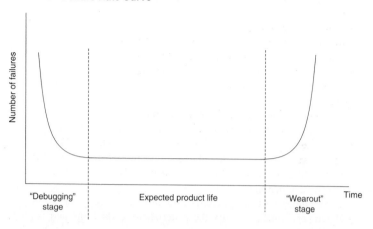

Note: Failure rates are high initially, usually due to manufacturing defects; then they level off to a low rate until the third stage, when components begin to wear out.

- Minimize the number of parts, or if possible, eliminate parts, especially fasteners.
- Attempt to use plastics to provide snap fits and combine parts that would be otherwise separate.
- Use parts such as integral hinges, springs, cams, and bearings.
- Attempt to eliminate steps requiring machining operations.
- Standardize parts.
- Use processible materials.
- Fit the product design to the present manufacturing process.
- Design each part to be easy to make.
- Design for the expected production quantity.
- Design parts so that they fit together easily.
- Minimize the number of production equipment adjustments that have to be made.

6. *The product should be designed to minimize its impact on the environment as a result of pollutants, disposal, and so on.* Bralla (1996) offers the following guidelines for environmental friendliness:

- Avoid as much as possible the use of toxic materials in the product and its manufacturing process.

- Design the product and its components to be reusable, refurbishable, or recyclable.
- Minimize the number of parts.
- Minimize the amount of material in the product.
- Avoid the use of separate fasteners, if possible.
- Use the fewest possible number of fasteners.
- Design the product to be easily disassembled, even if some parts are corroded.
- Minimize the number of different materials in a product.
- Choose materials that are compatible so they can be recycled together.
- Avoid the use of composite materials like metal-reinforced plastics.
- Standardize components to aid in eventual refurbishing of products.
- Use molded-in nomenclature rather than labels or separate nameplates for product identification.
- Use modular designs to simplify assembly and disassembly.
- Wherever feasible, identify the material from which the part is made right on the part.
- Make separation points between parts as clearly visible as possible so that disassembly and recycling are made easier.
- Avoid designs that require spray-painted finishes.
- Provide predetermined break areas, if needed, to allow easy separation of fasteners that may be incompatible with the recycling stream.
- Use a woven-metal mesh (which is more likely to be recyclable) instead of metal-filled material for welding thermoplastics.
- Design the product to utilize recycled materials from other sources.

7. *The product should be designed so that if returned for service, such service can be enacted easily, quickly, and efficiently.* Such service includes repair and regular maintenance. Bralla's (1996) guidelines for serviceability include:

- Increase the reliability of the overall product to reduce service requirements.
- Design the product so that components that will require periodic maintenance and those prone to wear or failure are easily visible and accessible.
- Design all high-mortality parts, or those that need replacement or removal for service to other parts, for easy detachment and replacement (e.g., with quick disconnects or snap fits for quick disassembly).
- Design high-mortality parts so that they can be replaced without removing other parts or disturbing their adjustment.
- Design with field replacement in mind.

- When tools are required, use standard, commonly available tools.
- Consider the use of modules—assemblies containing all components needed for a particular function—which are easily replaced when necessary and easily tested to verify their operability. A module is a group of components and subassemblies performing a particular function and packaged together in a self-contained unit so that they can be installed or replaced as one unit at the same time.
- Design the product for easy testability:
  — As much as possible, design the product and its components so that tests can be made with standard instruments.
  — Incorporate built-in test capability and, if possible, built-in self-testing devices in the product.
  — Make the tests themselves easy and standardized, capable of being performed in the field.
  — Provide accessibility for test probes (e.g., prominent test points or access holes).
  — Make modules testable while still assembled to the product.
- Use standard commercial parts as much as possible to further ensure their interchangeability and to simplify the problem of field stocking of replacement parts.
- Provide malfunction annunciation—that is, design the product with indicators that inform the operator that the equipment is malfunctioning and indicate which component is malfunctioning.
- Make sure that parts that may require replacement during service are clearly identified with part numbers or other essential reference designations.
- Design replacements parts to prevent their incorrect insertion during maintenance.
- Design for fault isolation.
- Utilize the minimum number of screw head types and sizes used in fasteners or portions of the product.
- Provide anticipated spare parts with the product.
- When access covers are not removable, make sure they are self-supporting when open.
- Make sure repair, service, and maintenance tasks pose no safety hazards, such as sharp corners or burrs.
- Incorporate automatic timing or counting devices in the product to signal the need for replacement of high wear or depletable parts.
- Provide clear and complete preventive maintenance manuals or instructions as part of the engineering specifications for the product.
- Provide room for drainage of fluids that must be periodically changed; make sure drainage plugs are accessible.

- Ensure that components that are apt to be replaced or are adjacent to those that are, are not too fragile.

8. *The product should be designed with the user in mind, including considerations relating to understanding how to properly install and operate the product.* Bralla's (1996) guidelines for user friendliness include:

- Fit the product to the user's physical attributes and knowledge.
- Simplify the structure of the user's tasks.
- Make the controls and their functions obvious.
- Use mappings so that the operator understands what the controls do.
- Utilize constraints to prevent incorrect actions.
- Provide user feedback.
- Display operating information clearly.
- Make controls easy to handle.
- Anticipate human errors.
- Avoid awkward and extreme motions for the user.
- Standardize arrangements and systems.

9. *The product should be appealing to customers and users.* Product planners must realize that sometimes the customer and the user are distinct and that different aspects of the product might appeal to each party. The classic example is diapers, where the customer is the parent and the user is the baby. Considerations of price and absorbability may be important to parents, while the feel of the diaper may be the most important to the baby. Both considerations are deserving and therefore necessary.

10. *Product accessories, attachments, and peripheral functions of the product should be given careful consideration.* Particular effort should be made to avoid extraneous accessories, attachments, or peripheral functions, which unnecessarily increase product price and may make the product more difficult to use (Nussbaum and Neff 1991).

11. *Product development speed is crucial.* Efforts to minimize design, tool-up, and manufacturing of the product should be given top consideration. Bralla's (1996) guidelines for minimizing time-to-market include:

- Use standard components rather than ones specially designed for the application.
- Use standard and existing systems, procedures, and materials.
- Use modules, especially if they are from existing products.

- Do not redesign more than necessary.
- Design conservatively.
- Design to do it right the first time.
- Design for processes that do not require long tooling lead times or could be completed with standard available tooling.

Key Techniques to Aid Technical Development:
Quality Function Deployment

To facilitate DFX activities, various computer systems exist. These include computer-aided design (CAD), computer-aided manufacturing, and computer-aided engineering. Another emerging technology is stereolithography, which is a computer-based system that takes a CAD drawing of a discrete part, translates it, and creates a three-dimensional prototype by guiding a laser through a resin material that hardens into the part. Stereolithography and other related technologies represent key technologies for rapid prototyping.

Another popular technique used in conjunction with DFX is quality function deployment (QFD). Developed in the 1960s for use in Japan's Kobe shipyards, QFD was later adopted by the Japanese and U.S. automobile industries and even later adopted by other industries. The attractive objective of the QFD methodology is that it purposely links customer needs with technical specifications in an attempt to create an "optimal" product configuration.

The original QFD methodology comprises four stages of evaluation, beginning at a top level with the linkage between customer benefits sought and product specifications. The next three levels detail product specifications down to the level of parts specifications and further down to the level of manufacturing process specifications (see Exhibit 7.3). In most cases, companies have found that managing the QFD process across these four levels is extremely complex and time-consuming. Thus, most companies find the most expeditious approach is to focus on the top level of evaluation, which links customer benefits sought to product specifications (technical specifications). This level is commonly referred to as the "House of Quality" (Hauser and Clausing 1988).

The "House of Quality" illustrates the relationships between the "voice of the customer" (VOC) and the "voice of the engineer" (VOE), where VOC emphasizes product benefits—that is, what the customer wants to get out of using the product—and VOE delineates the technical characteristics of the product. The relationships are shown in a matrix where the VOC is located in the rows of the matrix and the VOE is located in the columns (see Exhibit 7.4). For example, a customer describing a pencil may state that it should not

Exhibit 7.3 **The Four Stages of Quality Function Deployment**

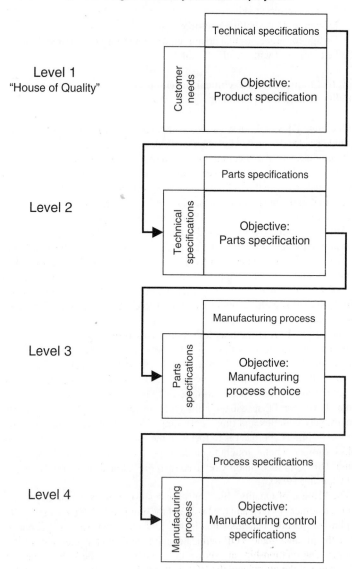

Level 1
"House of Quality"

Technical specifications

Customer needs

Objective:
Product specification

Level 2

Parts specifications

Technical specifications

Objective:
Parts specification

Level 3

Manufacturing process

Parts specifications

Objective:
Manufacturing
process choice

Level 4

Process specifications

Manufacturing process

Objective:
Manufacturing control
specifications

easily roll when placed on a hard surface, while an engineer would consider pencil hexagonality (a typical customer would not use the term "hexagonality"). The matrix indicates a strong relationship between these two issues and that hexagonality should be a design priority in order to reduce the roll of a pencil.

Customer information is collected through VOC studies. Each VOC study collects three important pieces of information: (1) the customer needs or benefits sought, (2) the importance of each of these needs or benefits relative to each other, and (3) evaluations of the company's and competitors' current offerings in satisfying these needs or benefits. For many companies, the VOC study in itself provides an ample amount of information. Consequently, a company may choose not to perform a full QFD analysis, but rather analyze the ample amount of data collected during the VOC study to clarify what specific needs or benefits the customers seek. This information is then used to frame the product's technical specifications. Other companies take the next step by attempting to match VOC data with technical data, thereby applying QFD methodology.

VOE data represent the specific technical characteristics (technical specifications) of the product. Such characteristics may derive from the product protocol or correspond to those characteristics that can be readily tested. In addition to specifying technical characteristics, VOE data will indicate a desired course of action for each respective characteristic in terms of reducing or increasing the magnitude of this characteristic. For example, the engineering team for a new car in specifying the technical characteristic of weight may indicate a desire to reduce weight. The third element of VOE data is specifying the relationships between the various technical characteristics—for example, how would reducing the car's weight affect wind resistance? These relationships are specified in a matrix above the technical characteristics called the "trade-off roof." Both negative and positive correlations between the technical specifications would be indicated. A fourth possible element that may be included in VOE data is benchmark data comparing the company's product with competitors' products on the given technical characteristics. Such data would provide quantitative benchmarks on each of the technical characteristics.

Exhibit 7.4 illustrates the QFD methodology in the case of a pencil. Customer needs (VOC data) are listed on the rows, and technical specifications (VOE data) are given in the columns. Four customer needs are specified: easy to hold, does not smear, point lasts, and does not roll. The importance of each of these needs is rated on a five-point scale, where 1 is "not important" and 5 is "very important," in the column following the technical specifications. The needs are also evaluated across the company's and its top competitors' products using a five-point scale, where 1 is "very weak on this need" and

Exhibit 7.4 The "House of Quality" Matrix

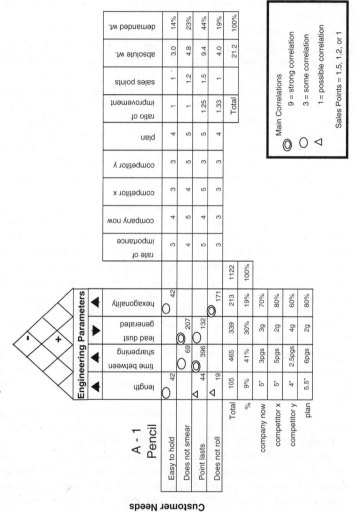

5 is "very strong on this need." As shown, "point lasts" is the most important need (rated 5 in importance); the company is evaluated as being below competitor X but above competitor Y on this need. The column after the competitor evaluation data is headed "plan." The plan represents what the company wants customers to perceive; the plan is therefore a management decision. The next column, "ratio of improvement," is the calculation of "plan" divided by the company now. As shown in Exhibit 7.4, the company scored a 4 on "point lasts" and has set a plan of 5, which calculates a 1.25 (or 5/4) ratio of improvement. This can be interpreted as meaning that the company wants to improve perceptions of "point lasts" by 25 percent (note that a ratio of 1 would represent 0 percent or no change). Sales points are incremental bumps to particular needs that management or the sales force sees as necessary to create a competitive advantage. Three sales points are possible: a score of 1 (no bump), a score of 1.2 (slight bump), or a score of 1.5 (bump). Absolute weight is calculated by multiplying the rate of importance by the ratio of improvement by the sales points. "Point lasts" has an absolute weight of 9.4 ($5 \times 1.25 \times 1.5$). The total absolute weight is the sum of the absolute weights for easy to hold, does not smear, point lasts, and does not roll, which is 21.2. Demanded weight is a relative percentage, calculated by dividing the absolute weight for each row by the total absolute weight. For example, the demanded weight for "point lasts" is 9.4 divided by 21.2, which is .44 or 44 percent. The use of demanded weight allows for the interpretation that 44 percent of product demand is based on the point lasting. Note that some QFD methodologies prefer not to use the sales point system as some product planners believe only the customer should dictate how needs are weighted. The sales point system is used in the present example because it can be used to emphasize needs that might become more important in the future (as will be discussed later). The series of calculations via a QFD provides a way of prioritizing customer needs, which can be clearly presented to engineering. In certain situations, the prioritizing of customer needs is sufficient to drive technical development, and this is why many companies do not apply the full QFD methodology.

Following the prioritizing of customer needs, the relationships between each of the customer needs and technical characteristics are examined. In most cases, an intense discussion ensues between marketing and engineering personnel to clarify these relationships. This highlights the key benefit of QFD as a tool for facilitating interdepartmental communication. Assuming that consensus is reached, which often takes time, the correlations between the respective need and characteristic are listed. In the given example, three types of correlations can be listed: a weak correlation, which is given the weight of 1; some correlation, which is given the weight of 3; and a strong correlation, which is given the weight of 9. Using these weights, the relationships between each customer need and technical specification can be weighted accordingly by multiplying the weight of the relationship by the demanded weight for the respective customer need. For example, the relationship between "point lasts" and "time between sharpenings" is indicated to be a strong correlation, which is a weight of 9. Multiplying this weight by "point lasts" demand weight of 44 percent equals a score of 396. Completing calculations across the cells and then totaling the columns provide a total score for each technical specification. Calculating the relative percentage of each column to the sum of the column scores suggests how much demand is predicated on each respective technical characteristic. As shown in Exhibit 7.4, "time between sharpenings" has a score of 465, which represents 41 percent of the total score. This can be loosely interpreted as suggesting that 41 percent of product demand is predicated on addressing the "time between sharpenings" characteristic. At this point, engineering has a priority list of which technical characteristics to focus on during development. The respective engineering benchmarks serve as milestones to drive the technical development process.

The Theory of Innovative Problem-Solving

Contradictions between technical characteristics can arise when performing the QFD methodology. A greater "time between sharpenings" leads to more "lead dust generated" even though the consumer desires greater "time between sharpenings" and less "lead dust generated." While one approach is to favor the higher weighted characteristic, a methodology called the theory of innovative problem solving (TIPS, also known by the Russian acronym TRIZ) has emerged from Russia.

TIPS was developed by Genrich Altshuller as part of a World War II initiative to develop new military technology for the Soviet Union by reviewing patents around the world. Altshuller determined that certain distinct principles are used to solve certain distinct problems. He subsequently developed a matrix linking forty common problems or contradictions with principles to resolve these contradictions. TIPS is therefore used by companies to identify potential principles for resolving technical contradictions. TIPS does not offer a specific solution; rather, it suggests a class of solutions that the company needs to investigate. In the case of the contradiction between "time between sharpening" and "lead dust generated," it is possible to classify "time between sharpening" as a "time of action of a stationary object" problem and "lead dust generated" as an "amount of substance" problem. Resolving a contradiction between these two problem areas may be achieved by looking at the principles of local quality, transformation properties, and porous materials.

Local quality encompasses the following considerations: (1) transition from homogeneous to heterogeneous structure of an object or outside environment; (2) different parts of an object should carry out different functions; and (3) each part of an object should be placed in conditions that are most favorable for its operation. Transformation properties include (1) changing the physical state of the system, (2) changing the concentration or density, (3) changing the degree of flexibility, and (4) changing the temperature or volume. And porous materials involve (1) making an object porous or using supplementary porous elements (inserts, covers, etc.); and (2) if an object is already porous, filling pores in advance with some substance. Based on these principles and their elements, a possible solution to the contradiction may be conceived. This example briefly illustrates how the TIPS methodology can be applied. See Altshuller (1997) for further reading.

The Kano Model

Another consideration in performing the QFD methodology is to go beyond developing products that just satisfy customers' needs and develop products that delight customers. According to the model proposed by Dr. Noriaki Kano in the 1980s, there are three types of product attributes or features that can be designed into a product to give customer satisfaction and work toward delighting the customer: assumed features, expected features, and delighting features. As shown in Exhibit 7.5, the differing degrees to which assumed features, expected features, and delighting features are incorporated into a product will have different effects on customer satisfaction.

Assumed features are basic product attributes that customers equate to the particular product. As shown, assumed features do not drive customer satisfaction, but rather minimize it. As more and more assumed features are designed into the product, a potential customer will be less and less dissatisfied but never satisfied.

Expected features are product attributes that by nature of their name are expected in the product. The distinction of expected features is that they have a linear relationship with customer satisfaction: if the expected features are better than customers' expectations, customers will be satisfied.

Delighting features are unexpected product attributes that surpass customers' expectations for what typically would be delivered in the product or service. Of course, such unexpected product attributes would need to be perceived as adding value to the product and not just superfluous product attributes.

Using the service provided by the American Automobile Association (AAA), the Kano model is illustrated. An assumed feature would be AAA

Exhibit 7.5 **The Kano Model**

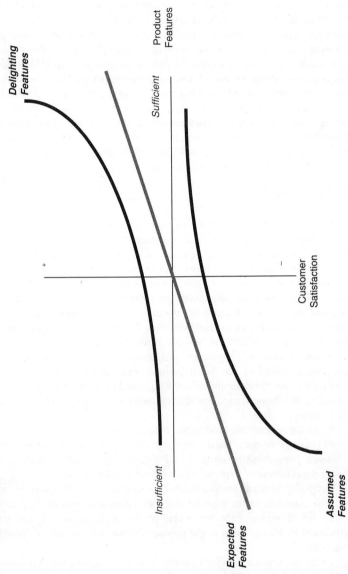

126

answering the telephone and sending out a tow truck for roadside assistance once a customer calls for a tow truck because of a flat tire. This is a basic service that AAA members pay for and would assume to be a standard feature. An expected feature would be the time that the tow truck takes to arrive. The sooner the tow truck arrives on the scene, the more satisfied the customer will be (as defined, expected features have a linear relationship with customer satisfaction). Naturally, the customer having a flat tire would expect the tire to be repaired (or the car towed for repair). However, if the tow truck personnel not only fixed the flat tire, but also in the same time washed the car and changed the oil at no extra charge, the customer would most likely be delighted; these represent delighting features.

An approach for incorporating the Kano model into the QFD methodology is to use sales points. That is, the weights of 1, 1.2, and 1.5 can be used to represent assumed, expected, and delighting features, respectively. Determining which features are which would stem from a process of customer interviews, managerial judgment, and company experience. When using the Kano model, product planners must realize that features identified as delighting in a current version of a product may be expected features in the next version of the product. It is recommended that only a few delighting features be used in each product design; otherwise customers will expect or even assume these features in future product versions. It is also possible that building too many delighting features into the product may make it too costly for customers to afford.

Quantifying the Kano Model

An approach for quantifying the Kano model has been presented by Stein and Iansiti (1995). Customers are asked a battery of positive and negative questions about product attributes and are requested to label their response to each question according to one of the following five statements:

- I like it that way.
- It must be that way.
- I am neutral.
- I can live with it that way.
- I dislike it that way.

For example, if an emergency automobile service like AAA was being evaluated, the product attribute of timely response time by the tow truck could be examined asking these two questions: (1) tow truck response time should be very timely, and (2) tow truck response time does not need to be timely. Based on customer responses to positive and negative questions about the same product attribute, a matrix shown in Exhibit 7.6 categorizes attributes as follows:

- *Delighter:* The delighter is not expected so its absence does not cause dissatisfaction. If the need is met, however, it will increase satisfaction.
- *Linear satisfier:* The better the product is at meeting the need, the better the customer likes it.
- *Must be/must have:* No matter how well the product meets the need, the customer simply accepts it as something that is expected. However, if the need is not met, the customer is very dissatisfied.
- *Indifferent quality element:* Produces neither satisfaction nor dissatisfaction in the customer, regardless of whether it is met in the product.
- *Reverse quality element:* Creates dissatisfaction when fulfilled or satisfaction when not fulfilled. This implies that either the survey question was not written correctly or that the trait is undesirable to the customer.
- *Questionable result:* The relationship does not make sense and should be investigated to determine whether the survey question was not written correctly or something unique is occurring.

For more information, refer to Stein and Iansiti (1995).

Product Use Testing

After the product concept becomes tangible, questions surrounding whether the product meets the given product protocol might arise. The primary question, of course, is whether the product actually works. Product use testing (also known as use testing or field testing) is used to evaluate a product's functional performance and examine the product protocol characteristics.

Three specific types of product use testing are possible:

- *Alpha testing:* in-house testing using employees as the basis for testing. The advantages of alpha testing are that it is often inexpensive and that competitors are not attuned to the new product. The disadvantage is that employees may not necessarily reflect customer views.
- *Beta testing:* seeing if the product works in customer operations. The basis for testing is therefore the customer site. The advantage of beta testing is that the customer provides insight into the product and its functioning. The disadvantages are that competitors can learn about the new product and that the customers who are testing the product are not necessarily indicative of the total market.
- *Gamma testing:* longer-term testing where the product is put through

Exhibit 7.6

Quantifying the Kano Model

		Result of negative question				
		Like	Must be	Neutral	Live with	Dislike
	Like	Q	D	D	D	L
Result of	Must be	R	I	I	I	M
positive	Neutral	R	I	I	I	M
question	Live with	R	I	I	I	M
	Dislike	R	R	R	R	Q

D = Delighter
. . . the delighter is not expected so its absence does not cause dissatisfaction. If the
need is met, however, it will increase satisfaction.

L = Linear Satisfier
. . . the better the product is at meeting the need, the better the customer likes it.

M = Must Be / Must Have
. . . no matter how well the product meets the need, the customer simply accepts it
as something that is expected. However, if the need is not met, the customer is
very dissatisfied.

I = Indifferent Quality Element
. . . produces neither satisfaction nor dissatisfaction in the customer, regardless of
whether it is met in the product.

R = Reverse Quality Element
. . . creates dissatisfaction when fulfilled or satisfaction when not fulfilled. This implies
that either the survey question was not written correctly or that the trait is undesirable to the customer.

Q = Questionable Result
. . . the relationship does not make sense and should be investigated to determine
whether the survey question was not written correctly or something unique is
occurring.

Source: Adapted from Kano, Seraku, Takahashi, and Tsuji (1984).

extensive use by the customer. Gamma testing is predominantly used by
pharmaceutical companies due to the regulatory requirements surrounding medicinal drugs. Most other companies will only pursue alpha and
beta testing.

Though there are risks, product use testing can be a beneficial exercise. In
particular, product use testing can provide consumers' first impressions of the

product. Being attuned to these first impressions can help a company ensure that the product is being perceived as intended and is understandable by consumers. Product use testing also can determine if the product is being used as intended or, perhaps, used for unintended (possibly incorrect) purposes. It can also reveal if there are inherent benefits that were not expected. All this information can be assessed, and a determination can be made of how well the new product meets the protocol. This information also can be assessed to help determine the potential success of the product and what is necessary for properly marketing the product.

Structuring a Product Use Test

Crawford (1997) provides a detailed structure for conducting a product use test. This structure contains five testing dimensions: test objectives, test group characteristics, product usage considerations, product form considerations, and measurement and analysis considerations. Prior to conducting a product use test, a written protocol outlining the product use test by these dimensions would be beneficial.

The first dimension, test objectives, specifies what a company wants or needs to learn by performing the product use test. Much of what will be driving the objectives will be key elements given within the product protocol. Other key issues not necessarily given in the product protocol but considered important by the development team or management should be listed too.

The second dimension, test group characteristics, concerns test group composition, mode of contact, company disclosure, and degree of product explanation to be given. Test group composition refers to whether customers and/ or noncustomers should serve as the test group. Noncustomers could include experts, industry opinion leaders, and employees. Mode of contact includes such issues as whether mail or personal interaction should be employed, whether an individual or group setting should be employed, and whether a central testing location (e.g., in-house at the company or at a market research facility) or multiple testing locations (e.g., at customer sites or multiple market research facilities) should be employed. Company disclosure pertains to whether users should be told the company name and the brand. It is possible that such information may introduce halo effects—that is, users' perceptions of the company and brand name will bias their views of the new product. The last issue is the degree of product explanation to be given—whether customers should be given full information about the product, given a limited amount of information, or given the new product without any explanation of use to see if they can figure out how to use the product. Degree of product explanation to be given will depend on the objectives of the test.

The third dimension, product usage considerations, concerns the degree of control to be given to users during the test, number of usage exposures to be allowed, and duration of each product use experience. Degree of control pertains to whether the company should control the users' experience with the product during the test (e.g., by using a laboratory setting) or whether users should be given freedom to use the product as they wish. Related to this is whether the users' experience with the product should be supervised or unsupervised. Another consideration is how many exposures to the product should be allowed. A monadic test would be a one-time experience, while a sequential monadic test would consist of a series of single experiences. A third consideration is the duration of each user's experience with the product—whether the experience should be timed or should last as long as the user wishes.

The fourth dimension, product form considerations, concerns the nature of the product to be given to users during the test. One issue in this dimension is the form of the product. Should the product be the best single product possible, or should multiple variations of the product be provided? Another issue concerning product form is the source of the product. Possible sources include engineering prototype, batch production, pilot production, and final production. Naturally, an engineering prototype may not be as refined as the product emerging from final production runs.

The fifth dimension, measurement and analysis, concerns the recording and assessment of test results. One issue is the mode for recording user reactions. Options for recording user reactions include paper documentation, audiotape, and videotape. With regard to paper documentation, consideration should be given to whether a standard form or questionnaire should be used or just note taking. A designation of whether the user or a test attendant will fill out the paperwork or talk on the audiotape or videotape needs to be made. Another issue is a designation of norms for the product use test. That is, there should be a designation of what constitutes a good test, assuming that comparative information from previous product use tests is available. A final issue concerns whether measurement and analysis should be performed in-house or by a consulting agency (i.e., should the product use test rely on internal versus external expertise).

It needs to be understood that product testing does not always go as planned. There are times when customers or users will provide contrary evidence or even conflicting data. In response to this situation, product planners should not change the data just because results were not what were expected. Rather, product planners need to examine the data closely to determine what is wrong or conflicting and why the discrepancy occurred. More importantly, product planners should be alert to strange results. Such results might indicate that a problem exists.

There are a few, select instances when a product use test would not be performed, perhaps because of time pressures or a fear of alerting competitors to the new product. In such a situation, the company would naturally continue toward launch, but give special attention to constructing a thorough set of contingency plans in case problems did arise. Overall, some type of product use testing is highly recommended to proof the product before launch.

Discussion Questions

1. What is a product protocol?
2. What is DFX?
3. What is quality function deployment?
4. What are the three types of attributes or features in the Kano model?
5. What are the three possible types of product use testing?

References

Altshuller, Genrich. 1997. *40 Principles: TRIZ Keys to Technical Innovation*. Worcester, MA: Technical Innovation Center.

Bralla, James G. 1996. *Design for Excellence*. New York: McGraw-Hill.

Crawford, C. Merle. 1997. *New Products Management*. 5th ed. Boston: Irwin.

Hauser, John R., and Don Clausing. 1988. "The House of Quality." *Harvard Business Review*, 66 (3) (May–June), 63–73.

Kano, Noriaki, Nobuhiku Seraku, Fumio Takahashi, and Shinichi Tsuji. 1984. "Attractive Quality and Must-be Quality." *The Journal of the Japanese Society for Quality Control*, 14 (2), 39–48

Nussbaum, Bruce, and Robert Neff. 1991. "High Tech Gone Haywire." *Business Week*, April 29, pp. 58–66.

Stein, Ellen, and Marco Iansiti. 1995. "Understanding Customer Needs." *Harvard Business School Case Note* # 9-695-051.

Ulrich, Karl T., and Steven D. Eppinger. 1995. *Product Design and Development*. New York: McGraw-Hill.

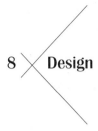

8 Design

Chapter 7 addressed technical development and technical design considerations. This chapter discusses design from an applied arts perspective—a perspective commonly employed by such disciplines as industrial design, graphic design, and interior design in the course of product planning. Embracing this perspective, design considers the aesthetic, functional, and human aspects of an object or process, accomplished through research, thought, modeling, interactive adjustment, and redesign.

The Meaning of Design

Design can be formally defined as the process of originating and developing a plan for a product, structure, system, or component with intention. Design also represents the organized arrangement of one or more elements and principles for the purpose of a proposal, drawing, model, description, or implementation of a product. Carnegie Mellon's School of Design defines design as the process of taking something from its existing state and moving it to a preferred state; this applies to new artifacts, whose existing state is undefined, as well as previously created artifacts whose state stands to be improved (www.design.cmu.edu).

Simple, easy-to-use, and attractive products should be focal goals in the course of design. These are not necessarily easy-to-attain goals because intuitive, easy-to-use, and beautiful design can be a complicated endeavor. A major emphasis on user interaction is essential to achieving these goals in the design endeavor and creating a true favorable product experience for the customer. The designer also needs to heed other various elements to underlie and frame the design process, regardless of the specific design discipline. Incorporating these elements into the product design endeavor, the designer strives to achieve an appropriate, acceptable, and market-ready design. While not an exhaustive list, the following elements present criteria to guide a holistic product composition.

- *Balance:* Balance, which can be either symmetrical or asymmetrical, refers to a sense that dominant focal points do not pull too much to any part of the design.
- *Color:* Color, the most expressive element, represents the occurrence of light hitting the surface of an object and being reflected back to the eye. Color can be used to draw attention to a particular part of the image and/or to increase visual appeal. Color also can affect thought and evoke emotions. There are the primary colors of red, blue, and yellow; the secondary colors of orange, purple (violet), and green; and the tertiary colors of red-orange, red-purple, blue-purple, blue-green, yellow-orange, and yellow-green. Complementary colors are used to create contrast. Analogous colors are used to create color harmony.
- *Contrast:* Contrast is the occurrence of contrasting elements, such as color, value, or size. It creates interest and pulls the attention toward the focal point.
- *Emphasis:* Emphasis guides the eye into, through, and out of the image through the use of a sequence of various levels of focal points: primary focal point, secondary, tertiary, and so on. The emphasis hierarchy may give direction and organization to a design, improving the design's visual appeal and style and avoiding subconscious confusion. The emphasis or dominance of an object can be increased by making the object larger, more sophisticated, or more ornate, placing it in the foreground, or making it stand out visually more than other objects in a project.
- *Form:* Form is any three-dimensional object than can be measured from top to bottom, side to side, and back to front (depth). Form also can be defined by light and dark. Geometric form is human-made, and natural form is organic. Form may be created by the combining of two or more shapes and enhanced by tone, texture, and color.
- *Functionality:* Functionality refers to meeting the specified needs of the user. Functionality can increase visual appeal and prestige.
- *Genuineness:* Genuineness in media and form is using real material for finishes rather than faux materials, providing style, prestige, glamour, or luxury rather than pretense. Genuineness in design is usually better functionally and aesthetically.
- *Harmony:* Harmony occurs when some or many of the design components achieve a sensitive balance of variety and unity and appear to belong together. Combined with unity, harmony generally makes designs more visually appealing, organized, and interesting. Design harmony may be used to produce a hidden or difficulty-to-see order or organization, and harmony of colors may be achieved using complementary or analogous colors.

- *Line:* Line refers to the continuous movement of a point along a surface and represents a basic shape component on paper. Lines and curves are the basic building blocks of two-dimensional shapes. Adding in length, thickness, and direction, line can be horizontal, vertical, diagonal, zigzag, wavy, parallel, dash, and dotted.
- *Proximity:* Proximity helps to produce harmony by grouping like objects.
- *Rhythm:* Rhythm is the recurrence of elements within a piece such as colors, lines, shapes, or values. Any element that occurs is generally echoed, often with some variation to keep interest.
- *Safety:* Alongside design aesthetics are the health and safety of a product. The design should heed all potential safety concerns stemming from the design.
- *Scale:* Scale represents the relationship of size between objects. Scale is a relative element comparing different surface areas in the product design.
- *Shape:* Shape is an area enclosed by lines to form a two-dimensional boundary space that may be geometric or organic in nature.
- *Space:* Space has the two dimensions of length and width and may have a third dimension of height. Space also addresses background, foreground, and middle ground, plus positive and negative space. Positive space refers to the space of a shape representing the subject matter. Negative space refers to the open space around the subject matter.
- *Style:* Style is how much an observer is attracted to a particular design. It involves individual psychological effects stemming from factors such as color and shape preferences.
- *Texture:* Texture is the way the surface of an object feels. Two types of texture are tactile and implied. Tactile texture is the way the surface of an object actually feels, whereas implied texture is the way the surface on an object looks like it feels.
- *Tone:* Tone refers to the shading relationship between light and dark on a surface or object. It gives objects depth and perception.
- *Type:* Type is the letterform that provides a message.
- *Unity:* Unity refers to the use of balance, repetition, and/or design harmony. Unity helps the objects belong together.
- *Variety:* The use of dissimilar element creates interest and uniqueness, reducing monotony.

Product Design Situations

Product design situations can be formulated into one of four general categories (Veryzer 1998, 2006). Each category reflects different considerations and challenges:

- *Renovative design:* Involves the updating or overhaul of an existing product with little change in the technology employed or the functionality delivered.
- *Adaptive design:* Involves adjusting an existing product to new circumstances or a changed situation (e.g., improvements in technological capabilities, reorienting the design direction of an existing product). In extreme cases, adaptive design can entail a drastic shift in the design direction of a product.
- *Evolutionary design:* Involves the design of new products where the progression from existing products is relatively continuous in terms of product capabilities delivered, technology employed, and design direction (e.g., form and appearance).
- *Discontinuous design:* Involves a dramatic break in the progression from the course of previous products. Discontinuous design situations may be further subdivided into three cases: (1) primarily technological discontinuity (products perceived as essentially the same as existing products even though they utilize revolutionary new technology); (2) primarily commercial discontinuity (products perceived as being highly innovative even though they utilize little new technology but uniquely package it for an unmet consumer need); and (3) both commercial and technical discontinuities.

Each design situation has an objective to help focus the design endeavor. A number of objectives are possible, but there are essentially five fundamental objectives to guide the execution of design.

1. *Achieve a cost advantage.* This design results in a product cost advantage. The emphasis is to minimize component and production costs while pursuing a cost domination objective.

2. *Achieve design eminence.* This design establishes an identifiable and unique product image. The emphasis is on differentiating the product using primarily ergonomics, innovative concepts, and aesthetics that embody both consumers' needs and brand values. Value is added through design elements that improve product usability, enhance perception (e.g., visual, tactile, auditory senses), evoke emotive reactions to reinforce the product's brand message (e.g., high performance, power, sophistication), and resonate with target consumer values. A design-eminence objective can involve establishing design styles, trends, or fashions, and/or changing brand perceptions.

3. *Achieve feature leadership.* This design introduces innovative, leading-edge products emphasizing new features. The emphasis is to pursue new solutions

and push the frontier of applying or developing technology. Being agile and forward-thinking and taking risks to move past and even cannibalize sales of previous products are required.

4. *Achieve a specific concentration.* This design focuses on delivering the optimal product for a narrow product space (e.g., product category or requirements of a particular type of user). The emphasis with the concentration objective is an integral understanding of the needs of specific customer segments relevant to the narrow product space. Developing significant points of difference that can be used to distinguish the product using improvements in the product's (or service's) fit and performance is also emphasized.

5. *Provide a desirable alternative.* This design competes with an established product category or category leader. Such an objective, which corresponds to a market challenger or market follower objective, is the reality for many product offerings. Competing in a particular category by offering alternatives that increase the available selection of products can be a viable and even profitable approach. This objective is more likely to succeed when there is sufficient room in the market, such as in a growth market. When the market becomes more competitive, such as when the market is no longer expanding and is stable, a firm pursuing this objective alone is likely to have to adopt or overlap with another objective to compete successfully. Pursuit of this objective relies on execution to attract customers and not necessarily on market leadership in terms of features, form, user interaction, semiotics (meanings and signs), or style.

Design Disciplines

There are different types of design disciplines. Three disciplines that may serve prominent roles in product planning are industrial design, graphic design, and interior design.

Industrial Design

Industrial design is a combination of applied art and applied science to create and execute design solutions for problems of form, usability, user ergonomics, engineering, marketing, brand development, and sales. Combining creative and intuitive elements of the visual arts with practical knowledge of markets, human behavior, materials, and manufacturing, industrial designers study function, form, and the connection between product and user to create product designs of high value. Industrial designers strive not simply to make a product that meets requirements, but also to create ideas that exceed expectations, delight the customer, and build brand equity for the company.

Industrial designers examine usability and form relationships as they partner with engineers and marketers to identify and fulfill customer needs, wants, and expectations by creating robust, appealing product forms that can be produced in quantity. Product characteristics specified by the industrial designer may include the overall form of the object, the location of details with respect to one another, colors, texture, sounds, and ergonomics. Production process aspects posed by the industrial design may concern the production process itself, the choice of materials, and how the product will be presented to the consumer at the point of sale.

The design methodologies that industrial designers employ may be considered "creative," but analytical processes take place too. Industrial designers are trained to analyze the problem and approach it from many angles—thinking in a broad "systems" manner. For example, a problem statement might be to "design a better chair." An industrial designer might broaden the problem statement to "design a better means of supporting a person in a sitting position." This restatement allows for a greater range of possible and potential solutions by exploring the boundaries of the problem and understanding constraints. Commonly employed methodologies include user research, sketching, comparative product research, model making, prototyping, and testing. Here concepts are developed as storyboards and flow charts to organize the sequence of operations and develop a diagram of choices. Three-dimensional computer-aided rendering and computer-aided design (CAD) software packages are often employed to move from concept to production. These technologies enable animations and simulations that model a virtual prototype to allow a fuller evaluation of concepts.

Industrial Design Through the Development Process

Industrial design can be employed in various ways and at various points in the product planning process, whether it is resourced from an in-house company department or outsourced from an industrial design consulting firm. Either way, the involvement of industrial design should be considered to provide unique views and possibilities for the product.

In the early stages of the product planning process, industrial designers can aid in the generation of initial concepts. Sketches, models, and CAD can be used to identify, develop, and refine preferred concepts. Further refinement to the concepts occur through reviews with engineering and marketing team members, individual user interviews, focus groups, and user testing of functional models.

In the middle stages of the product planning process, industrial designers work with engineers and technical experts to develop and validate product form and functionality, including aesthetics and packaging. Through an iterative exchange, industrial designers address key features and components to optimize the design by way of ergonomics, usability, and end-user appeal in order to ensure greater propensity for market success. Such exchange should go beyond surface alterations to the product. Industrial designers also participate in discussions with vendors, molders, fabricators, and assembly line personnel to address manufacturability issues.

During the commercialization stage, industrial designers work with marketing and support market launch activities. Industrial designers can contribute to refining and resolving issues pertaining to packaging, manuals, promotions, and marketing communication materials. Industrial design would champion user-centric and brand themes prior to and during the product launch.

After launch, industrial designers should stay involved to interpret the market response, watch the product in use, and continue to gather user feedback. Such data could serve as valuable input for revisions to the introduced product, line extensions, and other considerations regarding future product planning activities.

Graphic Design

Graphic design refers to a number of artistic and professional disciplines that focus on visual communication and presentation. Both the design processes by which the communication and presentation are created and the generated product designs represent considerations by graphic design.

The aim of graphic design is to enhance the transfer of knowledge. To do this, various methods are used to combine symbols, images, and/or words and thereby create a visual representation of ideas and messages. Typography, visual arts, and page layout techniques may be employed by a graphic designer to produce the final result. Readability is one of the most important features of graphic design and is enhanced by improving the visual presentation of text by way of composition.

Company identity elements—logos, colors, artwork, packaging, and text—will be addressed by the graphic designer as part of the branding initiative. Such branding relates to the identifying mark or trade name for a product or service. Corporate identity, which relates to the underlying values of a company and its external company image, can be addressed as well while working with marketing personnel, communications consultants, and commercial writers.

Graphic designers should be involved with the layout and formatting of educational and instructional materials to make the information accessible and readily understandable. Graphic design also aids in the presentation of opinion and facts through graphics and thoughtful compositions of visual information, which is called information design. Graphic designers could be employed to improve promotional material and electronic media to inform and even entertain—the latter garnering market attention and favorable awareness. Such design involves the stylization and presentation of text and imagery by the graphic designer, which would include organizing content into a reasonable layout and determining if any other graphic elements are required. Combining all print and electronic content into a meaningful communication vehicle represents multimedia design.

Before any graphic elements can be applied to a design, they must be originated by someone with visual art skills. Such graphic elements are often (but not always) developed by a graphic designer and would include primarily visual works, including traditional art media, photography, and computer-generated art. Graphic design principles may be applied to each graphic art element individually and/or to the final composition. These include typography, page layout, interface design, and chromatics.

Typography is the art and technique of type design, type character modification, and type arrangement. Type characters (called glyphs) are created and modified using a variety of illustration techniques. Type arrangement is the selection of typefaces, point size, line length, line spacing, and letter spacing.

Page layout is the part of graphic design that deals in the arrangement and style treatment of page content. With print media, elements usually consist of text, images (pictures), and occasionally place-holder graphics for elements that are not printed with ink.

Interface design pertains to web design and software design when end-user interactivity is predicated on the layout of information. Graphic designers will combine visual communication skills, interactive communication skills, icon design, and online branding. These will be presented by the graphic designer to software developers and web developers in order to create the website or software application that enhances the interactive experience by the website visitor or user.

Chromatics is the study of how eyes perceive color. Issues regarding light sensitivity, color sensitivity, and color perception would be considered. These contribute to understanding and organizing colors in print forms and electronic media.

Interior Design

Interior design is a multifaceted profession in which creative and technical solutions are applied within a structure to achieve a built interior environment (National Council for Interior Design Qualification). These solutions are functional, enhance the quality of life and culture of the occupants, and are aesthetically attractive. Designs are created in response to and coordinated with code and regulatory requirements and should encourage the principles of environmental sustainability.

The work of an interior designer draws upon many disciplines, including environmental psychology, architecture, product design, and traditional decoration (aesthetics and cosmetics). Planning the spaces of almost every type of building, interior designers rely on a multitude of technical, analytical, and creative skills and understandings of architectural elements. These skills address such architectural details as floor plans, home renovations, and construction codes. Some interior designers are architects.

Interior design encompasses residential and commercial contexts. Within residential design, kitchen design, bathroom design, universal design, design for the aged, multifamily housing, and so on would be considerations. Commercial design addresses these issues in the commercial market and might specialize in furniture design, medical care facility design, hotel design, retail store design, workspace design, and sustainability.

The aim of interior design is to improve the psychological and/or physiological well-being of clients. This is accomplished by following a systematic, coordinated methodology that includes research, analysis, and integration of knowledge into the creative process. Interior designers endeavor to understand and respect clients' social, physical, and psychological needs; seek appropriate solutions; and apply all these considerations in a safe and ecologically sensitive manner that promotes clients' health, safety, and welfare. Project goals surrounding the design of an interior space are met when the needs and resources of the client are satisfied.

Discussion Questions

1. What is meant by design?
2. What are some important design elements to be considered?
3. What is industrial design?
4. What is graphic design?
5. What is interior design?

References

Veryzer, Robert W. 1998. "Discontinuous Innovation and the New Product Development Process." *Journal of Product Innovation Management*, 15, 304–321.
———.2006. "Enhancing New Product Development Success Through Industrial Design

Strategy." In *The PDMA Handbook of New Product Development*, 2nd ed., ed. Kenneth B. Kahn, 378–388. Hoboken, NJ: John Wiley.

Additional Resources

The following websites are excellent sources for more information on design and design-related disciplines:

Carnegie Mellon School of Design. www.design.cmu.edu.
Design Council, UK. www.design-council.org.uk.
Industrial Design Society of America. www.idsa.org.
National Council for Interior Design Qualification. www.ncidq.org.

9 ╳ Market Planning

Another stream of activities within the technical development stage is market plan development. A subtle distinction between the present set of activities and those activities discussed in the previous chapter is that market plan development is not officially finalized until product launch, while, for the most part, the product's engineering and attribute design is finalized prior to initiating launch activities.

Market planning can be envisioned as a process involving two distinct sets of activities: the situation analysis and marketing mix development. The situation analysis involves an assessment of the 3 Cs: company issues, competitor issues, and customer issues. Marketing mix development involves identification and integration of the 4 Ps, the most appropriate product issues, place (distribution) issues, promotion issues, and price issues. Together the 3 Cs and 4 Ps represent a framework for market plan development, where the 3 Cs orient the 4 Ps and the 4 Ps represent the company's offering to the marketplace (see Exhibit 9.1).

The Situation Analysis

The purpose of the situation analysis is to assess competitors and customers within the marketplace, as well as evaluate the ability of the company to compete against these competitors and provide offerings to satisfy customer needs. Various types of analyses can be performed as part of the situation analysis, including an industry analysis, competitor analysis, company analysis, customer analysis, and sales analysis. Both internal and external data sources will be needed to properly conduct these analyses.

Industry Analysis

The purpose of an industry analysis is to assess the forces that impact doing business in a given marketplace. In this way, the company can determine whether the market is attractive enough to justify launching the particular product being developed.

Exhibit 9.1   **A Market Planning Framework: The 3 Cs and 4 Ps**

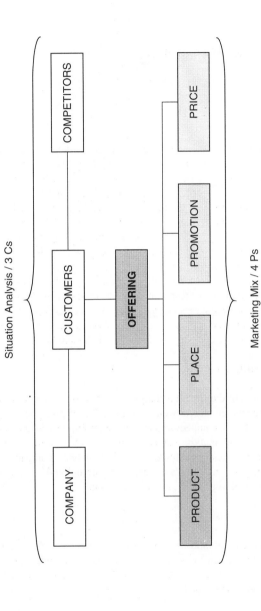

Situation Analysis / 3 Cs

Marketing Mix / 4 Ps

One popular framework for conducting an industry analysis is Michael Porter's five forces model (Porter 1980). His five forces are the power of buyers, the power of suppliers, the threat of substitute products, barriers to entry and exit, and competitive rivalry (see Exhibit 9.2). An attractive market generally would be one reflecting low levels of each of these five forces. The following characteristics are indications of high levels of each of the respective forces:

1. High bargaining power of the buyer exists when the buyer accounts for a large percentage of the industry's output, the product is undifferentiated, buyers are earning low profits, there is a threat by the buyer to backward integrate, and the buyer has full information.

2. High bargaining power of the supplier exists when suppliers are highly concentrated (only a few firms dominate the market), there is no substitute for the product supplied, and the supplier has differentiated its product and/or built-in switching costs.

3. High pressure from substitute products exist when valid, similarly priced substitutes are available and new and better technologies are emerging.

4. High (strong) barriers to market entry and exit exist when there are economies of scale, products are highly differentiated, there are extensive capital requirements, there are high switching costs, and a distribution network is necessary for success.

5. Intense rivalry exists when there are many balanced competitors, market growth is slow, fixed costs are high, and products are not well differentiated.

Along with the above five forces, an industry analysis should consider environmental factors and market-specific factors. An assessment of environmental factors would consider the technological environment, economic environment, social environment, political environment, and regulatory environment. The technological environment pertains to emerging technologies that could influence or replace current marketplace technologies, including product technologies and manufacturing technologies. The economic environment pertains to inflation rates and monetary fluctuations that could influence the market cost structure and/or customer demand. The social environment pertains to trends in demographics and psychographics (consumer lifestyles, values, attitudes) within the marketplace that would influence customer preferences and demand. The political environment pertains to the influence of local, state, national, and international politics on a company's ability to sell a product and the consumers' ability to buy the product, as well as the tax and tariffs

Exhibit 9.2 **Porter's Five Forces Model**

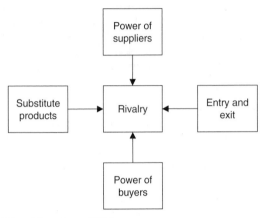

Source: Adapted from Porter (1980).

that would apply to the respective product. Related to political environment is the regulatory environment, which corresponds to the laws and regulations under which a product is to be developed, marketed, and purchased.

Market-specific factors are factors that describe the nature of market demand for a given product and the nature of profitability in satisfying such demand. Several factors that should be considered are market size, market growth, market life cycle, seasonality, cyclicity, marketing mix drivers, and profitability. Market size concerns the amount of potential demand for the product, given in terms of potential customers, unit sales potential, and/or revenue potential. Market growth is the rate at which the number of customers, unit sales, and/or revenue will increase (or possibly decrease) over time. Market life cycle recognizes whether the market is new and uncertain; growing and booming; mature, stable, but competitive; or declining and questionable. Seasonality pertains to the distinct buying patterns within a given year, while cyclicity pertains to the possible repetitive economic patterns for a given market in the past two years. Marketing mix drivers indicate the sensitivity of demand within the market to particular elements of the marketing mix—for example, a price-sensitive market, a promotion-sensitive market, or a technology-driven features market. And profitability indicates the profit potential of the given market or the degree to which current companies are profitable in the marketplace. One way of suggesting profitability is to identify the current or potential margin rate.

Combining Porter's model components with environmental factors and market-specific factors, an industry analysis can be performed by indicating whether conditions on a particular factor are favorable or attractive for entering the market with the new product. As shown in Exhibit 9.3, attractiveness can be simply noted as a plus or minus for each factor. A market with a majority of pluses would be characterized as an attractive market providing considerable opportunity for the new product.

Competitor Analysis

In analyzing competitors, two types of analyses can be performed. The first type of analysis is employed to identify immediate competitors and potential competitors. A second type of analysis then can be employed to assess the abilities of the most immediate competitors to formulate competitive strategies.

Identifying Competitors

One approach for identifying immediate and potential competitors is to evaluate four levels of competition: product form competition, product category competition, generic competition, and budget competition. Product form competition is the most specific view of competition: competitors are considered those products or companies in the product category that are going after the same segment with essentially the same product features. Product category competition is a broader view of competition, representing those products with similar features. Generic competition focuses on substitutable product categories—that is, those products or services fulfilling the same customer need. Budget competition is the broadest view of competition, where all products and services competing for the same customer dollars are identified as competitors. Aside from identifying competitors, the levels of competition can be used to identify potential complementary products as well. For example, bundling the product with a budget competitor may result in a better new product. However, identifying all budget competitors is difficult and complex due to the many potential competitors that might exist.

These four levels of competition are illustrated using the case example of dishwashers (see Exhibit 9.4). Assuming that the product being developed is a built-in dishwasher, its immediate competitors would be other built-in dishwashers; this represents the product form level of competition. Product category competition would result from other types of dishwashers, including portable dishwashers, countertop dishwashers, and specialty dishwashers (basically, all remaining types of dishwashers). Generic competition could include disposable plateware and handwashing—all potential substitutes for a built-in dishwasher. Potential budget competition could include televisions, clothes washers, clothes dryers, refrigerators, stoves, and even furniture; these

Exhibit 9.3

Evaluating Market Attractiveness

Market factors	Competitive factors	Environmental factors
• Size (+)	• Power of buyers (−)	• Technological (−)
• Growth (0)	• Power of suppliers (−)	• Economic (0)
• Life cycle stage (0)	• Rivalry (−)	• Social (+)
• Cyclicity (0)	• Substitutes (+)	• Political (+)
• Seasonality (0)	• Entries and exits (+)	• Regulatory (0)
• Financial ratios (0)		

Note: Given that there are five +s (favorable market situations), seven 0s (neutral market situations), and four −s (unfavorable market situations), it would appear that this market is attractive because the pluses outnumber the minuses.

are all items that a customer could buy for the same amount of money that a built-in dishwasher costs. Bundling product form and budget competition characteristics could suggest a potential product that integrates a dishwasher and stove, or a marketing promotion that could allow a customer to buy both a built-in dishwasher and refrigerator for reduced cost.

In addition to structuring competition, the four levels of competition can be useful in providing market definitions. In the dishwasher example, product form competition can be defined as "the common type of house dishwasher appliance" with the benefits of "being built into the kitchen cabinetry beneath the kitchen counter for discreet operation and connected directly to water and power sources for anytime use." Product form competitors would include the other types of dishwashers with the benefit of "an automated way to clean dishes." Generic competition is portrayed as different products that allow the benefit of "having clean dishes." By going through this exercise of creating definitions and establishing benefits, a greater understanding of the market may be achieved. This dishwasher example is fairly intuitive; in other market situations, creating distinct definitions may not be so easy if the lines between products are not as clear. The process of arriving at a market definition also is subjective in nature, and thus different individuals (work teams) may arrive at different market definitions and identified benefits. Nonetheless, arriving at a market definition is important because it provides a basis on which the company can build its market plan and launch the product.

Coupled with defining the market, it is valuable to consider how different market segments may appeal to different competitors. In this way, a company might find that what it perceived as an immediate competitor may not necessarily be one. For illustrative purposes, the market segments of college students, singles, married couples without children, and families are identified in Exhibit 9.5. As shown, the

Exhibit 9.4 **Evaluating the Four Levels of Competition:
A Dishwasher Example**

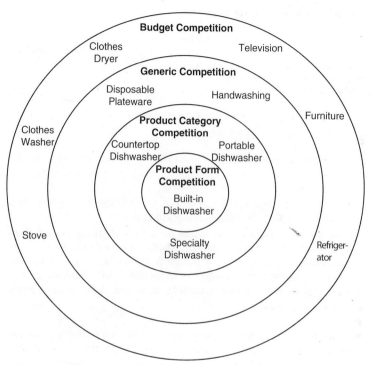

built-in dishwasher should be appealing to singles, married couples, and families. The portable and countertop dishwashers would be more of a competitor in the college students and singles market, and specialty dishwashers would become a competitor in the married couples and families segments. The construction of a table like the one in Exhibit 9.5 may be based on analytical market research or managerial intuition. Again, the value in undertaking this exercise is to provide market understanding and a basis on which the company can build its market plan and launch the product.

Assessing Competitor Abilities

Once a set of immediate and potential competitors is identified, an assessment of their abilities should be undertaken to determine their threat to the company.

Exhibit 9.5

Competition Across Market Segments

	College students	Singles	Married (no children)	Families
Built-in dishwasher		X	X	X
Portable/countertop dishwasher	X	X		
Specialty dishwasher			X	X

One approach is proposed by Lehmann and Winer (2008), who suggest the following five types of abilities:

- the ability to conceive and design (patent issues, research labs capabilities, research and development funding, technology strategy, development capabilities);
- the ability to produce (manufacturing capabilities, process flexibility, suppliers, plant locations, economies of scale);
- the ability to market (distribution network, advertising effectiveness, sales force effectiveness, marketing budget, customer service);
- the ability to manage (corporate culture, decision-making capabilities, number of employees, top management reputation, level of bureaucracy);
- the ability to finance (long-term debt, short-term debt, liquidity, profitability, revenue).

In a similar fashion to the previously discussed industry analysis, pluses and minuses can be used across criteria associated with each of the above abilities to determine the strengths and weaknesses of a particular competitor. Exhibit 9.6 illustrates a case example. Again, company intuition and judgment are the basis of this analysis.

Company Analysis

While assessing competitors, Lehmann and Winer (2008) recommend that the company evaluate itself on the list of abilities to see how it compares against competitors. Based on this assessment, strategies for marketing the product can be detailed capitalizing on company strengths and minimizing company weaknesses. This can be one way of analyzing the company.

A broader analysis is to conduct a SWOT (strengths, weaknesses, opportunities, threats) analysis. As implied by the name, the SWOT analysis identifies areas on which to capitalize and other areas to avoid. SWOT analysis goes beyond delineating a company's abilities by pointing out potential op-

Exhibit 9.6

Assessing Competitor Abilities

	Competitor A	Competitor B	The Company
Ability to conceive and design	+	+	0
Ability to produce	0	0	+
Ability to finance	0	0	−
Ability to market	+	+	0
Ability to manage	−	−	+

Note: Based on this assessment, there appears to be some degree of parity in the marketplace across the five types of abilities.

portunities and threats presented by these abilities—or lack of abilities (see Exhibit 9.7).

Customer Analysis

The purpose of a customer analysis is to clarify the market segments and identify the target markets for the product being developed. This analysis is critical to market plan development because any marketing plan will be predicated on the target market being served. Failure to identify a segment and subsequently a target market will lead to a misspecified (and in most cases, an ineffective) marketing plan. As previously discussed, the market will usually comprise market segments, and there are various approaches for market segmentation ranging from judgmental techniques to sophisticated statistical analyses. Once distinct market segments are identified, it is necessary to describe each of the segments and establish a profile. Lehmann and Winer (2008) offer eight general questions that are useful in establishing such a profile:

1. Who are the customer and user?

   - Describe by demographics: gender, age, education, income, etc.
   - Describe by psychographics: lifestyles, attitudes, etc.
   - Construct customer and user profiles.

2. What does the customer buy?

   - List important product and service characteristics.
   - Indicate the typical quantity purchased.

3. Where does the customer buy?

   - List purchase locations.

Exhibit 9.7

SWOT Analysis

Below are issues that should be considered while performing a company SWOT (strength, weaknesses, opportunities, threats) analysis.

Potential internal strengths	Potential internal weaknesses	Potential external opportunities	Potential external threats
• Core competencies in key areas • Adequate financial resources • Well-thought-of by buyers • An acknowledged market leader • Well-conceived functional area strategies • Access to economies of scale • Insulated from strong competitive pressures • Proprietary technology • Cost advantages • Better advertising campaigns • Product innovation skills • Proven management • Ahead on experience curve • Better manufacturing capabilities • Superior technological skills • Others?	• No clear strategic direction • Obsolete facilities • Subpar profitability • Lack of managerial depth and talent • Missing key skills or competencies • Poor track record in implementing strategy • Plagued with internal operating problems • Falling behind in research and development • Too narrow a product line • Weak market image • Weak distribution network • Below average marketing skills • Unable to finance needed changes in strategy • Higher overall unit costs relative to key competitors • Others?	• Serve additional customer groups • Enter new markets or segments • Expand product line to meet broader range of customer needs • Diversify into related products • Vertical integration (forward or backward) • Falling trade barriers in attractive foreign markets • Complacency among rival firms • Market growth • Others?	• Entry of lower-cost foreign competitors • Rising sales of substitute products • Slower market growth • Adverse shifts in foreign exchange rates and trade policies of foreign governments • Costly regulatory requirements • Vulnerability to recession and business cycle • Growing bargaining power of customers and/or suppliers • Changing buyer needs and tastes • Adverse demographic changes • Others?

Source: Adapted from Peter and Donnelly (1998).

4. When does the customer buy?

- Indicate time of year when purchased.
- Indicate time of day, week, and month when purchased.
- Consider special situations surrounding when a purchase is made (e.g., on sale versus regular price).

5. How do customers choose to buy what they buy?

- Are there opinion leaders?
- What are the purchase influences?
- List information sources used by customers.
- List key elements of the customer decision-making process.

6. What is value to the customer?

- List the benefits customers are seeking.
- Consider the links between these benefits and product or service attributes.

7. Will a customer buy again and why?

- Identify customer satisfaction drivers.
- Delineate customer complaints.
- Identify repurchase drivers.
- Consider the likelihood of repurchase.

8. Are customers sensitive to marketing mix elements? If yes, which ones?

- List sensitivities to product issues.
- List sensitivities to distribution issues.
- List sensitivities to promotion issues, including advertising, publicity, sales force, and special promotions.
- List sensitivities to price.

Answering these eight questions will help to identify which market segments (target markets) are most favorable and thus should be pursued. In addition, answering these eight questions should help identify the marketing mix activities that will be important to driving market awareness, market acceptance, and purchase.

Sales Analysis

Unlike the previous analyses, a sales analysis is focused on internal company data and represents an examination of existing product sales to identify demand patterns. A sales analysis also can pinpoint profitable versus less profitable products.

Companies can undertake various analyses of sales data. One analysis is to investigate the demand history of products by way of a forecastability analysis (refer to Kahn 2009). Such an analysis involves ascertaining the average level of sales, sales variability, sales trend (upward/growing sales or downward/ declining sales), and sales seasonality. This analysis is based on statistical analysis of a time series of data, typically a stream of two to three years (or longer) of monthly sales data. The mean or average can be calculated on the time series data to indicate the sales level; standard deviation and coefficient of variation (mean divided by the standard deviation) can be used to indicate sales variability; a simple time series regression where sales are regressed onto time can be used to indicate trend; and the autocorrelation between month or quarters in a given year to previous years can be used to suggest possible seasonality. Exhibit 9.8 illustrates various sales patterns as part of a sales analysis, including no trend, no seasonality (a level data pattern); trend, no seasonality (trended data); no trend and seasonality (seasonal data); and trend and seasonality.

A second useful analysis is to examine the margin per product. One way to conduct this analysis is to compare unit volume to revenue over time. If the pattern of unit volume is distinctly different from revenue, there may be need to investigate, especially if (1) the revenue line is decreasing while unit volume is increasing, or (2) the revenue line is decreasing at a faster rate than the rate of unit volume.

Marketing Objectives

Having conducting the various analyses constituting a situation analysis, it is necessary to outline marketing objectives and goals prior to framing marketing mix activities. The reason why a situation analysis should be conducted prior to outlining objectives and goals is that such analysis can be useful in outlining appropriate objectives and realistic goals.

While definitions can vary, objectives are defined as general statements concerning what the company wants to be or achieve. Such statements can

Exhibit 9.8 **Sales Pattern Recognition**

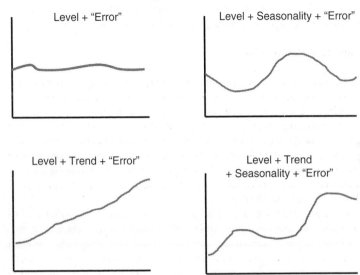

relate to financial criteria or nonfinancial criteria like image, innovativeness, and market standing. The following are examples of marketing objectives:

- to be the market leader
- to provide technologically innovative products
- to remain profitable
- to continue to increase sales
- to stand out with customer service

Goals are very similar to objectives and are very much linked to them. The distinction between goals and objectives is that goals are specific, measurable, time-specific criteria on which the achievement of objectives is measured. That is, objectives are broken down into specific, measurable criteria that are given as benchmarks to be achieved within a given time period. The following are examples of marketing goals:

- a minimum unit sales volume of 100,000 units per quarter
- a 10 percent increase in year 2012 sales
- a 5 percent increase in customer satisfaction ratings
- the introduction of five new products by year 2015

Only when marketing management and upper management agree to the objectives and goals for the product development project can work begin on identifying and organizing appropriate marketing mix activities.

Marketing Mix Activities

The identification and organization of marketing mix activities is called the marketing strategy process. This is because decisions concerning marketing mix activities have strategic ramifications and budget implications for the company.

The marketing mix is only one element of marketing strategy. The other critical element is the identification of the target market or markets to be served. In fact, identification of target market(s) must precede the identification of appropriate marketing mix activities. Failure to do so prohibits the tailoring of marketing mix activities and, in a broader sense, leads to an undefined or ill-defined marketing strategy.

Assuming that the target market is specified, four particular elements of the marketing mix need to be addressed: product issues, place (distribution) issues, promotion issues, and price issues (Ps). In general, product issues attempt to provide an offering that encapsulates customer needs and wants; place issues address availability of the product; promotion issues communicate the product to the customer; and price represents the "cost" to the customer. Many issues are conceivably associated with each of these Ps, as illustrated in Exhibit 9.9. Among the host of issues that deserve consideration, a sample of key issues inherent in each of the Ps is now detailed.

Key Product Issues

Positioning: the product's standing relative to other competitors' products, as well as other company products
Product attributes: product benefits, features, functions, and form
Branding: considerations of brand name, brand mark, trade character, trademark, trade dress:

- Brand name: a word, letter, letters, group of words, or number that can be spoken (e.g., Charmin, Sprint). A good brand name should be recognizable, short, easy to remember, easy to pronounce, easy to spell, and markedly different from the brand names of other similar products. If the intent is to eventually trademark the brand name, then by law the particular name cannot be immoral or misleading, cannot be very broad in description, cannot imply characteristics that the product

Exhibit 9.9

Marketing Mix Activities

	Product	Place	Promotion	Price
Objective	Customer needs and wants	Convenience	Communication	Cost to the customer
Activities	• Variety • Quality • Design • Style • Brand • Packaging • Size • Support • Warranty	• Channels • Coverage • Assortment • Locations • Inventory • Transportation	• Advertising • Sales force • Publicity • Special promotions • Direct marketing	• Price • Discounts • Allowances • Payment plans • Competition • Costs

does not possess, and should not be confusingly similar to any existing trademarks.

- Brand mark: a symbol, design, or distinctive coloring of lettering that cannot be spoken (e.g., Prudential's rock, Traveler's umbrella)
- Trade character: a brand mark that is personified (e.g., McDonald's Ronald McDonald, Disney's Mickey Mouse, Morton's girl holding an umbrella)
- Trademark: a brand name, a brand mark, trade character, or combination thereof that is given legal protection
- Trade dress: the color of the product and/or its packaging that distinguishes the product in the marketplace (e.g., Kodak film packaging is gold, Fuji film packaging is green)

Packaging: considerations of primary packaging, secondary packaging, and tertiary packaging for purposes of product containment, protection, safety, and display, as well to assist the customer or user:

- Primary packaging: a product's immediate packaging, such as the bottle in the case of aspirin
- Secondary packaging: the container for multiple units of the product, such as the carton containing multiple bottles of aspirin that the retail store receives
- Tertiary packaging: the pallet or slip sheet on which multiple cartons are secured and shipped; for example, multiple cartons of aspirin are palletized (placed onto a pallet), unitized (strapped, shrink-wrapped or stretch-wrapped), and then shipped to a distribution center serving individual retail stores

Key Distribution Issues

Channel type: consumer versus business-to-business
Channel structure: direct (manufacturer direct to the customer) versus indirect (through channel intermediaries)
Distribution strategy: exclusive, selective, or intensive distribution strategy:

- Exclusive: the product is offered in only a very few distribution outlets
- Selective: the product is offered in more than just a few distribution outlets, but not all outlets
- Intensive: the product is offered in as many distribution outlets as possible

Physical distribution and transportation: physical distribution and transportation options including rail, motor carrier, waterway, air, and pipeline

Key Promotion Issues

Advertising: a promotional message paid for by a sponsoring organization. Key advertising issues include objective, theme, and media:

- Objective: possible advertising objectives include awareness; reminder; changing attitudes about product use; changing perceptions about importance of brand attributes; changing beliefs about brand; attitude reinforcements; and corporate and product line image branding
- Theme: creative message to be promoted via the advertising
- Media: media types include newspapers, television, radio, direct mail, outdoor signs, magazines, Internet, and so on

Publicity: a promotional message *not* paid for by a sponsoring organization and not under the control of a sponsoring organization. Publicity includes activities related to public relations, press relations, and government relations for purposes of awareness, credibility, and relationship-building.
Personal selling: direct contact with the purchaser for purposes of prospecting for new business, information gathering, communication with the customer, order-taking, and/or account management. Key personal selling issues include the following:

- Sales force organization: decisions related to sales force size and territory design
- Sales force responsibilities: identification of sales managers and sales force supervision; sales force reporting structure

- Incentives and bonuses: compensation package; incentives to encourage selling of a new product versus current products
- Support materials: new product literature (e.g., brochures, handouts); other promotional materials
- Support staff: account management; customer database management; sales force automation functions; other support resources

Special promotions: a diverse set of customer incentives for stimulating purchase in the short term. Includes coupons, samples, point-of-purchase displays, rebates, two-for-one bundling, contests, premiums (gifts), and so on

Key Pricing Issues

Pricing strategy: premium, parity, or penetration pricing strategy:

- Premium: charging a higher price for the product for purposes of image or greater margin to recoup development costs (also known as a price-skimming strategy)
- Parity: charging a price that is equivalent to that charged by current competitors in the marketplace
- Penetration: charging a lower price to encourage higher sales volume

Bases for price calculation: considerations of how the price will be calculated, including the product cost to the manufacturer (cost-focus), range of prices that customers are willing to pay (customer-focus), and current price of similar offers (competitor-focus). Typically, all of these bases should be used in determining a product's market price.

Estimating the Marketing Strategy Budget

The next step after composing the marketing strategy is to calculate the budget necessary to implement the strategy. This is important because in many cases what may appear to be the best strategy can turn out to be cost-prohibitive. In those cases where the budget exceeds management expectations, a process of weighing the costs and benefits of each marketing mix activity is undertaken to construct an acceptable marketing strategy.

The ATAR model previously discussed in Chapter 6 can be used to determine whether the budget is acceptable. Expected sales revenue from the new product can be calculated and compared to the budget in the form of a profit and loss (P&L) statement. Obviously, if the budget exceeds the expected sales revenue, a revised marketing strategy is in order. This can mean one of two things: (1) a revised marketing mix or (2) a new target market and corresponding marketing mix. For example, assume that market potential is estimated to be 5 million, a 20 percent share is estimated, and the product selling price is $1.80; sales revenue is calculated to be $1,800,000. The corresponding marketing strategy to achieve this 20 percent share is estimated to cost $1,650,000, which comprises $750,000 for advertising and promotion; $800,000 for sales force and distribution initiatives; and $100,000 for other marketing activities like market research. Profit is therefore $150,000, or approximately a 9 percent rate of return on expenditures. Given this information, management would need to decide whether the estimated profit is in line with company policy and acceptable. Otherwise, a new strategy would be necessary, assuming that the company would still want to commercialize the product.

A break-even analysis can be conducted as well, using the following formula:

$$Break\text{-}even = \frac{fixed\ costs}{(price - variable\ costs)}$$

Break-even analysis indicates what break-even point (in units or dollars) is needed to ensure profitability. The use of the ATAR model will indicate what the total market potential is, whether the break-even point falls within this potential, and if yes, what the necessary penetration rate in the market is—too high a penetration rate may indicate the project is too costly or will not generate enough revenue.

Consider the example of a car theft deterrent device. A budget of $225,000 is expected for development and commercialization costs. Treating these as fixed costs and considering that the device will be priced at $250 and cost $175 to produce, the break-even point is 3,000 units ($225,000 / [$250 – $175]). Assuming that the market potential is 3,600 and the penetration rate is 10 percent, then only 360 units will be sold. It is obvious that the product concept will not be profitable in the first year nor in subsequent years (in fact, the break-even calculation does not take into account that there will be additional funding for marketing costs in the second year and beyond). Assuming that the market potential is correctly calculated to be 3,600, a market penetration rate (market share) of 83 percent would be necessary! In most cases, an 83 percent market penetration rate is improbable.

Marketing Strategy Control

After an acceptable budget is constructed, it is necessary to determine the metrics by which the success of the proposed marketing strategy will be measured. This helps to track and ensure that the strategy is indeed on budget and on course to meeting the given objectives and goals.

Appropriate metrics to employ are ones that are directly linked to the given objectives and goals. For instance, if profitability is a key goal, then profitability, not sales revenue, should be tracked. In addition, how a particular metric is to be measured should be specified. So if market share is to be tracked, then a definition of market share will be useful—for example, total category market share, total subcategory market share, or segment market share.

Each metric should help in evaluating the performance of the respective marketing strategy across the given objectives and goals. If a metric is below expectations or a predetermined target value, then a course of action remedying the situation will be necessary. Action may include increasing the budget to emphasize a particular marketing mix element or revising the proposed set of marketing mix activities. If the product performs very poorly across each metric for a given period of time, even after several marketing mix revisions, this may be an indication that the product is poorly conceived, market demand has shifted, or market demand did not exist as originally thought, and so the product should be removed from the marketplace.

Entrepreneurship Thinking and Business Plan Development

Market planning normally does not require consideration of business plan development because the product planning initiative is within an existing company. There are times, however, when business plan development is necessary, particularly in the case of a spin-out or business start-up situation.

Starting a new business from the point of conception requires additional considerations beyond the marketing plan, including the financial plan (how are financial resources to be secured?), management team (who has what management responsibilities?), and the operations plan (what are the physical necessities of the business pertaining to location, facilities, and equipment?). To solidify thinking about whether to pursue a start-up, *Forbes* (Nelson 2007) suggests that one keenly answer the following twenty questions and understand what they mean for starting a business (note that these questions and their answers are beneficial for solidifying product planning consideration as well):

Question 1. What is your value proposition?
Explain why customers need your product in three, jargon-free sentences or less.

Question 2. Does your product address a viable market?
Confirm that there is a viable market for the new product.

Question 3. What differentiates your product from competitors'?

Establish what is tangibly valuable for the customer and that the competition does not yet offer.

Question 4. How big is the threat of new entrants?
Consider that any profitable business opportunity will attract competition.

Question 5. How much start-up capital do you need?
Figure out how much is needed, and then add plenty of extra cushion.

Question 6. How much cash do you need to survive the early years?
Mind the cash.

Question 7. How will you finance the business?
Match the timing of cash inflows from assets with the outflows due to liabilities; a mismatch can sting.

Question 8. What are your strengths?
Figure out what you are good at and stick to it.

Question 9. What are your weaknesses?
Stick to core competencies and find trusted partners to handle the rest.

Question 10. How much power do your suppliers have?
Remember that the fewer the number of suppliers, the more sway they have. On the flip side, beware getting hooked on low-cost providers who do not keep an eye on quality.

Question 11. How much power do your buyers have?
It is no fun to be in a business where a few big customers can demand price cuts with each passing year.

Question 12. How should you sell your product?
Whatever sales method you choose, make sure it aligns with the overall business strategy.

Question 13. How should you market your product?
Get the word out, but do not go broke doing it.

Question 14. Does the business scale?
Being able to drop variable costs as volume increases is called scale, and it can make a big difference to the bottom line.

Question 15. What are your financial projections?
Be reasonable with financial projections.

Question 16. What price will consumers pay?
The price decision can make the difference between profitability and huge losses.

Question 17. How do you protect your intellectual property?
Think about patents and confidentiality and nondisclosure agreements.

Question 18. How do you keep employees happy?
Attracting and retaining talent is critical to the business.

Question 19. How committed are you to making this happen?
Realize that if you want to run the show, get ready to give everything—and then some.

Question 20. What is your end game?
Running a business with an eye toward flipping it to a strategic buyer is a lot different than digging in for the long haul.

Discussion Questions

1. What are the two sets of activities that constitute market planning?
2. What are the four levels of competition?
3. What issues are relevant for product considerations?
4. What issues are relevant for place considerations?
5. What issues are relevant for promotion considerations?
6. What issues are relevant for price considerations?
7. How is entrepreneurship or start-up activity different from corporate product planning?

References

Kahn, Kenneth B. 2009. "Benchmarking Forecast Error with Your Own Data." *Journal of Business Forecasting*, 28 (2), 20–23.

Kotler, Philip. 1997. *Marketing Management: Analysis, Planning, Implementation, and Control*. 9th ed. Upper Saddle River, NJ: Prentice-Hall.

Lehmann, Donald R., and Russell S. Winer. 2008. *Analysis for Market Planning*. 7th ed. Chicago: McGraw-Hill/Irwin.

Nelson, Brett. 2007. "The 20 Most Important Questions in Business." *Forbes*, November 21. www.forbes.com/2007/11/21/walmart-microsoft-apple-ent-manage-cx_bn_1121importantquestions.html.

Peter, J. Paul, and James H. Donnelly Jr. 1998. *Marketing Management: Knowledge and Skills*. Boston: McGraw-Hill/Irwin.

Porter, Michael E. 1980. *Competitive Strategy: Techniques for Analyzing Industries and Competitors*. New York: Free Press.

10 Commercialization and Launch

At the end of the technical development stage, the developed product and its marketing plan will be assessed. If everything is in order and approval is given, the product then enters the last stage of product development. This last stage, characteristically called the commercialization stage, consists of initiatives that commercialize and ultimately launch the product. Various activities will be undertaken in this stage, such as market testing, launch preparation, and new product forecasting.

Market Testing

Market testing is employed to evaluate the marketing plan. While it is presumed that much of the marketing plan will be set, market testing is useful for refining the marketing plan to ensure that it is comprehensible to the marketplace. Market testing also can be useful for identifying problems in the marketing plan that would lead to a revision of the marketing plan. Market testing can provide feedback that can be used to calculate revenue and unit volume forecasts as well.

In general, market testing can be broken down into three categories of techniques: pseudo-sale testing, controlled sale testing, and full-scale testing. The distinctions between these categories are what is sold (or not sold) and the extent of the selling effort (exclusive versus selective distribution). The pseudo sale is not a real selling situation, while the controlled sale and full-scale are. Pseudo and controlled sale market testing are targeted to an exclusive customer base, while full-scale market testing is a selective or even intensive distribution scenario.

Pseudo-Sale

Pseudo-sale market testing represents artificial selling situations that are akin to role-playing or hypothetical selling situations. The actual product is *not* available for sale. There are basically two types of pseudo-sale market testing techniques: the speculative sale and premarket testing.

Speculative sales rely on the sales force and are typically associated with

164

business-to-business products. During a speculative sale situation, a salesperson will approach a customer, make a full pitch about the product, and then see if the customer would likely buy the product. Situations where the speculative method fits include the following:

- when industrial firms have very close downstream relationships with key buyers;
- when new product work is technical, entrenched within a firm's expertise, and little reaction is needed from the marketplace;
- when the venture has little risk, and thus a costlier method is not defendable;
- when a firm has a tight patent;
- when the item is new and key diagnostics are needed.

More appropriate for consumer product goods and services, premarket testing often represents final consumer intercepts, when a market research firm will survey shoppers at a store, shopping center, or other shopping experience (such as online). Typically, participants during a premarket test will be asked to provide demographic information, answer various investigative questions, and provide feedback on one or more hypothetical products, and sometimes advertising samples will be shown. The survey information is summarized and can be incorporated into proprietary market research models like Bases II, Assessor, Litmus, and ESP to determine new product forecasts. Overall, premarket testing attempts to predict the likelihood of commercial success for a given new product.

Controlled Sale

The second category of market testing techniques is the controlled sale. The distinction of the controlled sale category is that the product is available for purchase in an exclusive market setting. There are basically three types of controlled sale market testing techniques: informal selling, direct marketing, and minimarkets.

Informal selling is typically performed at trade shows, where salespeople can show the product, informally approach customers, make the pitch, and see if the customer will actually buy the product.

Direct marketing focuses selling efforts on a particular market segment or target market; this segment or target market will receive information about the product and be able to purchase the product. For example, some catalog shopping companies may add a new product to a special catalog that is sent only to a particular segment or target market. The response that this new product generates in this market segment or target market is evaluated. A variation on this approach is to use "vapor" products. Manufacturers add high-resolution, photo-quality, computer-aided drawings of new product concepts to their catalogs. Any such product will be produced only when a certain number of orders come in; otherwise, the customer will be informed that the product is "out of stock" and offered another option.

The third technique is minimarkets: only certain stores in a specific geographic location sell the product and are supported with promotional materials. When Black and Decker introduced its Snakelight, only certain Ace Hardware stores supported by in-store advertising sold the product initially in order to gauge interest in the product.

Full-Scale

The third category, full-scale market testing techniques, represents the actual selling of the product in a selective or intensive distribution environment. Two techniques associated with full-scale market testing are test marketing and rollout.

Test marketing is mostly used to fine-tune the product and the marketing campaign. In this kind of extensive initiative, a representative piece of the market receives the total marketing program. In many cases, test marketing is applied on a city-by-city basis. One benefit of test marketing is that it provides an abundant supply of information and can verify production. However, test marketing is not without problems: test marketing is expensive, competitors can mess up test marketing results by introducing new promotions or pricing strategies, and there is always the risk that the test market city will not reflect the behavior of the overall market.

The second full-scale technique is rollout, which represents an actual launching of the product. A rollout occurs when a subset of the intended target market receives the product. The company then slowly introduces the new product to other parts of the target market until the entire market is receiving the product. In many cases, a rollout will be geographic in nature with the smallest region receiving the product first and other individual regions receiving the product in a predetermined order, often smallest to largest. This sequence allows production to ramp up to meet the demands of large regions and the overall total market. Serving smaller regions initially keeps volume down and offers manufacturing time to work problems out of the system, if any. While rollout sounds good, it too has risks: the company needs to have full production capabilities ready and needs buy-in from channel members to accept the product; there will be a competitive response, and rollouts tend not to get the media attention that national launches get.

Conceivably, the three types of market testing may be employed to build on each other. The key in using each of the techniques is to carefully examine the market testing results, determine if refinements or revisions are necessary, and then effect such changes. In sum, market testing will signal if the product and corresponding marketing plan are indeed market acceptable and ready for launch.

Understanding the Launch Phenomenon

Assuming that all signals indicate a "go" condition, efforts to launch the product will begin. These efforts can comprise a variety of activities, all requiring proper management. Such activities aim to increase awareness, trial, availability, and repeat purchase—akin to the previously discussed ATAR model. Prescriptions for addressing these issues are:

- *Awareness:* Let customers know about your company and what you are offering; a key way of getting awareness is through preannouncing.
- *Trial:* Encourage customers to try either through promotions that generate self-interest or interest that is vicarious in nature (trying the product because others have tried the product). Barriers to trial that must be overcome include the following:
  - Lack of interest in the product
  - Lack of belief in the product
  - Rejection of something negative about the product
  - Complacency about the product
  - Competition
  - Doubts about trying the product
  - Lack of usage opportunities
  - Product cost
  - Customers' loyalty to other products
  - Customers' perceived risk of rejection or product failure
- *Availability:* Make sure that distributors, dealers, and resellers can offer your product to the market. Trade discounts and incentives are often used as a way to ensure availability in the channel.
- *Repeat purchase:* Encourage customers to purchase again, if applicable. Promotions are popular mechanisms in the final consumer channel, while contracts may be useful for getting repurchase in business-to-business channels.

The ATAR model (discussed in previous chapters) is an extension of diffusion theory (see Rogers 1995), which provides understanding of the launch phenomenon. By definition, diffusion is the accumulation of all individual

167

adoption processes. Adoption is the process that an individual (or group or business) undergoes in making a decision of whether to purchase or not purchase a new product.

Rogers's work indicates that in general, consumers (individual or business-to-business) will transition through a five-stage process:

1. *Knowledge:* The customer receives physical or social stimuli.
2. *Persuasion:* The customer weighs risks versus benefits.
3. *Decision:* The customer adopts or rejects the product. There are two types of rejection: active rejection, when a customer considers adoption and may even try the product, but decides not to adopt, and passive rejection, when the customer never considers use of the product (also referred to as nonadoption).
4. *Implementation:* The customer purchases the product and puts it to use.
5. *Confirmation:* The customer seeks reinforcement of the innovation decision (to reduce possible cognitive dissonance, i.e., second thoughts about the purchase).

Rogers's research has found that five key product characteristics can facilitate the adoption process, thereby facilitating the overall diffusion process. The prescription is to consider how the new product can reflect these characteristics, if not have these characteristics integrated into the product design and/or marketing plan. In short, a new product needs to

- reflect a relative advantage: the new product must be superior to current product offerings;
- have compatibility with the customer's environment: the product needs to fit with current product usage and customer activity;
- minimize complexity: the product should be easy to understand and not confusing;
- be divisible (trialability): if possible, the innovation should be divided into trial samples and have trial opportunities available;
- be communicable (observability): the product should be easy to communicate, not only in promoting the product, but also by customer word-of-mouth; the product also should be able to be observed publicly.

Rogers's work also illustrates that adoption is a staggered phenomenon across customers. In other words, adoption will occur at different points in time for different types of customers. Rogers specifies five types of customer with respect to adoption of new products: the innovators (or lead users, as previously mentioned), generally composing 2.5 percent of the market; early adopters, composing 13.5 percent of the market; early majority, composing 34 percent of the market; late majority, composing another 34 percent of the market; and laggards, composing 16 percent of the market (see Exhibit 10.1).

These percentages can be useful not only for conceptualizing market segments, but also for estimating market penetration (market diffusion) of discontinuous innovations. For example, if forecasts for a new emerging technology suggest a market potential of 100,000 units, conceivably only the innovators and early adopters will purchase the product in the first year. Hence, market potential may be really only 16 percent of 100,000 units or 16,000 units. From this, a company market penetration rate of 20 percent will only generate 3,200 unit sales.

Another way to look at these relative percentages is to total them and generate a cumulative percentage curve. As shown in Exhibit 10.2, this curve takes the shape of an S and thus is commonly referred to as the S-curve or diffusion curve. The purpose of this curve is to exhibit the rate of diffusion that a new product will have within the marketplace. In particular, at what point in time will 50 percent of consumers in the market adopt the product (50 percent represents a majority of the market, comprising innovators, early adopters, and the early majority)? This point is called the inflection point, or the point at which the rate of diffusion (market growth) is increasing at a diminishing rate. Prior to the inflection point, the rate of diffusion is increasing at an increasing rate. The S-curve is helpful in planning strategy on how to expedite customers' purchasing the product in order to penetrate the majority of the market as soon as possible. The S-curve also can suggest different scenarios based on different rates of diffusion and help identify which scenario is most preferred and most likely to occur.

The Launch Cycle

Upon management approval, the launch cycle will begin. By definition, the launch of a product proceeds in four phases: (1) prelaunch preparation, (2) announcement, (3) beachhead, and (4) early growth (see Exhibit 10.3).

Prelaunch preparation comprises the activities that precede the actual point at which the product is officially offered for sale in the market. These activities typically will include making preannouncements (public company statements about the pending launch of the product), building marketing capability, establishing service capability, promoting the new product via public relations, and filling the distribution pipeline. Together these activities have the purpose of building excitement and ensuring that the company is ready to meet market demand.

Exhibit 10.1 **Customer Types Associated With Product Diffusion**

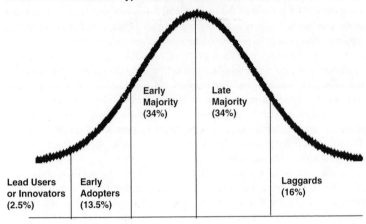

Exhibit 10.2 **The S-Curve**

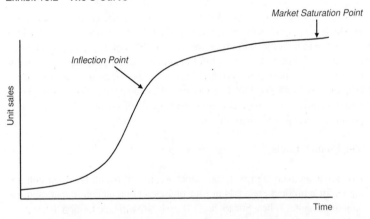

The second phase is announcement, which is not really a phase. Announcement is the point at which the product is officially offered to the complete market. It is at the point of announcement that all decisions are finalized.

The third phase is beachhead. Here efforts focus on achieving market awareness and generating an initial stream of sales.

The fourth phase of launch is early growth. Hopefully, sales will grow as interest in the new product grows. If sales are not growing, a decision needs

Exhibit 10.3 **The Launch Cycle**

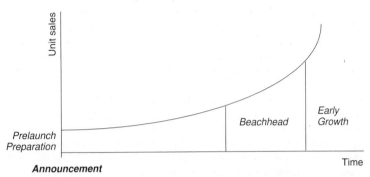

to be made quickly. In general, there are five decision options: (1) increase spending; (2) revise the launch or marketing strategy; (3) revise the product (a costly, timely, and potentially risky endeavor); (4) pull the product temporarily from the marketplace (a risky option, which often does not lead to success the second time around); or (5) abandon the product (given the amount of resources expensed during the product development process, this should be considered the last option). Note that options 1 and 2 should be considered initially. If these two options do not work, then options 3, 4, and 5 should be considered, with option 5 representing the last resort.

Prelaunch Preparation: Launch Control Protocol

One tool that is useful during prelaunch preparation is the launch control protocol. In the same vein as the product protocol during the technical development phase, the launch protocol is used to monitor and control activities during the launch cycle by identifying key "deliverables" or success measures during product launch. Such measures can correspond to a variety of issues, including sales volume, profitability, market awareness, or other designated issues. Along with these success measures, the launch control protocol establishes trigger points to indicate at what point action needs to be taken. The launch control protocol further specifies what type of action should be taken to avoid unnecessary confusion during launch.

Constructing a launch control protocol follows four steps. The first step is to identify potential problems that might occur during a particular product's launch. Three ways to identify such problems include reviewing the situation analysis from the marketing plan to outline potential threats, looking at the company's product launch history to indicate problems from previous product launches,

171

and role-playing, with employees representing various channel members and competitors. Role-playing is especially powerful for revealing problems. After several iterations of a role-playing exercise, one company successfully generated a list of foreseeable problems and established remedies for these problems. As it turned out, the company was able to stay one step ahead of competitors because it had foreseen competitor responses and potential market problems.

The second step in a launch control protocol is to select the problems that should be monitored and controlled. Selection should be based on the impact of the potential problem on the commercial success of the product. Those problems that could severely hamper success should be selected.

The third step in a launch control protocol is to design a system for monitoring and controlling each of the selected problems. To do this, it is necessary to identify a measurable variable that corresponds to each problem. For example, if one of the selected problems is "sales lower than expected," two possible variables to measure would be unit sales volume and revenue sales volume. It is necessary to specify which variable is most appropriate to get at the selected problem: unit sales, revenue sales, or both. In addition to identifying the measurable variable, it is necessary to identify the trigger point for that variable, which designates the boundary at which a problem should be recognized. If "sales lower than expected" is the problem, what would represent a situation of lower sales than expected: unit sales less than 100,000 units? revenue sales less than $1,000,000?

The fourth step in a launch control protocol is to develop remedies or contingency plans for each of the selected problems. These remedies or contingency plans would set out a course of action that the company would undertake in the event that the problem arose.

Exhibit 10.4 presents a sample of a launch control protocol. As shown, the problem of "overall sales lower than expected" is tracked by unit shipments, with the trigger point of less than 1,000 unit shipments per month signifying a problem. The remedy for the problem is implementation of an instantaneous redeemable coupon campaign.

During the launch control protocol, some consideration should be given to unforeseen and nontrackable problems. These will be difficult to conceive, but a good launch control protocol will specify what to do in case something not identified in the launch control protocol occurs. In this way, the launch team knows ahead of time what it may need to do just in case something does happen.

Plotting the Launch Process

Another tool that is useful during launch is construction of a path diagram to spell out the launch cycle. A path diagram portrays the activities to be

Exhibit 10.4

The Launch Control Protocol

Potential problem	Tracking	Contingency plan
Customers are not making trial purchases of the new product.	Look at point-of-sale reports. At minimum, 100 purchases per retail outlet are expected.	Install point-of-purchase displays.
Overall sales volume lower than expected.	Track monthly unit shipments. Shipments of less than 1,000 per month signify a problem.	Implement an instantaneous redeemable coupon campaign.
Competitor has similar new product.	Difficult to track, but conduct surveys with retailers and final consumers.	Offer 2-for-1 program. Consider bundling new product with other products.

undertaken during the launch cycle to ensure that all activities are performed and that the launch is on time. A path diagram specifically illustrates the network of activities during launch, with each distinct activity represented by a node (circle) and the order in which these activities must be undertaken represented by arrows.

To construct a path diagram, it is first necessary to list all the launch activities to be undertaken. Next, the launch activities are organized into sets of activities, where each set represents the sequencing of the activities within the given set. Those activities that do not need to be sequenced and/or not predicated on any other launch activity serve as their own set. For example, ten launch activities may initially be listed in random order: pilot production, approve advertising copy, produce brochures, purchase air time for advertising, train sales force, procure raw materials, build initial finished goods inventory, hire advertising agency, prepare final production, and notify key accounts of pending new product. These activities are then organized into three sets of activities and ordered accordingly, as shown below:

1. Manufacturing-related activities: Procure raw materials → pilot production → prepare final production → build initial finished goods inventory
2. Promotion-related activities: Hire advertising agency → approve advertising copy → purchase airtime for advertising → produce brochures

3. Sales-related activities: Train sales force → notify key accounts of pending new product

These three sets of activities are combined into the path diagram presented in Exhibit 10.5. A key benefit of this diagram is to identify critical activities that predicate other necessary activities. Also, the diagram identifies activities that can be undertaken in the event that a particular "critical" activity is not yet completed. As shown in Exhibit 10.5, it is apparent that hiring an advertising agency is critical to all promotion-related activities. However, a delay in purchasing airtime for advertising does not prevent the company from producing brochures, which can occur simultaneously.

Once a path diagram is completed, it can serve as a roadmap for the launch cycle. A path diagram also can be used in two advanced forms of scheduling analyses: critical path method (CPM) and program evaluation and review technique (PERT). Both techniques are similar in their logical structure; however, CPM is deterministic in nature in that it gives a specific time to complete each activity and, based on this information, identifies a set of critical activities (called the critical path). In short, the critical path represents those launch activities that have no slack time (scheduling flexibility): that is, these activities cannot be delayed or the overall launch will be delayed. PERT is probabilistic in nature and provides optimistic, most likely, and pessimistic times of completion for a given launch activity and the overall launch cycle. Based on these times, it can be reasonably determined if the launch will be on time, early, or late. Microsoft Project is a common software package for conducting CPM and PERT.

New Product Forecasting

While employed throughout the product development process, new product forecasting becomes particularly important during the launch cycle. This is because a company's production and distribution systems rely predominantly on the output of new product forecasting (i.e., new product forecasts) to properly prepare for launch. The interest and aim is to generate new product forecasts during the launch cycle that are as accurate as possible.

It is important to recognize that there are four general types of new product forecasts, which can be broken down by potential versus forecast, and market versus sales. Potential represents a maximum attainable estimate; forecast represents a likely attainable estimate. Market represents all companies within a given industry marketplace; sales pertains only to the respective focal company. The general types of new product forecasts are defined as:

Exhibit 10.5 **Path Diagram**

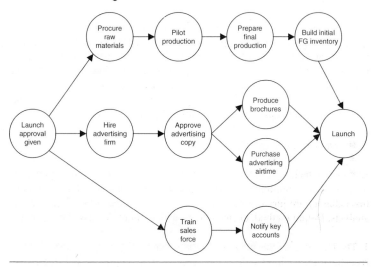

- *Market potential:* the maximum estimate of total market volume reasonably attainable under a given set of conditions
- *Sales potential:* the maximum estimate of company sales reasonably attainable within a given market under a given set of conditions
- *Market forecast:* a reasonable estimate of market volume attainable by firms in that market under a given set of conditions
- *Sales forecast:* a reasonable estimate of company sales attainable within a given market under a given set of conditions

During the new product forecasting effort, one or all of the above may be of interest. Early in the process, the forecasting focus will be market potential. These forecasts are normally in dollars and used to address the question of whether this is a good opportunity to pursue. During the concept generation and concept evaluation stages, forecasts investigate sales potential in answering the question of whether this is a good idea for the company to pursue. Entering the technical development and launch phases, unit sales forecasts would become critical in order to plan for the launch and ensure adequate supply through the channel. Product testing during technical development and market testing during the commercialization would help to qualify key assumptions and better estimate unit demand and sales revenue.

CHAPTER 10

New Product Forecasting Techniques

Along with the ATAR and ECV models previously discussed, there are a variety of techniques available for new product forecasting. Although there are multiple ways to categorize forecasting techniques, one useful way is to divide them into the three categories of company judgmental techniques, company data quantitative techniques, and customer or market research techniques. Albeit showing only a sample of techniques, the text below and Exhibit 10.6 list the most popular techniques associated with each of these three categories.

Judgmental Techniques

Judgmental techniques represent techniques that attempt to turn experience, judgments, and intuition into formal forecasts. Six popular techniques within this category are jury of executive opinion, sales force composite, scenario analysis, Delphi method, decision trees, and assumptions-based modeling.

1. The *jury of executive opinion* is a top-down forecasting technique that derives the forecast through the ad hoc combination of opinions and predictions made by informed executives and experts.

2. The *sales force composite* is a bottoms-up forecasting technique where individuals (typically salespeople) provide their forecasts, which are then aggregated to calculate a higher-level forecast.

3. *Scenario analysis* involves the development of scenarios to predict the future (e.g., Huss 1988; Huss and Honton 1987). Two types of scenario analysis are exploratory and normative approaches. Exploratory scenario analysis starts in the present and moves out to the future based on current trends. Normative scenario analysis leaps out to the future and works back to determine what should be done to achieve what is expected to occur.

4. The *Delphi method* is a technique based on subjective expert opinion gathered through several structured anonymous rounds of data collection (e.g., Gordon 1994; Woudenberg 1991). Each successive round provides consolidated feedback to the respondents, after which the forecast is further refined. The objective of the Delphi method is to capture the advantages of multiple experts in a committee, while minimizing the effects of social pressure to agree with the majority, ego pressure to stick with an original forecast despite new information, the influence of a repetitive argument, and the influence of a dominant individual.

Exhibit 10.6 **New Product Forecasting Techniques**

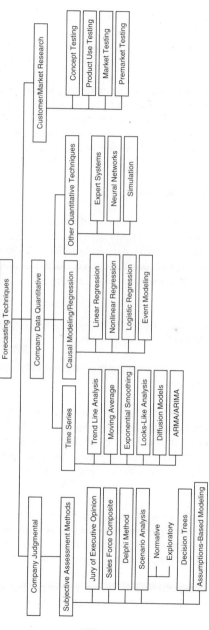

177

5. *Decision trees* are a probabilistic approach to forecasting where various contingencies and their associated probability of occurring are determined—typically in a subjective fashion. Conditional probabilities are then calculated, and the most probable events are identified (e.g., Ulvila 1985).

6. *Assumptions-based modeling* is a technique that attempts to model the behavior of the relevant market environment by breaking the market down into market drivers. Then, by assuming values for these drivers, forecasts are generated. These models are also referred to as chain models or market breakdown models (e.g., Crawford and diBenedetto 2003; Kahn 2002, 2006).

Quantitative Techniques: Time Series

Quantitative techniques are broken into the three subcategories of time series, "causal"/regression modeling, and other quantitative techniques. Time series techniques analyze sales data to detect historical sales patterns and construct a representative graph or formula to project sales into the future. Time series techniques used in association with new product forecasting include the following.

1. In *trend line analysis*, a line is fit to a set of data. This is done either graphically or mathematically.

2. *Moving average* is a technique that averages only a specified number of previous sales periods.

3. *Exponential smoothing techniques* are a set of techniques that develop forecasts by addressing the forecast components of level, trend, seasonality, and cycle. Weights or smoothing coefficients for each of these components are determined statistically and applied to "smooth" previous period information (e.g., Makridakis, Wheelwright, and Hyndman 1997; Mentzer and Bienstock 1998).

4. *Looks-like analysis (analogous forecasting)* is a technique that attempts to map sales of other products onto the product being forecast. Looks-like analysis is a popular technique applied to line extensions by using sales of previous product line introductions to profile sales of the new product.

5. *Diffusion models* estimate the growth rate of product sales by considering various factors influencing the consumer adoption process. Considerations

taken into account include the rate at which mass media (the coefficient of innovation) and word of mouth (the coefficient of imitation) affect lead users, early adopter, early majority, late majority, and laggard customer segments. The Bass model, the Gompertz curve, and the logistic curve are examples of popular diffusion models. Diffusion models are also referred to as technology S-curves (e.g., Lilien, Rangaswamy, and Van den Bulte 1999; Mahajan, Muller, and Bass 1990; Mahajan, Muller, and Wind 2000).

6. *Autoregressive moving average (ARMA)* and *autoregressive integrated moving average (ARIMA) models* are a set of advanced statistical approaches to forecasting that incorporate key elements of both time series and regression model building. Three basic activities (or stages) are considered: (1) identifying the model, (2) determining the model's parameters, and (3) testing and applying the model. Critical in using any of these techniques is understanding the concepts of autocorrelation and differencing. ARMA/ARIMA models are also referred to as Box-Jenkins techniques (e.g., Makridakis, Wheelwright, and Hyndman 1997).

Quantitative Techniques: "Causal"/Regression Modeling

"Causal"/regression modeling techniques use exogenous or independent variables and, through statistical methods, develop formulas correlating these with a dependent variable. The term "causal" is very loosely used because these models are predicated on correlational relationships and not true cause-and-effect relationships. Four popular techniques within this subcategory are as follows.

1. *Linear regression* is a statistical methodology that assesses the relation between one or more managerial variables and a dependent variable (sales), strictly assuming that these relationships are linear in nature (e.g., Neter et al. 1996). For example, price may be an important driver of new product sales. The relationship between price and the quantity sold would be determined from prior data of other products within the product line and then used to predict sales for the forthcoming product.

2. *Nonlinear regression* is a statistical methodology that assesses the relation between one or more managerial variables and a dependent variable (sales); these relationships are *not* necessarily assumed to be linear in nature.

3. *Logistic regression* is a statistical methodology that assesses the relation between one or more managerial variables and a binary outcome, such as

purchase versus nonpurchase. A logistic regression model calculates the probability of an event occurring or not occurring.

4. *Event modeling* is often a regression-based methodology that assesses the relation between one or more events, whether company-initiated or nonaffiliated with the company, and a dependent variable (sales). For example, a promotion used with prior product launches would be analyzed and the bump in sales caused by this promotion statistically determined. The expected bump in sales would be correspondingly mapped to the sales of the new product.

Quantitative Techniques: Unique Methodologies

The third category of quantitative techniques contains those techniques that employ unique methodologies or represent a hybrid of time series and regression techniques. Three samples of these forecasting techniques are given below.

1. *Expert systems* are typically computer-based heuristics or rules for forecasting. These rules are determined by interviewing forecasting experts and then constructing "if-then" statements. Forecasts are generated by going through various applicable "if-then" statements until all statements have been considered.

2. *Neural networks* are advanced statistical models that attempt to decipher patterns in a particular sales time series (e.g., Adya and Collopy 1998). These models can be time-consuming to build and difficult to explain; many of these models are proprietary.

3. *Simulation* is an approach to incorporate market forces into a decision model. "What-if" scenarios are then considered. Normally, simulation is computer-based. A typical simulation model is Monte Carlo simulation, which employs randomly generated events to drive the model and assess outcomes.

Customer or Market Research Techniques

Customer or market research techniques include those approaches that collect data on the customer or market and then systematically analyze these data to draw inferences on which to make forecasts. Concept testing, product use testing, market testing, and premarket testing are the four general classes of customer or market research techniques.

1. *Concept testing* has current and/or potential customers evaluate a new product concept and give their opinions on whether the concept is something that they might have interest in and be likely to buy. The purpose of concept testing is to proof the new product concept.

2. *Product use testing* has current and/or potential customers evaluate a product's functional characteristics and performance. The purpose of product use testing is to proof the product's function.

3. *Market testing* has targeted customers evaluate the marketing plan for a new product in a market setting. The purpose of market testing is to proof the proposed marketing plan and the "final" new product.

4. *Premarket testing* uses syndicated data and primary consumer research to estimate the sales potential of new product initiatives (e.g., Fader and Hardie 2001; Urban et al. 1983). Assessor and Bases are two proprietary new product forecasting models associated with premarket testing. Bases is commonly employed in the consumer products goods industry (see www.bases.com).

While there are a number of forecasting techniques available, not all are appropriate for every forecasting situation. Qualitative techniques are quite adaptable, but very time-consuming; they would not be appropriate in situations with severe time constraints. Quantitative techniques require data and rely on the critical assumption that current data will correspond to future states; if these requirements are not feasible, quantitative techniques would not be meaningful. Customer or market research tools are time-consuming and expensive to perform. Budget constraints could seriously hamper the degree of customer or market research that may be applied. A "toolbox" approach is therefore recommended for applying new product forecasting techniques.

To assist in decisions related to new product forecasting, Kahn (2006) provides a variation of the product-market matrix to reveal four new product forecasting situations (see Exhibit 10.7). Mapping market uncertainty and product technology uncertainty on the two dimensions of "current" and "new" reveals four cells, each of which represents one of the four new product forecasting strategies: sales analysis, life cycle analysis, customer or market analysis, and scenario analysis.

A new product forecasting strategy of sales analysis is associated with the situation of current market and current product technology, where the uncertainties of market and product technology are lowest. Cost reductions and product improvements would populate this cell. The nature of these products

Exhibit 10.7   **New Product Forecasting Strategy Framework**

Product Technology

		Current	New
Market	**Current**	**Sales Analysis** Cost reductions, product improvements	**Product Line/ Life Cycle Analysis** Line extensions
	New	**Customer and Market Analysis** New markets, new uses	**Scenario Analysis (What-if)** New-to-the-company, new-to-the-world

would signify that sales data are available because the product has previously existed. Analysis would focus on looking for deviations and deflections in sales patterns based on previous cost reductions and improvements in the product. Quantitative techniques such as times series and regression could be quite useful in achieving objective forecasts.

A product life cycle analysis strategy is associated with the situation of current market and new technology. Line extensions are associated with this cell and represent higher product technology uncertainty. Because there is already an understanding of the current marketplace, analyses would attempt to overlay patterns of previously launched products in the product line onto the new line extensions. These patterns would characterize a launch curve or life cycle curve by way of looks-like analysis or analogous forecasting.

A customer or market analysis strategy would be necessary in the case of current technology and a new market due to higher market uncertainty. The purpose of this forecasting strategy is to understand the new market, reduce uncertainty, and manifest greater understanding about the new market. Various customer or market research studies might be engaged along with the use of assumptions-based models in an attempt to specify market drivers, which would be validated by the customer or market research performed. Products in this cell include new use and new market products.

A scenario analysis strategy corresponds to the situation of new market and new product technology, representing high market and product technology uncertainties akin to new-to-the-company (new category entries) and new-to-the-world products. Scenario analysis would be employed to paint a picture of the future and future directions to be taken. A scenario analysis strategy should not be confused with simply the use of scenario analysis; rather the intent of forecasting in this situation is to develop various scenarios on which to base the new product development decision. Given a lack of data, the potential difficulty in identifying the specific target market, and questions regarding technology acceptance, subjective assessment techniques would play a major role in this cell.

Forecasting techniques can have applicability across all of the cells, but depending on the specific situation, some techniques are better suited for the task at hand. The resources necessary and outcome desired also will dictate which techniques are better suited for the task at hand. For example, customer or market research could greatly benefit market understanding related to cost reductions, product improvements, and line extensions. These techniques can consume resources in terms of cost, personnel, and time, however. Managerial judgment techniques can be readily applied to all types of new products. Yet often these techniques will not provide enough lower-level detail, as in the case of a product improvement. The new product forecasting framework of Exhibit 10.7 intends to offer viable strategies to facilitate the new product forecasting effort by suggesting those techniques that would be most appropriate and readily applicable.

New Product Forecasting Accuracy

Even with a plethora of techniques, new product forecasting is characteristically associated with low accuracy (high forecast error). Research shows that the overall average accuracy across the six types of new products is about 58 percent, with cost improvement forecasts generally 72 percent accurate; product improvement forecasts 65 percent accurate; line extension forecasts 63 percent accurate; market extension forecasts 54 percent accurate; new category entry (new-to-the-company) forecasts 47 percent; and new-to-the-world products 40 percent accurate (Kahn 2002); these mean values of new product forecasting accuracy were collected by asking respondents to indicate the average forecast accuracy achieved one year after launch. The nature of these accuracy data reaffirms that new markets (i.e., market extensions, new category entries, and new-to-the-world products) are more troublesome to forecast than those situations where a current market is being served (i.e., cost improvements, product improvements, line extensions; see Exhibit 10.8).

One of the underlying reasons for low accuracy is the multiple organizational biases that impinge on the new product forecasting endeavor and cause unnecessary error. Naturally a new product forecast should be developed with

Exhibit 10.8

New Product Forecasting Accuracy Achieved

Type of new product	Average percent accuracy achieved	Forecast horizon in months
Cost reductions	72	21
Product improvements	65	20
Line extensions	63	21
New markets	54	24
New category entries	47	35
New-to-the-world	40	36

Source: Kahn (2002).

a keen eye toward realism and presented to management regardless of the outcome shown, but seldom does this happen. Various research studies have documented the impact of organizational biases on new product forecasting (e.g., Bolton 2003; Forlani, Mullins, and Walker 2002; Tyebjee 1987). Examples of these biases include the Accountability/Management Commitment Bias, Advocacy Bias, Anchoring, Confirmation Bias, "Hard" Data Bias, Optimism Bias, Overconfidence Bias, Planning Fallacy, Post-decision Audit Bias, and Sunk Cost Fallacy (see Kahn 2010). While it is very unlikely that new product forecasting will be free of all biases due to the need to rely on judgment, understanding the persistent types of biases can allow for necessary procedures that enable transparency of new product forecasting figures and sounder new product decision-making. When systematic biases are identified and properly mitigated, the chance for a new product forecast to be on target increases.

The New Product Forecasting Process

Applying techniques appropriately while addressing organizational biases that surround new product forecasting mandates a process approach toward new product forecasting. The new product forecasting process should highlight critical uncertainties inherent in developing the new product forecast, such as cannibalization effects and market penetration. The process also should designate what data need to be collected to address these uncertainties. A process approach to new product forecasting further mandates the continuous building on experiences from prior new product forecasts, cross-functional communication (especially with marketing), and customer feedback, thereby enabling organizational learning and understanding on which to make a credible and realistic forecast.

Assumptions management is an important part of the new product forecasting process. Accordingly, the new product forecasting process should clearly specify assumptions and make them transparent so that there is company understanding of what underlies these assumptions. After launch, a tracking system would closely monitor and control these assumptions to determine if forecasts will come to fruition or deviate significantly.

As part of a successful new product forecasting endeavor, successful companies have realized that new product forecasts should not be point forecasts, but rather be presented as ranges. These ranges typically become more narrowed as the product approaches and enters the launch phase. For example, pessimistic, likely, and optimistic cases could be connected with the monitoring and control of assumptions to determine which scenario is playing out. Best-in-class companies also construct databases to collect, track, and reflect on new product rollouts, especially those in consumer packaged goods industries. Such internal databases are crucial for the validation of new product forecasting assumptions, as well as documenting new product forecasting accuracy. Tying the internal database with syndicated data, market share, and competitor data can enable more robust analyses related to brand preference, price elasticities, and geographic rollout scenarios.

Recommendations for implementing a better and more satisfying approach to new product forecasting also should consider the following:

- technical business functions like market research, research and development, and sales forecasting in the new product forecasting process;
- use of customer or market research studies to obtain a view from outside the company and satisfy the apparent need for customer and market information on which to base new product forecasts;
- use of sophisticated, analytical techniques like experience curves, exponential smoothing, linear regression, moving average, scenario analysis, and simulation in conjunction with qualitative techniques like jury of executive opinion, looks-like analysis, and sales force composite method;
- reliance on interdepartmental communication, especially with the marketing and sales departments;
- reconciliation of new product forecasts by using multiple techniques, including both analytical/quantitative and judgmental/qualitative techniques.

See Kahn (2002, 2006) for more discussion of new product forecasting practices.

Discussion Questions

1. What are the three categories of market testing?
2. What are the five stages of Rogers's diffusion model?
3. What are the five types of customers when it comes to the adoption of new products?
4. What are the four stages of the launch cycle?
5. What is a launch control protocol?
6. What are the three general categories for new product forecasting techniques?

References

Adya, Monica, and Fred Collopy. 1998. "How Effective Are Neural Nets at Forecasting and Prediction? A Review and Evaluation." *Journal of Forecasting*, 17, 451–461.

Bolton, Lisa E. 2003. "Stickier Priors: The Effects of Nonanalytic and Analytic Thinking in New Product Forecasting." *Journal of Marketing Research*, 40 (February), 65–79.

Crawford, Merle, and Anthony diBenedetto. 2003. *New Products Management*. 7th ed. Boston: McGraw-Hill/Irwin.

Fader, Peter S., and Bruce G.S. Hardie. 2001. "Forecasting Trial Sales of New Consumer Packaged Goods." In *Principles of Forecasting: A Handbook for Researchers and Practitioners*, ed. J. Scott Armstrong, 613–630. Norwell, MA: Kluwer.

Forlani, David, John W. Mullins, and Orville C. Walker Jr. 2002. "New Product Decision Making: How Chance and Size of Loss Influence What Marketing Managers See and Do." *Psychology and Marketing*, 19 (11), 957–981.

Gordon, Theodore Jay. 1994. "The Delphi Method." AC/UNU Millennium Project, Futures Research Methodology, Summary Report.

Huss, William R. 1988. "A Move Toward Scenario Analysis." *International Journal of Forecasting*, 4 (3), 377–388.

Huss, William R., and Edward J. Honton. 1987. "Scenario Planning: What Style Should You Use?" *Long Range Planning*, 20 (4), 21–29.

Kahn, Kenneth B. 2002. "An Exploratory Investigation of New Product Forecasting Practices." *Journal of Product Innovation Management*, 19 (March), 133–143.

———. 2006. *New Product Forecasting: An Applied Approach*. Armonk, NY: M.E. Sharpe.

———. 2010. "Identifying the Biases in New Product Forecasting." *Journal of Business Forecasting*, 28 (2), 34–37.

Lilien, Gary, Arvind Rangaswamy, and Christophe Van den Bulte. 1999. *Diffusion Models: Managerial Applications and Software*. Institute for the Study of Business Markets Report #7–1999.

Mahajan, Vijay, Eitan Muller, and Frank M. Bass. 1990. "New Product Diffusion Models in Marketing: A Review and Directions for Research." *Journal of Marketing*, 54 (1), 1–26.

Mahajan, Vijay, Eitan Muller, and Yoram Wind, eds. 2000. *New-Product Diffusion Models*. Volume 11, International Series in Quantitative Marketing. Boston: Kluwer.

Makridakis, Spyros G., Steven C. Wheelwright, and Rob J. Hyndman. 1997. *Forecasting: Methods and Applications*. New York: John Wiley.

Mentzer, John T., and Carol C. Bienstock. 1998. *Sales Forecasting Management*. Thousand Oaks, CA: Sage.

Neter, John, Michael H. Kutner, Christopher J. Nachsheim, and William Wasserman. 1996. *Applied Linear Regression Models*. Chicago: Irwin.

Rogers, Everett M. 1995. *Diffusion of Innovations*. 4th ed. New York: Free Press.

Tyebjee, Tyzoon T. 1987. "Behavioral Biases in New Product Forecasting." *International Journal of Forecasting*, 3, 393–404.

Ulvila, Jacob W. 1985. "Decision Trees for Forecasting." *Journal of Forecasting*, 4 (4), 377–385.

Urban, Glen L., Gerald M. Katz, Thomas E. Hatch, and Alvin J. Silk. 1983. "The ASSESSOR Pre-Test Market Evaluation System." *Interfaces*, 13 (6), 38–59.

Woudenberg, Fred. 1991. "An Evaluation of Delphi." *Technological Forecasting and Social Change*, 131–150.

11 ╳ Life Cycle Management

After launch, the product begins what is termed "the product life cycle." The product development team is discharged at this point, if it has not already been discharged prior to launch, and a product management team (which in many cases had launch responsibility) takes over responsibility for the product.

The product management team will focus on the life cycle management of the product—that is, ensuring that the product reaches its full potential as a particular product item or emerging product line in the company's product mix. Associated with reaching this potential are decisions about fine-tuning the product's marketing strategy, defending against competitors, and continuous innovation of the product, if feasible. Brand management considerations also will persist after product launch.

The Product Life Cycle

The product life cycle is a concept that attempts to describe a product's unit sales postlaunch through its eventual termination. The curve parallels the diffusion or S-curve, suggesting product diffusion into the marketplace.

The theory underlying the product life cycle is that unit sales will transition through four distinct product life cycle stages: introduction, growth, maturity, and decline (see Exhibit 11.1). The introduction stage represents the launch cycle. Here sales slowly emerge as the company tries to establish a beachhead and then early growth. The focus of the marketing effort is to create awareness and get trial. During the growth stage, sales rise steadily, and the focus becomes to maximize market share. The maturity stage represents a leveling of sales, and the focus is profit maximizing and market share maintenance. The decline stage is the final stage characteristic of decreasing unit sales. In the decline stage the focal marketing strategy is to harvest the product, which represents a reduction in marketing expenditures while revenues are sustained for as long as possible.

The product life cycle also can be used to describe the possible development of an emerging market. In particular, the framework suggests that competi-

Exhibit 11.1 **The Product Life Cycle**

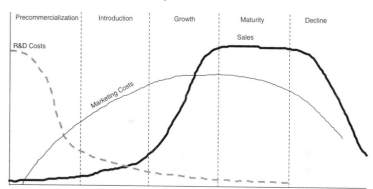

tion will be low in the introduction stage, but fierce during the growth stage as competitors see the growth potential of the respective market. During the maturity stage, the number of competitors will be reduced through mergers, acquisitions, and companies dropping out of the market. Market share at this point will be pretty much determined, with intense efforts needed to make headway into securing additional market share. The decline stage represents a declining number of competitors as companies leave the market.

It is important to use the product life cycle concept as just a guideline, not a definitive model. By inappropriately using the product life cycle, various companies have incorrectly determined that their product was declining, pulled resources from the product, and prematurely terminated their product. In one case, a toothpaste manufacturer saw sales decline over a period and concluded—based on the product life cycle theory—that the product was in the decline stage. The company consequently reduced the amount of resources going to the product, which contributed to a further reduction in sales. The manufacturer then sold off its product to another company, which refreshed the marketing campaign, put ample marketing resources into the product, and grew the market (Dhalla and Yuspeh 1976). It is therefore necessary to keep in mind the following facts:

- The stages of the product life cycle, the time span of the entire life cycle, and the shape of the life cycle will vary by product.
- External factors can impact the performance of a product, shortening or lengthening its life cycle.
- A company can influence a product's life cycle.
- The product life cycle can become a self-fulfilling prophecy—a tendency

to believe that something will happen and thus to do things that ensure that it will happen. For example, a company that expects sales to decline may reduce the promotion budget, which, in turn, will typically reduce sales.

Another issue with the product life cycle is the different variations of the product life cycle curve, depending on the level of analysis performed. The product-form level represents a view at the specific product-form level. The product-class level represents a view at the product-type level; and the generic-need level portrays an overall industry view. For example, an herbal tea manufacturer can see three different perspectives when using the product life cycle concept, depending at what level of analysis is the focal perspective. At the beverage industry view, an analyst for the company may see a very mature market. Using tea as the product-class, the analyst may see a slightly declining market. But at the herbal tea level, the market suggests growth. This highlights a need for proper definition of the market to be analyzed and careful interpretation of the product life cycle curve.

Overall, the product life cycle should be viewed as a managerial planning tool for developing strategy (see Exhibit 11.2) and not a market forecasting tool for making unit sales predictions. The product life cycle can provide insight into possible changing consumer composition, competition, and support requirements, as well as provide insight into what may be a balanced portfolio based on these market dynamics.

Strategic Considerations During the Maturity Stage

In conjunction with any analysis that may be done using product life cycle, a company will need to decide on a strategy to enact late in the growth stage and that will carry into the maturity stage. There are three strategic options that may be enacted.

The first strategy is a maintenance strategy. This strategy focuses on fine-tuning the marketing mix to ensure product profitability. Minor changes are made to the marketing mix to minimize marketing expenses to keep costs low and sustain a reasonable margin.

The second strategy is a defense strategy. The company concentrates on an issue perceived to be important from the customer perspective—for example, price, product quality, or service quality. The product differentiates itself from competitors by being superior on this important issue. There is a great risk, however, in using price as a differential advantage; price is the easiest marketing mix element to copy, and there is always someone willing to match price.

The third strategy is an innovation strategy. This strategy emphasizes new

Exhibit 11.2

Strategic Considerations Across the Traditional Product Life Cycle

	Product life cycle stage			
	Introduction	Growth	Maturity	Decline
Market characteristics				
Sales	Low sales	Rapidly rising sales	Peak sales	Declining sales
Costs	High cost per customer	Average cost per customer	Low cost per customer	Low cost per customer
Profits	Negative	Rising profits	High profits	Declining profits
Customers	Innovators	Early adopters	Middle majority	Laggards
Competitors	Few	Growing number	Stable number beginning to decline	Declining number
Strategic considerations				
Marketing objectives	Create product awareness and trial	Maximize market share	Maximize profits while defending market share	Reduce expenditures and milk the brand
Product strategies	Offer a basic product	Offer product extensions, service, warranty	Diversify brand and models	Phase out weak items
Distribution strategies	Build selective distribution	Build intensive distribution	Build more intensive distribution	Go selective; phase out unprofitable outlets
Promotion strategies	Build product awareness among early adopters and dealers; use heavy sales promotions to entice trial	Build awareness and interest in mass market; reduce sales promotions to take advantage of heavy consumer demand	Stress brand differences and benefits; increase sales promotions to encourage brand switching	Reduce promotion activity to the level needed to retain hard-core loyal customers
Price strategies	Charge cost-plus	Price to penetrate market	Price to match or best competitors	Cut price

Source: Kotler (2000).

191

products as a way to sustain a competitive advantage. These new product include flankers or line extensions, new uses or users (market extensions), and/or significant innovations (next-generation or new-to-the-world products); product improvements would be associated with the first two given strategies. The flanker option is a common approach but can lead to product proliferation (too many similar products). The significant innovations option is a valid but risky endeavor because it makes the current product obsolete. With regard to this option, the adage goes as follows: "If you're going to have cannibals, you may as well keep the cannibals in the family."

Product Families, Product Platforms, and the Product Mix Map

Product families are a life cycle management consideration if the respective company decides to expand beyond a single product offering. Such a decision may derive from an interest in expanding width or depth of a product line or from an inherent need to introduce next-generation products to keep up with the pace of technology in the industry. If a decision to expand is made, consideration also is given to the notion of product platforms and product families.

Product platforms are typically an underlying basis for a product family. Product platforms provide a common foundation upon which new products (line extensions or next-generation products) can be built. Specifically, product platforms represent the sharing of essential design elements and critical components by a set of products to make production, distribution, and service processes more effective and efficient. For example, Chrysler used the same basic car frame, suspension, and drive train for the Chrysler Concorde, Eagle Vision, and Dodge Intrepid, thereby reducing overall production costs. Chrysler later introduced its New Yorker model based on a longer version of the platform (Meyer and Utterback 1993).

By definition, product families are "products that share a common platform but have specific features and functionality required by different sets of customers" (Meyer and Utterback 1993). A product family can be conceived as serving a market segment or set of market segments, while the individual products within the family serve specific target markets with the segment(s). In terms of the product mix hierarchy, product families are an assortment of "similar" product lines, which, in turn, are an assortment of "similar" product items. "Similarity" in this case is based on the common platform used across the product lines, and each of the individual features and functionality would designate the individual items within each line. The assortment of product families would represent the company's product mix.

A driver for using product families is a need for greater effectiveness and efficiencies in the manufacturing process. Among other things, effectiveness and efficiencies stem from (1) less inventorying of specialized parts because products would share parts; (2) less production downtime related to production line turnover because products would share common processing steps; and (3) greater responsiveness to customer requests because the standard product platform would allow for staging of the production process such that a significant portion of the manufacturing process could take place up-front, and tailoring of the product would take place only when an order was received. Product families also offer the benefit of providing structure to a complex product mix. These or other reasons would encourage use of a product family structure.

With respect to the later issue of structure, mapping of the product mix can help identify product family groupings, identify gaps in product lines, and illustrate the product development history of the company. Product mix maps also can suggest core competencies of a company by linking the structure of the product mix and product successes based on the assumption that successes would reflect where the company was strongest.

To build a product mix map, the company or a particular strategic business unit (SBU) of the company would list its current product items. These items are then grouped according to product line. Taking each product line, the historical product offerings of the line are listed in chronological order to show a perspective of product development for the line. This would be repeated across the other product lines. Next, similar product lines are grouped according to various characteristics to suggest a possible product family. Those products sharing a common platform would characteristically be a product family. Upon completion, the map would show the structure of the product mix and historical perspective of how each of the lines developed. Other data used in conjunction with the product mix map could include market segments served by each product line to offer a market perspective when assessing each potential product family.

Exhibit 11.3 presents an example of a product mix map for a hypothetical shoe manufacturer. The map shows an evolution of the product mix from an even distribution of business and casual shoes to a greater number of casual shoes, suggesting an inherent company leaning toward the casual shoe market.

Brand Management

Another area during life cycle management is brand management, which is increasingly recognized as a key element of life cycle management in addition

Exhibit 11.3 **Sample Product Mix Map**

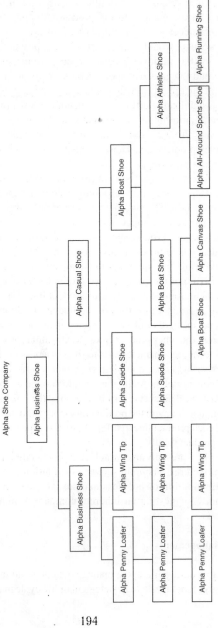

to product launch. The driver of brand management's emerging recognition is the fact that the brand can help customers interpret and process information about the product, feel more confident in their decision to buy the product, and/or feel more satisfied after purchase. Brands thus offer much value to companies by way of improving the efficiency and effectiveness of marketing campaigns. As the product transitions to other life cycle stages, brands can offer a strong competitive advantage, provide a basis for an improved profit margin, solidify brand loyalty, and assist in developing other new products via brand extensions.

Although simplified in the discussion of marketing plans in Chapter 9 as consisting of considerations of brand name, brand mark, trade character, trademark, and trade dress, brand management is much more. It focuses on the establishment and maintenance of, if not growth of, brand equity.

As defined by David Aaker (1996, 7), brand equity is "a set of assets and liabilities linked to a brand's name and symbols that adds to or subtracts from the value provided by a product or service to a firm and/or that firm's customers." Such value translates to a bottom-line (financial) impact. Indeed, the potential financial benefits of brand equity spurred the U.S. Internal Revenue Service in the early 1990s to consider the notion of taxing corporations on their brand equity as an intangible asset. However, the idea never materialized because of the complexity surrounding what brand equity is and how it could be measured.

A Brand Equity Framework

In his popular framework, Aaker (1996) argues that brand equity is a function of five key components: brand loyalty, brand awareness, perceived quality, brand associations, and other proprietary brand assets (see Exhibit 11.4).

Brand loyalty is defined as "a measure of the attachment that a customer has to a brand" (Aaker 1996, 21). Such attachment can be categorized into five distinct levels of loyalty. The lowest level of loyalty is no loyalty at all. These customers are indifferent about the brand and very responsive to price such that they will switch products often based on price. The next level of loyalty comprises customers who have no reason to change because they are satisfied, habitual buyers. However, these customers will change if given a compelling reason to change. The third level of loyalty is a satisfied buyer who will incur switching costs upon switching products. This buyer will change if given a compelling reason, but because of the switching cost is less likely to do so. The fourth level of loyalty is the customer who likes the brand and considers it a "friend." At this point, the customer is developing a "personal" relationship with the brand. The ultimate level of loyalty is the committed

Exhibit 11.4 **Aaker's Brand Equity Framework**

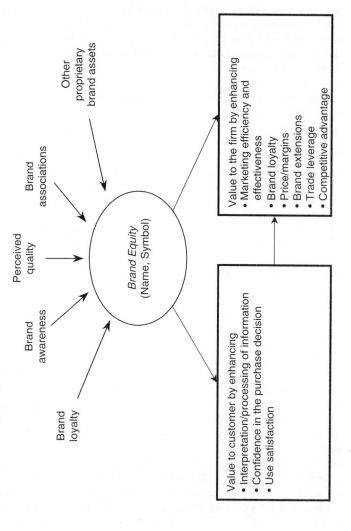

buyer, who buys the product regardless of any reason to change. Aaker recommends that in order to drive customers up to the higher levels of loyalty, companies must treat customers right, stay close to the customer, measure and manage customer satisfaction, create switching costs, and provide extras to delight the customer (see Exhibit 11.5).

Brand awareness is defined as "the ability of a potential buyer to recognize or recall that a brand is a member of a certain product category" (Aaker 1996, 10). Four distinct levels of awareness are given, as shown in Exhibit 11.6. The lowest level of awareness is no awareness at all. Basically, customers are unfamiliar with the brand. The next level of awareness is recognition of the brand. When prompted or cued, customers can remember what product category the product falls into after thinking about it. The third level of awareness is brand recall. Customers can readily recall a respective product's category after just seeing the brand's name or symbol. The highest level is top-of-mind awareness. When given a product category, customers will immediately recall the brand. For example, if asked to name a brand in the product category of cola soft drinks, a particular customer might immediately reply "Coca-Cola." To create and maintain brand awareness, it is recommended that the brand be memorable and different from other competitors' brands, associated with a slogan or jingle, connected to a symbol, regularly publicized, in full view at sponsored events, and used in conjunction with cues.

Perceived quality is defined as "the customer's perception of the overall superiority of a product or service with respect to its intended purpose" (Aaker 1996, 17). Perceived quality is portrayed as a continuum from low or indistinguishable perceived quality to high perceived quality. The key influence driving perceived quality is product quality and service quality meeting the expectations that customers have based on what the company says it is going to deliver. When expectations are not met, perceived quality will be judged as low; when met or exceeded, perceived quality will be judged as adequate or higher. As portrayed in Exhibit 11.7, at the lowest level is a commodity product, where the product is considered a commodity that is indistinguishable from competitors' products. The next level is where the product meets expectations. The third level is superior services and features, which allow the product to draw consumer appeal. The highest level is delighting services and features, which clearly distinguish the product in the marketplace and go beyond just meeting expectations to surpassing expectations.

Brand associations are items in a customer's memory that are linked to the brand (Aaker 1996). These associations include personal experiences, promotion activities, and/or any other "signal" connecting to the brand. For example, a motorboat manufacturer conducted extensive market research to find underlying themes for why people buy boats. It found that a segment of

Exhibit 11.5 **Brand Loyalty Pyramid**

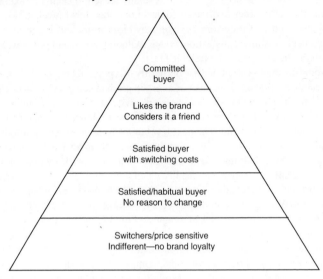

Exhibit 11.6 **Brand Awareness Pyramid**

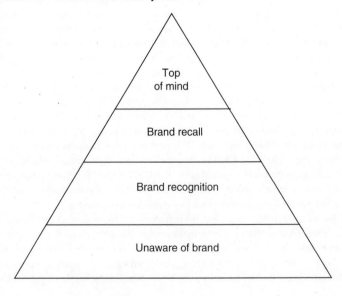

Exhibit 11.7 **Perceived Quality Pyramid**

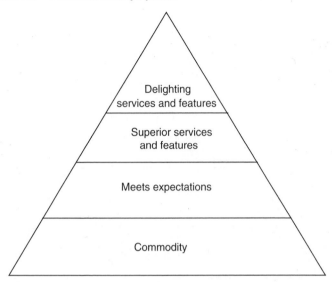

those interested in purchasing boats associated the childhood experience of fishing with their fathers and grandfathers. This association was subsequently employed in advertising to elicit customers' favorable thoughts about how buying the company's motorboat would allow customers to relive the experience and share it with their family. In particular, advertising showed a young boy fishing with his grandfather on one of the company's new boats. As suggested in Exhibit 11.8, the lowest level of brand associations is no product experience and thus no brand association. The next level is some experience, but no ties to the product. The third level is an ability to recall associations, but some associations are not predominant. The highest level of brand association is a strong link to memories, which become predominant when the customer interacts with or experiences the product. To establish brand associations, Aaker recommends that the company must be consistent over time and consistent over elements of the marketing program.

The last component is other proprietary brand assets, such as patents, trademarks, and channel relationships (Aaker 1996, 8). These assets inhibit or prevent competitors from eroding a customer base.

In the course of establishing and maintaining brand equity, efforts of measurement need to be undertaken. Aaker proposes eight variables that should be measured directly from customers to track each of the components of

Exhibit 11.8   **Brand Associations Pyramid**

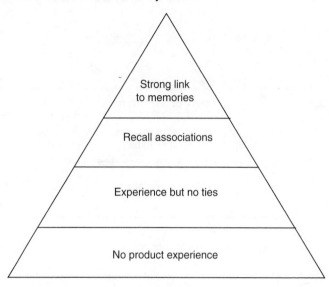

brand equity, except other proprietary brand assets. Three additional market behavior measures are also recommended to provide a broader market view. These eleven measures and corresponding definitions are as follows:

Brand Loyalty

- Price premium: What amount are customers willing to pay for the brand in comparison to competitor offerings?
- Customer satisfaction: Are customers really happy with the company's product and related services?

Brand Awareness

- Brand awareness: Is the brand salient in the minds of customers?

Perceived Quality

- Perceived quality: To what degree are customers' expectations for performance and benefits met?
- Leadership: How popular is the brand based on such characteristics as

top-selling brand in the category, customer acceptance, and recognition as technologically innovative?

Brand Associations

- Perceived value: What are the underlying reasons for why customers view the brand as a good value for the money, given competitors' offerings and brands?
- Brand personality: What evoked images, elicited traits, and expressed interests do customers have with or connect to the brand?
- Organizational associations: What are customers' opinion of the company and its bearing on the brand?

Market Behavior Measures

- Market share: What is the respective branded product's performance relative to the performance of competitors' products?
- Market price: What is the market price of the branded product over time relative to the price of competitors' products?
- Distribution coverage: How many outlets provide customer access to the branded product?

Multiple statistics and question items could be employed to measure each of the above variables. The key is to establish some level of tracking and regular reporting to uncover potential issues with the brand, either positive or negative in nature. Through a course of tracking and reporting, an improved understanding of that brand's equity would be realized, enabling better managerial decisions related to the branded product (branded product line).

A Brand Decision Framework

Various decisions surround brand management. Exhibit 11.9 presents a framework that outlines these decisions, including the branding decision itself, the brand-sponsor decision, the brand-name decision, the brand-strategy decision, and the brand-repositioning decision.

The branding decision concerns whether to brand or not to brand a product or service. The purpose of giving a brand to a product is to give it a distinguishable identity in the marketplace. However, a distinguishable identity is not necessary in certain cases like generic and no-name products.

The brand-sponsor decision concerns the channel level at which the brand will be given. A manufacturer brand is a brand that the manufacturer

Exhibit 11.9 **Brand Decision Framework**

Branding Decision
- Brand
- No brand

Brand-Sponsor Decision
- Manufacturer brand
- Distributor brand
- Licensed brand

Brand-Name Decision
- Individual names
- Blanket family name
- Separate family name
- Company-individual name

Brand-Strategy Decision
- Line extensions
- Brand extensions
- Multibrands
- New brands
- Cobrands

Brand-Repositioning Decision
- Repositioning
- No repositioning

Source: Adapted from Kotler (2000).

designates and that retains its brand characteristics (e.g., name, marks, trade characters, trade dress) throughout the channel. Examples of manufacturer brands are Oreo (Nabisco), Tide (Procter and Gamble), and Colgate Toothpaste (Colgate-Palmolive). Manufacturer brands are sometimes referred to as national brands. A distributor brand, sometimes referred to as a private label brand, is a brand that a distributor designates and sells at its outlets. Examples of distributor brands are Arizona jeans (J.C. Penney), Craftsman tools (Sears), and Sam's Choice (Wal-Mart). Associations and professional groups are associated with licensed brands. Such a group gives permission so that products can be sold with the group's name or brand on them—for example, merchandise sold with logos of sports teams from college athletics, the National Football League, National Basketball Association, and Major League Baseball.

The brand name decision concerns the approach for choosing a brand name. Four possible approaches include individual names, blanket family name, separate family name, and company-individual name. An individual name gives the product its own identity, so, if the product fails, the company name and other company brands are not affected. The drawback is that additional resources are necessary to develop and proof a new brand name. General Mills uses this strategy with its offerings—for example, Betty Crocker, Bisquick, Gold Medal, Nature Valley. The blanket family name emphasizes a core name connected with all new products. This name is typically the manufacturer's name. Heinz uses this brand name strategy to identify its products—for example, Heinz Ketchup, Heinz 57 Sauce, Heinz Mustard. The separate family name uses different names for different categories of products. Sears uses this strategy for its Craftsman tools and Kenmore appliances. The company-individual name highlights both the company brand and the product brand. The intent of this strategy to use the company brand name to accentuate the individual brand name. Kellogg Company uses this approach with its products—for example, Kellogg's Rice Krispies, Kellogg's Corn Flakes, Kellogg's Raisin Bran.

The brand-strategy decision concerns the establishment of the brand in the marketplace. Five approaches are possible: line extensions, brand extensions, multibrands, new brands, and cobrands. Line extensions take the existing brand name and apply it to a new size or flavor in an existing product category. For example, Kimberly Clark's Kleenex line comprises many line extensions, including Kleenex Facial Tissue, Kleenex Coldcare, Kleenex Expressions, and Kleenex Specialty Packs. Brand extensions apply an existing brand name to new product categories. Honda's use of its brand across various industries such as automobiles, motorcycles, lawn mowers, marine engines, and snowmobiles is characteristic of a brand extension strategy. Multibrands are the introduction of new brand names to the same product category currently served by the company. In this way, the company can serve multiple market segments. Procter & Gamble's Pamper and Luvs brands in the diaper market are indicative of a multibrand strategy. Marriott's use of multiple hotel brand names like Marriott Resorts, Courtyard by Marriott, Residence Inn, and Fairfield Inn indicates a multibrand strategy as well. A new brand strategy is simply developing a new brand name for every new product category entered. The use of a new brand strategy would be predicated on the belief that the present brand would not be well associated with the new category. Apple's introduction of the iPod and iPad illustrate a new brand strategy. The cobrand strategy is used when a product bears two or more well-known brand names. In ingredient cobranding, the ingredients of a product include another product, like Betty Crocker Brownies with Hershey's Chocolate. In same company cobranding, a company connects two or more of its brands into a new product, such as General Mills offering Trix-flavored Yoplait yogurt. In multiple-sponsor cobranding, brands of two or more companies are equally represented, such as in the case of Dow Corning.

After a brand has been introduced into the marketplace, a brand-repositioning decision might emerge. This decision concerns whether to change a brand or maintain the brand as is. Brands performing as expected would obviously remain unchanged or be given resources to strengthen their current image or identity. Brands performing below expectations could be repositioned to meet a different market or better target the intended market. A brand continuing to perform below expectations would obviously be a candidate for harvesting.

The Brand-Switching Matrix

An analytical method useful in brand management is the brand-switching matrix. This matrix classifies purchase behavior so as to reflect certain characteristics about the marketplace and customers' brand loyalty.

The simplest way to construct a brand-switching matrix is to survey customers about their previous brand purchase and current brand purchase. The data is then classified in the form of percentages of customers buying each of the different brands. For example, it might be found that 33 percent of customers that bought brand A during their last purchase once again buy brand A. This would suggest that brand A's brand loyalty is approximately 33 percent. An effective way to organize the data collected is a matrix format as shown in Exhibit 11.10.

Exhibit 11.10 specifically shows three different scenarios in a brand-

Exhibit 11.10

Brand-Switching Matrix

Exhibit 11.10a. Two Clear Submarkets

		Brand bought in the current period (t + 1)			
		A	B	C	D
Brand bought in the	A	.60	.35	.02	.03
previous period (t)	B	.25	.70	.03	.02
	C	.01	.04	.65	.30
	D	.03	.02	.20	.75

Exhibit 11.10b. Dominant Brand

		Brand bought in the current period (t + 1)			
		A	B	C	D
Brand bought in the	A	.90	.03	.02	.05
previous period (t)	B	.40	.40	.10	.10
	C	.30	.05	.60	.05
	D	.40	.04	.06	.50

Exhibit 11.10c. Equivalent Brands

		Brand bought in the current period (t + 1)			
		A	B	C	D
Brand bought in the	A	.40	.20	.18	.22
previous period (t)	B	.20	.35	.20	.25
	C	.27	.19	.30	.34
	D	.17	.18	.35	.30

Source: Data adapted from Lehmann and Winer (1997).

switching matrix format. As shown in Exhibit 11.10a, 60 percent of customers that bought brand A previously bought brand A again; 35 percent of customers that bought brand A previously bought brand B; 2 percent of customers that bought brand A previously bought brand C; and 3 percent of customers that bought brand A previously bought brand D. Exhibit 11.10a thus illustrates a scenario where two clear submarkets exist because it is apparent that brand A's competition is primarily from brand B, and vice versa, while brand C's competition is primarily from brand D, and vice versa. Exhibit 11.10b illustrates a scenario where a dominant brand exists. Exhibit 11.10c illustrates a scenario where all brands are relatively equivalent. The use of a brand-switching matrix illustrates these scenarios in a concise fashion.

Another way to read the data in the brand-switching matrix is to consider the columns as the percentage of customers gained from a respective competitor and the rows as the percentage of customers lost to a respective competitor. For example, in brand A's column of Exhibit 11.10a, brand A gains 60 percent of its own sales (keeps 60 percent of its sales), gains 25 percent of sales from brand B, gains 1 percent of sales from brand C, and gains 3 percent of sales from brand D. In brand A's row of Exhibit 11.10a, brand A "loses" 60 percent of its sales to itself (keeps 60 percent of its sales), loses 35 percent of sales to brand B, loses 2 percent of sales to brand C, and loses 3 percent of sales to brand D. Note that each row adds up to 100 percent. Also note that the cell where brand A gains from/loses to itself represents the amount of sales that brand A keeps. This cell can be construed as representing, if not quantifying, brand loyalty, and thus, the diagonal of the matrix can be interpreted as brand loyalty. Exhibit 11.10a suggests that brand loyalty for brands A, B, C, and D is 60 percent, 70 percent, 65 percent, and 75 percent, respectively.

An additional use of the brand-switching matrix is to estimate market share over time. To do this, the current market share of the different competitors must be first given. The brand-switching matrix can then provide the probabilities of keeping or losing share over time. As shown in Exhibit 11.11, a brand-switching matrix is constructed based on customers' purchase of the competing brands X and Y. The current market share for brands X and Y is 45 percent and 55 percent, respectively. After the next purchase, brand X's market share is estimated to decrease to 43.5 percent, and brand Y's market share is estimated to increase to 56.5 percent. These are calculated as follows: brand X gains/keeps 60 percent of its share (.60 × .45) and gains 30 percent of brand Y's share (.30 × .55), which summed equals 43.5 percent; brand Y gains 40 percent of brand X's share (.40 × .45) and gains/keeps 70 percent of its share (.70 × .55), which summed equals 56.5 percent. Subsequent purchase iterations would proceed in the same fashion using the newly calculated market share estimates.

The brand-switching matrix also can be used to estimate long-run market share as well. Using the matrix of Exhibit 11.11, a set of simultaneous equations can be set up and then solved to estimate market share for brands X and Y based on the given brand-switching probabilities. As shown, brand X's market share is equal to 60 percent of its own share plus 30 percent of brand Y's share. Brand Y's market share is equal to 40 percent of brand X's share plus 70 percent of its own share. Given that brand X's share plus brand Y's share equal 100 percent, the long-run market share estimates (steady-state market share estimates) are a 42.9 percent share for brand X and a 57.1 percent share for brand Y (see Exhibit 11.11).

These estimates assume that the brand-switching probabilities remain fairly constant. This assumption may or may not apply given the degree of marketing initiatives employed by the respective competitors. However, the

Exhibit 11.11

Market Share Estimation Using the Brand-Switching Matrix

		Brand bought in the current period $(t+1)$	
		X	Y
Brand bought in the previous period (t)	X	.60	.40
	Y	.30	.70

Initial market share: brand X = 45%, brand Y = 55%

After the next purchase iteration (t + 1):
Brand X market share = (.60*.45) + (.30*.55) = .27 + .165 = .435 or 43.5%
Brand Y market share = (.40*.45) + (.70*.55) = .18 + .385 = .565 or 56.5%

After another purchase iteration (t + 2):
Brand X market share = (.60*.435) + (.30*.565) = .261 + .1695 = .4305 or 43.0%
Brand Y market share = (.40*.435) + (.70*.565) = .174 + .3955 = .5695 or 56.9%

Estimating long-run market share:
Brand X market share = (.60*brand X market share) + (.30*brand Y market share)
Brand Y market share = (.40*brand X market share) + (.70*brand Y market share)
Total market = brand X market share + brand Y market share

or mathematically expressed as
X = .6X + .3Y
Y = .4X + .7Y
1 = X + Y

Solving for X,
Y = 1 − X
X = .6X + .3(1 − X) or X = .3X + .3 or X = 3/7 or X = .429
Y = 1 − .429 = .571

brand-switching matrix can serve as a useful what-if analysis tool in determining if a marketing program designed to change brand-switching behavior is cost-effective. For example, if a company knows that every 1 percent of market share represents $100,000 profit, is it worthwhile to implement a campaign to increase brand X's loyalty by 5 percent at a cost of $250,000? As shown in Exhibit 11.12, a 5 percent increase in brand loyalty will increase brand X's long-run market share by approximately 3.3 percent (the new market share would be 46.2 percent versus the previous market share of 42.9 percent). The new campaign would conceivably generate $330,000 in profit (3.3 × $100,000) and sufficiently cover the $250,000 budget. It therefore appears that the campaign is worthwhile to implement.

Exhibit 11.12

What-If Analysis Using the Brand-Switching Matrix: An Example

Current brand-switching behavior		Brand bought in the current period ($t + 1$)	
		X	Y
Brand bought in the	**X**	.60	.40
previous period (t)	Y	.30	.70

Initial market share: brand X = 45%, brand Y = 55%

Estimated long-run market share (current brand-switching behavior):
brand X = 42.9%, brand Y = 57.1%

Every 1% of market share = $100,000 profit

Proposed impact on brand-switching behavior after implementing new campaign		Brand bought in the current period ($t + 1$)	
		X	Y
Brand bought in the	**X**	**.65**	**.35**
previous period (t)	Y	.30	.70

Brand X market share = (**.65***brand X market share) + (.30* brand Y market share)
Brand Y market share = (**.35***brand X market share) + (.70*brand Y market share)
Total market = brand X market share + brand Y market share

or mathematically expressed as
X = .65X + .3Y
Y = .35X + .7Y
1 = X + Y

Solving for X,
Y = 1–X
X = .65X + .3(1–X) or X = .35X + .3 or X = 30/65 or X = .462
Y = 1–.462 = .538

Market share increase is 46.2% – 42.9% or 3.3%. So 3.3 × $100,000 = $330,000 profit.

Given that $330,000 sufficiently covers the $250,000 budget, implementation of the campaign would seem appropriate.

Discussion Questions

1. What are the four stages of the product life cycle?
2. What are some underlying issues with the product life cycle concept?
3. What is a product platform?

4. What are the components of brand equity?
5. What are some important brand decisions?

References

Aaker, David A. 1996. *Building Strong Brands*. New York: Free Press.

Dhalla, N.K., and S. Yuspeh. 1976. "Forget the Product Life-Cycle Concept." *Harvard Business Review*, 54 (1) (January–February), 102–112.

Kotler, Philip. 2000. *Marketing Management: Analysis, Planning, Implementation, and Control*. 10th ed. Upper Saddle River, NJ: Prentice-Hall.

Lehmann, Donald R., and Russell S. Winer. 1997. *Analysis for Market Planning*. 4th ed. Chicago: Irwin.

Meyer, Marc H., and James M. Utterback. 1993. "The Product Family and the Dynamics of Core Capability." *Sloan Management Review*, 34 (3) (Spring), 29–47.

12 ✕ Global Issues in Product Planning

Global considerations are prevalent in product planning. Among the many global issues that touch product planning, this chapter discusses four topics: global culture and language, global product development teams, sustainable product development, and base of the pyramid product development.

Overview of Global Considerations

A useful framework for product planning in global settings is given by Keegan (1995). This framework (see Exhibit 12.1) considers any necessary product changes and/or promotion changes to distinguish five strategies for introducing products to foreign (global) markets. These five strategies include straight extension, communication adaptation, product adaptation, dual adaptation, and product invention.

Straight extension is simply the introduction of the product into a foreign market without any change to the product itself or the promotion campaign. As a result of the North American Free Trade Act (NAFTA), many U.S. grocery product firms introduced their products into Canada and Mexico as straight extensions from the U.S. market. The packages of these companies' products already included both English and Spanish labels so there was literally no change to the product.

Communication adaptation is the introduction of the same product with changes to the product's promotion campaign. Four types of promotion changes are possible. The first is use of the same promotion message, varying only the language, colors, and name. However, this is not as simple as one would expect. As shown in Exhibit 12.2, the product name or slogan when translated meant something completely different than intended, often resulting in an embarrassing situation for the company. Colors too can have different meanings in different culture, especially with regard to cultural taboos. For example, purple is associated with death in Burma and some Latin American cultures, white is a mourning color in India, and green is associated with disease in Malaysia (Kotler 2000).

Exhibit 12.1 **Product Planning Strategies for International Settings**

		Product	
		Do not change product	Adapt product	Develop new product
Promotion	Do not change promotion	Straight extension	Product adaptation	Product invention
	Adapt promotion	Communication adaptation	Dual adaptation	

211

Exhibit 12.2

Slogans and Marketing Initiatives That Failed in International Settings

- GM's Chevy Nova was marketed in Central and South America. *No va* in Spanish means "it doesn't go."

- The Dairy Association's huge success with the "Got Milk?" campaign prompted it to expand advertising to Mexico. It was soon brought to the association's attention that the Spanish translation read "Are you lactating?"

- Coors put its slogan "Turn It Loose" into Spanish, where it was read as "Suffer from Diarrhea."

- Scandinavian vacuum manufacturer Electrolux used the following slogan in an American campaign: "Nothing sucks like an Electrolux."

- Clairol introduced the Mist Stick, a curling iron, into Germany only to find out that *mist* is German slang for manure.

- When Gerber started selling baby food in Africa, it used the same packaging as in the United States, with the smiling baby on the label. Later the company learned that in Africa, where many people cannot read, companies routinely put on package labels pictures of what's inside.

- Colgate introduced a toothpaste in France called Cue, the name of a notorious porno magazine.

- An American T-shirt maker in Miami printed shirts for the Spanish market that promoted the pope's visit. Instead of "I saw the Pope" (*el Papa*), the shirts used *la papa*, meaning "I saw the potato."

- Pepsi's "Come Alive with the Pepsi Generation" translated into "Pepsi Brings Your Ancestors Back from the Grave" in Chinese.

- The Coca-Cola name in China was first read as *Kekoukela*, meaning "Bite the wax tadpole" or "female horse stuffed with wax," depending on the dialect. Coke then researched 40,000 Chinese characters to find a phonetic equivalent *kokou kole*, which translated into "happiness in the mouth."

- Frank Perdue's chicken slogan, "It takes a strong man to make a tender chicken," was translated into Spanish as "It takes an aroused man to make a chicken affectionate."

- When Parker Pen marketed a ballpoint pen in Mexico, its ads were supposed to read, "It won't leak in your pocket and embarrass you." The company thought that the word *embarazar* (to impregnate) meant "to embarrass," so the ad read, "It won't leak in your pocket and make you pregnant!"

- When American Airlines wanted to advertise its new leather first-class seats in the Mexican market, it translated its "Fly in Leather" slogan literally, which meant "Fly naked" (*vuela en cuero*) in Spanish.

The second type of promotion change is to employ the same promotion theme, but adapt the promotion copy to the local market. For example, Camay soap varied its commercial content across countries by showing a woman in U.S. commercials, a man in Venezuela, and a man's hands in Italy and France (Kotler 2000).

The third type of promotion is the use of a global pool of promotions (e.g., advertisements) from which each local market chooses the most appropriate one. Allowing local market managers to design their promotions to meet country-specific needs within a given set of guidelines is also characteristic of this type of adaptation.

The fourth type of promotion is specifically designing a promotion campaign to target the local market. This essentially treats the foreign market as separate target market in regard to the promotion strategy. A driver for using a distinct promotion campaign is the fact that different cultures respond differently to promotion outlets. For example, magazines play a major role in Italy, but a minor role in Austria. Another driver for a distinct promotion campaign is country restrictions placed on promotion. Greece prohibits coupons, France prohibits games of chance and limits premiums, Saudi Arabia discourages the use of women in advertising, and Norway prohibits cigarette and alcohol advertising.

Product adaptation is an altering of the product to meet local conditions or preferences, but the general promotion campaign remains basically the same. For example, cellular telephone manufacturers must alter their telephone technologies to meet the cellular system specification in different global regions (e.g., GSM in Europe; CDMA, 3G, and 4G in the United States). These changes would represent a regional product adaptation. Product adaptation also can be much more specific, depending on the situation. A country-specific product adaptation is Kraft's blending of different coffees for different European countries, as the British prefer to drink coffee with milk while the French prefer to drink coffee black (Kotler 2000).

Dual adaptation is the altering of both the product and promotion campaign. In this way, the product and its associated promotion are tailored to meet the local conditions or preferences. As previously discussed, four types of promotion changes are possible. In the end, such promotion would likely promote the specific product features preferred by the local market.

Product invention is the development of a new product to meet the local conditions or preferences. Two types of product invention are possible. Backward invention is the reintroduction of earlier product forms that are well adapted to a foreign country's needs. National Cash Register reintroduced its crank-operated cash registers at half the price of modern cash registers and sold substantial numbers in technology-deficient areas of Latin

213

America and Africa. Forward invention is the creation of a new product to meet a need in another country. Such is the case of automakers, which develop vehicles to meet the local conditions of the marketplace. Vehicles designed for Europe and Asia are typically smaller than those designed for the United States. In certain cases, forward inventions developed by a U.S. company for a foreign market can be introduced to the U.S. market. Häagen-Dazs's dulce de leche flavored ice cream was originally developed for Argentina, but was subsequently rolled out in the United States and Europe with much success.

Understanding Global Culture and Language

If a decision is made to take a product to a foreign market, careful consideration of that foreign market's culture and language is essential. Otherwise, a failure to understand the foreign market can be a frustrating experience, if not a major fiasco, as Exhibit 12.2 suggests.

Copeland and Griggs (1985) suggest an intriguing set of themes that company planners should consider when trying to understand a foreign market. These themes, or "languages of the world," as Copeland and Griggs call them, provide a useful context on which to base a strategy for going into a foreign market with a given product or service. These five "languages" concern time, space, things, friendships, and agreements.

The language of time recognizes that the perceptions of time differ across country cultures. People in the United States do not like to wait, whereas people in Latin America have a greater tolerance for longer wait times. Waiting also has different meanings for cultures. A U.S. businessman visiting an executive in a Brazilian company had to wait a long time. The visitor thus thought that the Brazilian was not interested in seeing him, since in the United States long wait times are associated with stalling or trying to put people off. However, the Brazilian was trying to clear his agenda in order to avoid interruptions during the visit, so from his point of view, the longer wait time meant that he valued the U.S. businessman's visit very much.

The language of space recognizes that space has different meanings across country cultures. In the United States, personal space is valued; the typical comfort zone between people talking together is one to two feet. In other countries, people stand much closer to each other. Another facet of the language of space is being alone or with other people. In the United States, individual success is valued, but in Sri Lanka, the individual is not as valued as the social collective. This discrepancy hurt an American Express foray into Sri Lanka, which highlighted individual financial success in an advertisement showing a person alone on a beach. The Sri Lankan response to this advertisement was negative because the culture perceived the individual as a social outcast since he was alone on the beach.

The language of things highlights that cultures value different types of things. Japan is a culture of minimalism. Japanese homes typically do not have a lot of objects in them compared to the typical U.S. home. Another facet of things is gift-giving. Japanese culture values gifts at the beginning of a business relationship, whereas U.S. firms do not generally exchange gifts until after a relationship has been established. Furthermore, how to present the gift and what gift to give are very important. In Japan, a person presenting a gift should be sure to allow time for the group to gather before making the presentation and should present the gift with both hands. Also, a visitor should either present a group gift or a gift to each individual within the organization; it is extremely rude to present a gift to only one individual in a group. Appropriate and inappropriate types of gifts in various countries include the following: for Chinese colleagues, give modest gifts such as coffee-table books, ties, and pens, but never give clocks or anything from or made in Taiwan; for Indian colleagues, give sweets, nuts, fruit, elephant carvings, and candleholders, but never give leather objects and snake images; for Japanese colleagues, give items of Americana, scotch, brandy, or round fruits, but never give gifts that come in sets of four or nine; for Mexican colleagues, give desk clocks, fine pens, and gold lighters, but do not give sterling silver items, logo gifts, or food baskets; and for Saudi Arabian colleagues, give fine compasses and cashmere, but never give alcohol or pigskin products (Murphy 1999).

The language of friendships indicates the differences across culture with respect to personal relationships. For example, in nonmobile societies where there is limited travel between communities, individuals are less likely to want to expand their personal network. Mobile societies are more likely to welcome newcomers.

The language of agreements recognizes that the way people contract with each other differs across cultures. In the United States, agreements are often finalized through the use of lawyers. In Japan, people bow on an agreement. In Mediterranean cultures, a contract is not an end point, but shows that people are now serious about working with each other.

In addition to these "expressed" languages, there is a silent language involving signs, colors, and numbers. Translation of product names and promotion copy and the colors used need to be carefully monitored to ensure that there is no misinterpretation and that local taboos are not being violated. In the same way, numbers can have different meanings in different cultures. To reiterate, companies need to truly understand the given foreign market. Blindly entering a foreign market without careful study of that market will undoubtedly result in problems.

CHAPTER 12

Global Product Development Teams

The "languages of the world" can be useful for managing another global consideration—global product development teams (hereafter referred to as global teams). These teams are distinguished from other types of teams in that team members come from different countries around the world. Factors driving the need for global teams are the global dispersion of company resources, expansion of corporate facilities around the world, and the difficulty and expense associated with relocating individuals to a central location.

Global teams have their challenges. They pose greater behavioral challenges than co-located teams (teams whose members are all at the same physical location) or distributed teams (teams whose members are from different locations, but within the same country), and greater project management challenges than co-located teams. Behavioral challenges include generating trust between team members, achieving effective interpersonal relationships, and achieving effective communication among team members. Project management challenges include identifying customer needs, ensuring that project goals remain stable, staying on budget, keeping on schedule, and having sufficient resources.

Research suggests that companies need to devote greater effort and time to meeting these challenges, providing more training to the managers of these teams, and putting into place organizational infrastructures to support these efforts (McDonough, Kahn, and Barczak 2001). This is because global teams have been shown to perform less well than virtual or co-located teams, which is not surprising given the greater project management and behavioral challenges they face. Limited company experience in managing global teams also might contribute to an inability to effectively manage these greater challenges and to these teams' lower performance.

Communication appears to be one important factor for successful global teams. The work of McDonough, Kahn, and Griffin (1999) distinguishes that global teams have keen requirements for rich information, large volumes of information, and information speed. Regular use of telecommunications between global team members appears to mitigate problems and achieve levels of communication that satisfy these three dimensions. More successful global teams also employ an "affiliated set" of communication mechanisms that include fax, teleconferencing, email, and company databases. This affiliated set of communication mechanisms has complementary capabilities across the three communication dimensions, and firms that use these mechanisms jointly appear to better meet the three need dimensions. McDonough, Kahn, and Barczak (2001) also determined that a face-to-face meeting of the global project team at the beginning of the project is important to global team success.

Such a meeting appears to provide a focus and direction for the global team. The recommendation is that team leaders and senior management allocate time and resources so that global team members can get together face-to-face in one location at the beginning of the project. In summary, global teams present unique challenges that product planners should be prepared to deal with; global team communication is a must for addressing these challenges.

Sustainable Product Development

Much attention has been paid to sustainable product development globally. By definition, sustainable design concerns the balancing of economic, environmental, and social aspects in the creation of products and services. In doing so, sustainable product development looks to minimize adverse sustainability impacts and maximize sustainable value throughout the life cycle of the product, building, or service being developed. If done properly, sustainable products and services aim to increase stakeholders' quality of life, reduce resource and energy use, and stimulate higher levels of creativity and innovation in the course of product development.

Green product development is related to the topic of sustainability. While its roots are in regulatory compliance, green product development is driven by a response to satisfy market interest for environmentally friendly products. Companies find that green product development goes beyond environmental goodwill and can result in lowered operating costs stemming from improved energy efficiency and better product materials. Developing green products is not without cost, though, because it often requires high investment and research costs. Companies therefore should select their strategies on the basis of an environmental assessment and broad analysis of the product and market (Lewis et al. 2001).

Strategies for green product development include the following:

- Avoid toxic or hazardous materials.
- Choose clean production processes.
- Design products that are efficient in natural resources or energy consumption.
- Design products for regulatory compliance.
- Design products with low or zero emissions and minimal waste.
- Develop and brand energy efficient technology.
- Employ ways to reuse, recycle, and remanufacture.
- Maximize energy and water efficiencies.
- Select product and packaging materials that have no or minimal impact on the environment, such as natural versus synthetic materials and abundant versus rare materials.

Base of the Pyramid Product Development

Whereas traditional product development initiatives target customers at the upper end of the economic pyramid, "base of the pyramid" (BoP) product development refers to initiatives by companies to provide essential products and services, new jobs, and economic opportunities to economically disadvantaged populations at the bottom of the economic pyramid (Prahalad 2005; Prahalad and Hart 2002). Traditionally viewed as inaccessible and unprofitable markets, BoP markets are now seen as unexplored opportunities to supply the needs and wants of low-income consumers.

To tap the vast markets at the BoP, product development focuses on low-cost, quality products and services. This can be accomplished by altering existing product offerings or making new products at lower cost. Not only can serving BoP customers become a profitable opportunity for companies, but also it represents a social imperative given that two-thirds of the human population, or about 4 billion people, are at the bottom of the economic pyramid (Prahalad 2005; Prahalad and Hart 2002). BoP product development aims to curtail poverty and improve the living conditions of the world's poorest people.

Examples of BoP product development include the following:

- Unilever developed a shampoo product that works best with cold water and is sold in small packets to reduce barriers of up-front costs for the poor.
- Hindustani Lever Limited (HLL), a subsidiary of Unilever, developed an improved, eco-friendly detergent, which reduced the water-to-oil ratio, decentralized production, and took advantage of a large labor pool and social networks in rural markets, all of which slashed cost structures and enabled a lower price for the product.
- HLL rethought the refrigeration platform to provide ice cream to the BoP market. The result was a novel, salt-based heat shield that improved insulation methods and dropped the price of ice cream to an affordable level.
- The nonprofit group KickStart developed a manually powered irrigation pump that was engineered to be light and portable.
- Citibank's Suvidha, a consumer-banking product with a low deposit limit ($25), was an unqualified success when launched in Bangalore, with over 150,000 new accounts opened in the first year.
- Ericsson developed a low-cost cell phone (the MiniGSM) that can operate as a stand-alone device or as a networked data or voice system for up to 5,000 users in a thirty-five-kilometer (twenty-mile) radius.

- Voxiva, a start-up partnered with Telefonica, is automating business transactions over the phone in Latin America. Peru's Ministry of Health is using Voxiva's service to fill prescriptions and link people with health-care workers.

Discussion Questions

1. What are five strategies for introducing products to foreign markets?
2. Based on Copeland and Griggs, what are the five "languages of the world"?
3. What are some challenges faced by global product development teams?
4. What is sustainable product development?
5. What is "base of the pyramid" product development?

References

Copeland, Lennie, and Lewis Griggs. 1985. *Going International: How to Make Friends and Deal Effectively in the Global Marketplace*. New York: Random House.

Keegan, Warren J. 1995. *Multinational Marketing Management*. 5th ed. Upper Saddle River, NJ: Prentice-Hall.

Kotler, Philip. 2000. *Marketing Management: Analysis, Planning, Implementation, and Control*. 10th ed. Upper Saddle River, NJ: Prentice-Hall.

Lewis, Helen, John Gertsakis, Tim Grant, Nicola Morelli, and Andrew Sweatman. 2001. *Design + Environment: A Global Guide to Designing Greener Goods*. Sheffield, UK: Greenleaf.

McDonough, Edward F., Kenneth B. Kahn, and Gloria Barczak. 2001. "An Investigation of the Use of Global, Virtual, and Colocated New Product Development Teams." *Journal of Product Innovation Management*, 18 (2), 110–120.

McDonough, Edward F., Kenneth B. Kahn, and Abbie Griffin. 1999. "Managing Communication in Global Product Development Teams." *IEEE Transactions on Engineering Management*, 46 (4) (November), 375–386.

Murphy, Kate. 1999. "Gifts Without Gaffes for Global Clients." *Business Week*, December 6, p. 153.

Prahalad, C.K. 2005. *The Fortune at the Bottom of the Pyramid: Eradicating Poverty Through Profits*. Upper Saddle River, NJ: Wharton School Publishing.

Prahalad, C.K., and Stuart L. Hart. 2002. "The Fortune at the Bottom of the Pyramid." *Strategy + Business*, 26, 54–67.

13 Legal and Public Policy Considerations for Product Planning

Legal and public policy issues are important aspects of product planning and deserve the same, if not more, consideration than other aspects. Because of these issues' importance, it is not uncommon for a legal representative to be a member of the core team overseeing the product planning initiative. The legal representative provides counsel and direction on issues related to the topics of intellectual property, product liability, business entity formation, and even public policy, which are discussed in this chapter.

Intellectual Property

Intellectual property is critical in the course of product planning, especially when new technology development is involved, and understanding how to protect such intellectual property is essential in order to ensure a competitive advantage. Depending on the nature of the offering being developed, protection can come via a patent, trade secret, trademark, or copyright (www.uspto.gov).

Patent

A patent represents the government's granting of a property right to an inventor in exchange for disclosure of the invention. Through a patent, the inventor is given the right to exclude others from making, using, offering for sale, selling, or importing the invention for a specified duration. In the United States this duration can be twenty years from the date of the patent application. While a patent is the right to exclude others from making, using, or selling the invention, it is not the right to make, use, or sell the invention, nor can a patent conflict with state or federal laws prohibiting the making, use, offering to sell, selling, or importing such an invention.

There are various reasons for obtaining a patent. A patent can exclude others from the market, provide impediments to competition, serve as a defensive device in the case of cross-licensing, be a marketing device, or represent a source of revenue. Revenue can come from a patent by way of licensing arrangements or infringement suits; because a patent is considered a unique kind of personal property, it can be bought, sold, mortgaged, given, or willed to another person nearly as easily as any other personal property.

To obtain the protection afforded by a patent, inventors must make a full and complete disclosure of their invention. The invention or discovery not only must be new or previously unrecognized, but also must be something extraordinary. The specific criteria applied to any patent application is whether the invention is new, useful, and nonobvious, and stems from or pertains to a process, machine, article of manufacture, composition of matter, and new and useful improvements. An obvious or normally predictable result or something that an ordinary skilled person in the field could reasonably be expected to do is not patentable. Physical phenomena, abstract ideas, mere ideas, or suggestions are not patentable either, though the machine, process, or thing into which these may have been incorporated may be patentable.

There are three different types of patents:

1. *Utility patents* protect the functional aspects of an invention (i.e., the way something works or the structure that makes it work).
2. *Design patents* protect ornamental aspects of an article of manufacture.
3. *Plant patents* protect new types of plants.

A patent application has three main components: the petition, the specification, and the oath. The petition, addressed to the commissioner of patents, is essentially a request for a grant of letters patent to be issued to the applicant. The patent specification serves to clearly describe the invention, with drawings required in all cases to the point that they are meaningful. The oath is then taken by the applicant affirming that he or she is the originator of the thing for which the patent is being requested. Only inventors or joint inventors applying jointly can obtain a patent; if a noninventor applies, the patent is invalid.

Although not required, a provisional patent application is a preliminary step in the patent process, giving one-year period of protection. A provisional patent application allows filing without any formal patent claims, oath or declaration, or any information disclosure about what information might have been already available to the public. It provides the means to establish an early effective filing date in a nonprovisional patent application and allows the term "Patent Pending" to be applied. This year's protection provides enough time to evaluate the patentability and marketability of the respective invention before investing in the cost of a regular patent.

Trade Secret

A trade secret is a formula, practice, process, design, instrument, pattern, or compilation of information that is not generally known or reasonably ascertainable and by which a business can obtain an economic advantage over competitors or customers. An example of a trade secret is the formula for Coca-Cola Classic. Trade secrets correspond to "confidential information" or "classified information," though the precise language by which a trade secret is defined varies by jurisdiction. In general, the definition includes the following elements: information associated with a trade secret is not generally known nor readily accessible to the public; reasonable measures are taken to protect the information and maintain its secrecy; and the information has economic value for its holder by not being generally publicly known.

Characteristics of a trade secret are as follows. The duration of a trade secret is perpetual as long as the secrecy of the trade secret is maintained. There is no fee to establish a trade secret, though there may be costs necessary to ensure secrecy. A trade secret cannot be claimed if the trade secret is disclosed to others without restriction of confidentiality. There also must be either a written or an implied agreement to keep information secret. It is further important that the company put in place policies to protect trade secrets. Such policies would involve confidentiality agreements with employees and third parties; restricted access and disclosure of trade secrets to employees who need to know; security of building and facilities to prevent inadvertent disclosure; limitations of plant tours, sales displays, and so on; computer security and limited access; and controlled disposal of trash.

Trademark Protection

A trademark is any word, phrase, symbol, or design, or a combination of words, phrases, symbols, or designs, that identifies and distinguishes the source of goods or services of one party from those of others. A trademark differs from other property in that part of its value is in its unique design, which is usually classified in one of four ways: arbitrary/fanciful, suggestive, descriptive, or generic. Examples of trademarks are:

- *Brand names* identify goods such as Kodak® film or Tropicana® orange juice.
- *Trade dress* consists of distinctive traits, such as the color or shape of goods and/or packaging as in the shape of a glass Coca-Cola® bottle or the color and design of the Tide® detergent package.

- *Collective marks* identify goods, services, or members of a collective organization such as SAE® (Society of Automotive Engineers) or the AFL-CIO® (American Federation of Labor and Congress of Industrial Organizations).
- *Certification marks* identify goods or services meeting certain qualifications, such as UL® (Underwriters Laboratories) or the Good Housekeeping Seal®.

Trademarks for products should be used only as proper adjectives and should be followed by a generic noun, such as "Pampers® diapers"; trademarks should not be used as a verb.

Trademark registration continues for twenty years. Federally registered trademarks use the ® designation; unregistered trademarks use the ™ designation. If the trademark is still in use after the twenty-year period, the company may renew it by filing an application to renew. Nonuse of a trademark for a two-year period is prima facie evidence of abandonment of the trademark. A trademark also can be lost for a product name if, after time, the product name becomes established as the descriptive term for products in the category. Such was the case for Aspirin and Cellophane, which lost their trademark status when they became generic nouns.

Copyright Protection

The copyright is a form of legal protection for original works of authorship that is fixed in a tangible form. Examples of items that can receive copyright protection are software (source code and graphics), music, video, photography, manuals, books, compilations, brochures, website artwork, and architectural works.

A copyright gives exclusive right to copy, publicly perform, or display to the holder of the copyright. A copyright also gives the right to control reproduction, preparation of derivative works, distribution of copies, public performance, and public display. A copyright protects the language used, but it does not preserve the ideas presented in the material.

A copyright represents a property right that can be transferred to another party. In the case of a single author, the duration of the copyright is the life of the author plus seventy years. When there are joint authors, the copyright expires seventy years after the death of the last surviving author. Work-made-for-hire is copyrighted for ninety-five years from first publication or 120 years from creation, whichever is less, given that the work-made-for-hire was created within the scope of employment and the parties have agreed in writing to the arrangement before the work begins.

223

Product Liability

Product liability represents the vulnerability of a company to lawsuits because of inherent risks with the product, design defects within the product, manufacturing defects, a failure to provide adequate instructions, or after-use dangers. While inherent risks generally cannot be avoided, efforts can and should be taken to minimize flagrant design defects that would either present a dangerous condition to the user, overlook an essential safety device, and/or incorporate inadequate materials into the product. Efforts should be taken to minimize design defects through superior quality control procedures, as well as provide adequate instructions for use or warnings against harmful uses. With respect to warnings, it is imperative that any warnings be placed conspicuously on the product, communicate danger, and instruct how to avoid danger during and after use.

Should a lawsuit be filed against a company because of one of these issues or some other issue, four types of legal bases are possible. The first legal basis is negligence, which is defined as a personal wrong due to fault. The claim of negligence is that the product is defective by design and/or manufacture and that the company has failed to warn the public. The defense to this claim would be that the company is not negligent and that the product is not defective. A case where a company used substandard fasteners and, subsequently, the product broke apart could be open to a lawsuit based on negligence.

The second legal basis is warranty, which is the situation where the company breaks a promise or does not fulfill a promise. There can be implied warranty, which is the fitness of the product for a particular purpose, and expressed warranty, which is a statement of fact made by the manufacturer (including any employee of the manufacturer). The defense to this claim would be that the "supposed promise" is not implied by common usage of the product or that the "supposed promise" was not actually stated. A warranty case could surround promises by a salesperson about a product when, in fact, the product does not have features that satisfy those promises.

The third legal basis is strict liability, or the responsibility of not putting a defective product on the market. In a strict liability claim, negligence does not need to be shown, no direct sale needs to occur, and no statement by the manufacturer will relieve the liability. Rather, strict liability centers around the issue of whether the company knew the product could cause harm in any way. The defense against strict liability is one of three possible responses: the customer assumed the risk upon purchase, there was unforeseeable misuse, or the product is not defective. An explosives manufacturer would be held strictly liable for any unintended detonations and resulting material and physical harm.

The fourth legal basis is misrepresentation of the product in the marketplace. That is, the company portrays the product as something that it is not, and based on this claim, the user gets injured. For example, a helmet manufacturer in one of its advertisements showed an individual wearing one of its helmets while sitting on a motorcycle, even though the helmet was not a motorcycle helmet. A motorcyclist who subsequently was injured while riding and wearing one of the company's helmets sued on the basis that he was misled to believe that the helmets were appropriate for motorcycle use. The plaintiff won the case and was awarded compensation. Possible defenses to the claim of misrepresentation are that the way the company portrayed the product was truthful and/or that the buyer should have known better.

Business Entity Formation

As mentioned in Chapter 9, product planning does not normally require consideration of business entity formation because the activity occurs within and will directly benefit an existing company. Sometimes, however, opportunities for new business formation are possible during product planning. This is particularly the case if the company wishes to spin out technology it views as not fitting the existing company's strategy or when the respective technology emerges from a government or university laboratory. These and other start-up opportunities portray traditional entrepreneurship versus corporate entrepreneurship, where the latter is akin to product planning.

There is no "one size fits all" answer when it comes to choice of legal business entity. The decision of which legal entity to choose depends on the company's goals and expectations, industry norms and expectations, regulatory factors, tax consequences, and liability issues. Other considerations include functionality and maintenance costs, management and control, continuity of existence, and transferability of equity interests. In the United States, there are the following general types of entities:

- Sole proprietorships
- Incorporated entities such as the C corporation and S corporation
- Unincorporated entities such as the general partnership, limited partnership, limited liability partnership, and limited liability company

Sole proprietorship is run by one individual and there is no legal distinction between the owner and the business. All profits and all losses from the business go to the owner (subject to taxation), all assets of the business are owned by the proprietor, and all debts of the business are the responsibility of the owner to be paid from personal resources. The owner in a sole proprietorship has unlimited liability, meaning the owner is directly and personally liable and creditors and tort claimants can reach the owner's personal assets.

A C corporation is a corporation in the United States that, for federal income tax purposes, is taxed under Subchapter C of Chapter 1 of the Internal Revenue Code. Most major companies (and many smaller companies) are treated as C corporations for federal income tax purposes. The purpose of a C corporation is to separate management from the ownership of the firm, and shareholders are given limited liability. C corporations have perpetual duration; the power to sue and be sued in the corporate name; the power to acquire, own, and dispose of property in the corporate name; the power to incur liabilities in the corporate name; a centralized management structure (board of directors); limited liability of shareholders; and transferability of shares reflecting ownership without affecting corporate existence. C corporations face various tax consequences, including "double taxation," where corporate income tax is imposed on net earnings and distributed earnings are taxed when distributed to shareholders. In fact, virtually every transaction with shareholders has tax consequences.

An S corporation is a corporation that makes a valid election to be taxed under Subchapter S of Chapter 1 of the Internal Revenue Code. S corporations are almost identical to C corporations. Unlike a C corporation, an S corporation is treated as a pass-through entity, which means that the S corporation's tax items are passed through to the shareholders and taxed solely at the shareholder level. S corporations have the following limitations: the number of shareholders cannot exceed 100; certain types of shareholders are prohibited (i.e., nonresident aliens and entities other than estates and certain types of trusts); only one class of stock is permitted; it must be a domestic company and it must file Form 2553 (S election) before the fifteenth day of the third month after the beginning of the tax year in order for the election to be retroactive to the date of incorporation.

The general partnership is the basic noncorporate form for multiple owners, representing an association of two or more persons to carry on as co-owners of a business for profit. Partners can be individuals or entities. No formal organizational documents are required, but there is implied agreement on joint ownership of property and joint receipt of share of profits. Each partner has complete and equal control and is an agent of the partnership. General partnerships have unlimited liability, meaning that there is no limitation of liability; the partnership is not a legal entity separate from its owners; each partner is personally liable for partnership debts, liabilities, and obligations; and there is liability for acts of partners within the scope of the partnership business. General partnerships are taxed as a "pass-through" entity because the general partnership entity is not considered a distinct entity for tax purposes.

A limited partnership is a form of partnership similar to a general partnership, except that in addition to one or more general partners, there are one or more limited partners. A limited partnership can have an unlimited number of partners across two classes of partners: one class comprises one or more limited partners who may not participate in management; the other class comprises one or more general partners who manage the partnership. Unlike in a general partnership, there must be a partnership agreement. Limited partners are not personally liable for the debts, liabilities, or obligations of the limited partnership. Limited partners also are passive investors, generally liable only to the extent of the money contributed to the partnership together with any contractual liability of the limited partners. The general partner remains personally liable for partnership debts, obligations, and liabilities. The general partner may be an entity with limited liability, providing a layer of protection. Limited partnerships are taxed as a "pass-through" entity.

Limited liability partnerships are a variation of the general partnership, providing for limitation of liability without the restriction on active participation. Limited liability partnerships require the filing of a registration with the secretary of state in the state where the limited liability partnership will reside. Partners are not liable just because they are a partner. However, partners do remain liable for their own acts, and generally any partner will not have personal liability for the negligence or misconduct by another partner. The partner would have to be directly liable, for example through negligent supervision, and may be liable to the extent that rules hold them vicariously liable. Limited partnerships are taxed as a "pass-through" entity.

A limited liability company (referred to as a LLC) is a legal business structure that reflects characteristics of a corporation and a partnership or sole proprietorship (depending on the number of owners). The key benefit of a LLC is the limited liability that the owners have, though limited liability does not imply owners are always fully protected from personal liabilities. Such limited liability is akin to that of a C corporation in that members have protection from personal liability, but like a partnership or sole proprietorship, an LLC is taxed as a "pass-through" entity. The LLC is established by filing articles of organization with the respective state's secretary of state and governed by an operating agreement between the LLC and members. An unlimited number of individuals and/or entities can be owners of a LLC. The form of consideration exchanged for an equity interest may include cash, noncash property, and services, and members can allocate and distribute profits and losses of a LLC in accordance with the members' percentage interests or in accordance with another agreed-upon formula. Management powers can be retained by the members or centralized with a board of managers who themselves may or may not be members.

Exhibit 13.1 presents a table summarizing the different types of business entities. For more information about business entity formation, refer to the U.S. Small Business Administration's website at www.sba.gov.

Public Policy Issues

Public policy is a course of action, regulatory measure, law, judicial decision, or funding priority that addresses a contemporary topic. Issues associated with public policy must be keenly considered by product planners because such issues have bearing on whether a new product offering will succeed commercially or whether an existing product will continue to be offered in the marketplace. Public policy actions—such new legislation, regulatory agency decisions, media coverage, and even public opinion pertaining to a pressing issue—can influence and affect a new product's commercial success. Three issues commonly associated with public policy are environmental concerns, product or service performance, and morality.

Environmental Concerns

Environmental concerns are a growing public policy issue for companies. Growing concern surrounds the raw materials going into products, pollution caused by manufacturing the product, pollution caused by using the product, and product disposal. Printed circuit board manufacturers have been criticized for the use of acid and chlorofluorocarbons (CFCs) in etching their boards. Legislation has eliminated the use of CFCs, but the proper disposal of the acid remains controversial. Car manufacturers have historically been criticized for vehicle emissions, but a particular criticism has arisen concerning the reemergence of large, gas-consuming sport utility vehicles. And computer manufacturers have been criticized for their lack of attention to disposal problems; many of the components in computers are inert materials that cannot be recycled. The computer industry has responded by engaging in efforts to recycle components. Overall, efforts toward making products more environmentally friendly are a timely consideration and may serve as a competitive advantage.

Product Performance and Customer Service

Product performance concerns the assurance that a product or service will perform as specified. Extensive quality control and quality assurance programs have been implemented and monitored by many companies. Any quality problems are documented and remedied, with documentation on how the

Exhibit 13.1

Types of Business Entities

Type of business entities in the United States

	Sole proprietorship	C corporation	S corporation	General partnership/ Limited liability partnership (LLP)	Limited partnership	Limited liability company
Description	Run by one individual; there is no legal distinction between the owner and the business.	Taxed under Subchapter C of Chapter 1 of the U.S. Internal Revenue Code.	Entity makes a valid election to be taxed under Subchapter S of Chapter 1 of the U.S. Internal Revenue Code.	Represents two or more persons as co-owners. LLPs limit liability without a restriction on active participation.	Similar to a general partnership, except there are one or more limited partners.	Reflects characteristics of a corporation and a partnership or sole proprietorship.
Management	Owner	Directors and officers	Directors and officers	Partners	General partners only	Managers or officers
Number of owners/ investors	One	One or more	No more than 100	Two or more	Two or more	One or more
Personal liability	Yes	No	No	Yes	Yes for general partners; no for limited partners	No
Taxes	Taxed at the individual level	Net and distributed earnings taxed	Pass-through entity	Pass-through entity	Pass-through entity	Pass-through entity
Life span	Based on owner	Perpetual duration	Perpetual duration	Based on owners	Based on owners	Perpetual duration unless otherwise specified

229

remedy was enacted. This is especially true for medical products companies, which must document all product manufacturing and testing procedures to satisfy FDA requirements. Customer service and support are also essential. The company must be customer accessible and willing to listen to customers. Customer complaints need to be acted upon and customer questions answered to ensure proper use of the product. Together, all these initiatives will help to achieve customer satisfaction, possibly generating customer delight, and ultimately leading to customer loyalty.

Morality

Morality deals with controversial products and the issue of whether it is justified to sell a given product. Two examples of very controversial products are assault weapons and pornography. The general public's view of controversial products coupled with their societal impact influences product planning decisions surrounding these products. Assuming that the products are deemed legal, particular care is needed for how the product should be sold and used.

Managing Public Policy Issues

While public policy issues should be addressed during the situation analysis, unforeseen circumstances will arise. To minimize such circumstances, it is recommended that upper management be involved with product strategy and policy to ensure that the company image will not be negatively impacted by the product planning effort and that any potential shortcomings of the product offering are recognized before product launch. Concept, product, and market testing should be pursued to identify potential shortcomings as well. Even though testing may slow down the product development process, in the long run, such testing may be well worth the effort.

In the event that an unforeseen situation arises, a crisis management program should be in place to address the situation. Upper management should be readily visible to relax customer fears and preserve the product's or company's image. In some companies, safety czars are used to plan the crisis management program and ensure product safety. Ongoing education and public relations efforts by the company will also reassure customers and preserve the company's image. Such education is most often directed out of an external affairs department.

Discussion Questions

1. What is a patent, trade secret, trademark, and copyright?
2. What is a provisional patent?

3. What is meant by product liability?
4. What are some general types of business entity?
5. What are some public policy issues to consider during product planning?

References

U.S. Patent Office. www.uspto.gov.
U.S. Small Business Administration. www.sba.gov.

14   Product Planning Best Practices

A *best practice* is defined as that technique, method, process, or activity that is more effective at delivering a particular outcome than any other technique, method, process, or activity within that domain (Camp 1989). In the case of product planning, best practices are those product development practices that promote the greatest success in developing and launching new products and services. To date, various studies have been undertaken to search for best practices. The present chapter discusses results from a variety of sources, including two noteworthy studies by the American Productivity Quality Center (APQC) (Cooper, Edgett, and Kleinschmidt 2002, 2004a, 2004b, 2004c) and the Product Development & Management Association (PDMA) (Adams-Bigelow 2005; Barczak, Griffin, and Kahn 2009).

In Search of Product Development Best Practices

A starting point for understanding product development best practices is the 1993 *Business Week* article titled "Flops" (Power et al. 1993). This article discusses product development failure and presents ways to think about improving a company's chances to avoid such failure. The article presents data showing the costs incurred by some phenomenal failures, including the following:

- Ford's Edsel = loss of $250 million
- DuPont's Corfam = loss of $100 million
- RCA's Videodisc = loss of $500 million
- Time's TV *Cable Week* = loss of $47 million
- IBM's PCjr = marketing cost of $40 million

These data exemplify the costs and amount of resources involved in the product planning endeavor. The magnitude of these data further illustrates the major, strategic impact that product planning can have in corporations.

The "Flops" *Business Week* article lists six particular themes for how a company might improve its success rate in new products (Power et al. 1993, 78–79). These themes still resound today:

1. *Ask your customers:* Do not develop a product just because the engineering department loves a new technology. Consult users and customers at every step from idea generation to commercialization.
2. *Set realistic goals:* A new product might be sure to produce $20 million in sales. So do not make it a loser by aiming for $40 million.
3. *Break down walls:* Passing off a new product from one department to another risks potentially disastrous foul-ups. Instead, have research and development, marketing, and manufacturing work together from the start.
4. *Create gateways:* Do not let a product gather dangerous momentum. At each stage of a product's development, make sure it meets specific criteria of manufacturing viability, customer acceptance, sales support, and budget planning.
5. *Watch those tests:* A test market may succeed just because customers are sampling a new product out of curiosity. Do not get carried away by initial results. Test long enough to get a real sense of a product's potential.
6. *Do your postmortems:* Managers tend to run away from their flops. Do not. Formally review what went wrong and apply those lessons to the next launch. Reward managers who learn from their mistakes.

A similar set of best practice themes is provided by Urban and Hauser in their 1993 book, *Design and Marketing of New Products.* They prescribe the incorporation of the following themes to ensure a greater likelihood of product development success:

- Listen to potential users early
- Evaluate opportunities
- Generate creative ideas
- Develop a core benefit proposition (e.g., product innovation charter)
- Integrate marketing, engineering, production to deliver customer benefits (customer-oriented)
- Carefully design communication (collaboration versus communication)
- Forecast and evaluate profit potential before go/no go decisions
- Test the product and the marketing strategy
- Monitor customers and competition to assure continued improvement in the delivery of customer satisfaction/customer delight

Urban and Hauser (1993) also provide lists of reasons for why products fail and succeed. Reviewing these lists, companies can be attuned to and identify potential pitfalls in the product planning process. Products fail, the authors say, for the following reasons:

- The market was too small
- The product was a poor match for company
- The product was not new/not different from competitors' products
- The product offered no real benefit
- The product was poorly positioned versus competition
- There was inadequate support from the channel of distribution
- There was a high degree of forecasting error
- The product had poor timing
- There was a strong competitive response
- There were major shifts in the existing technology base
- There were changes in customers' tastes
- There were changes in environmental constraints
- There was poor repeat purchase or no diffusion of sales
- There was poor after-sales service
- The product provided an insufficient return of investment
- There was a lack of coordination between organizational functions
- There were organizational problems, including personality conflict within the company and the organizational structure, not conducive to product development

Products succeed, according to Urban and Hauser, for the following reasons:

- The product matched customer needs
- The product offered high value to the customer
- The product was innovative
- The product was technically superior
- There was ample screening and analysis supported by an effective decision support system
- The competitive environment was favorable
- The product fit internal company strengths
- There was effective communication among company functions
- There was top management support
- There was an enthusiastic champion
- There was a new product organization
- A new product development process provided structure, but there was some flexibility to adapt to unexpected difficulties

- The new product development effort avoided unnecessary risk
- The time from strategic commitment to launch was short
- There was a worldwide strategy surrounding the new product
- Quality was reflected throughout the product development process, and correspondingly, there was a commitment to customer satisfaction

APQC Benchmarking of Product Development Practices

The APQC study built on research by Dr. Robert Cooper, who found that the following pitfalls contribute to new product failures and a mediocre new product program:

- A lack of market orientation, including inadequate market analysis, a failure to understand customer needs and wants, and insufficient attention to the market
- Poor quality of execution during the product development process
- Moving too quickly, forcing the company to avoid doing or short-cutting certain key tasks
- Not enough homework on market and product definition
- A lack of product differentiation from competing products
- No focus, leading to a situation of too many projects, forcing a dispersion of limited resources, which, in turn, undersupports deserving projects

Relying on Dr. Cooper and Drs. Scott Edgett and Elko Kleinschmidt as subject matter experts, APQC conducted a new product development (NPD) best practices study in the early 2000s. The aim of the study was to discover practices that lead to better new product performance. Among the more than 100 "best" practices identified, the four major themes of strategy, focus on people, process, and resources emerged as important elements underlying superior NPD performance.

- *Strategy* emphasizes having an articulated product innovation and technology strategy for the business. This strategy should be closely linked to the overall business strategy and spell out NPD goals, delineate strategic arenas (arenas of focus), define strategic buckets and resources, and establish a roadmap for new product initiatives.
- *Focus on people* emphasizes that the company should organize effective cross-functional teams and establish the right climate and culture for innovation. An appropriate engagement role for senior management needs to be determined as well.
- *Process* corresponds to implementing a world-class, systematic new

product process that drives new product projects from idea through to launch quickly and effectively. This process should incorporate notable best practices and be implemented and executed accordingly.

- *Resources* emphasizes putting necessary resources in place across functional areas. These resources should be allocated via an effective portfolio management system that provides resources to the right innovation areas and to the right projects.

For more information about the APQC research study, see Cooper, Edgett, and Kleinschmidt (2004a, 2004b, 2004c), visit the APQC website at www.apqc.org, or call APQC at 1–800–232–5241.

PDMA Research on Product Development Practices: The Comparative Performance Assessment Study (CPAS) or PDMA Best Practices Study

Since 1990, the PDMA has sponsored best practice research projects to identify trends in NPD management practices and to discern which practices are associated with high degrees of success. The objective of this ongoing research is to assist managers in determining how to improve their own product development methods and practices. Topics covered by the CPAS, also known as the PDMA Best Practices Study, are varied, including process stages used, success statistics, techniques used, and issues.

The 2009 study found that since the earlier 1995 PDMA study, companies have become slightly more conservative in the portfolio of projects, with lower percentages of the total number of projects in the new-to-the-world and new-to-the-firm categories. Although success rates and development efficiencies have remained stable, a more conservative approach to product development seems to have had a negative impact on the sales and profits of the new products that have been commercialized. Formal processes for product development are now the norm, indicating that attention is moving to managing the multiple projects across the portfolio in a more orchestrated manner. Firms also are implementing a wide variety of software support tools for various aspects of product development and product planning. Below is a summary of results from the 2009 PDMA Best Practices Study:

- Success rates and efficiencies (projects started per commercial success) remain stable, although new products are contributing a lower percentage of revenues and profits than previously. Data suggest that 14 percent of the initial ideas generated actually become commercial successes, about 54 percent of commercialized new products are successful from a profit perspective, and 28 percent of sales and profits come from new products.

- Cycle times continue to drop dramatically, especially for more radical projects. New-to-the-world products now average 104 weeks (two years) for development, major line revisions average sixty-two weeks, and incremental projects average twenty-nine weeks.
- Formal processes are now the norm, with 69 percent of companies reporting a formal, cross-functional product development process. Having a formal process is no longer a differentiator, and many firms have moved to third-generation types of NPD processes. Processes for radical projects are more complex than for incremental projects.
- Firms have moved from implementing NPD processes to help manage individual projects to implementing portfolio management processes to help manage multiple projects simultaneously.
- Most firms use multiple market research tools to gather information about customer needs. The top three market research tools are beta testing, customer site visits, and voice of the customer. Other established market research tools used by firms include alpha testing, lead user analysis, concept tests, and focus groups.
- Firms are starting to use a wide variety of software support tools for engineering design and project management and support. Team online support tools are just starting to come into use in firms.
- The top engineering design tools are design for manufacturability, concurrent engineering, and failure mode and effect analysis. Other technology tools often used by firms are computer-aided design, computer-aided engineering, project management systems, document management systems, and rapid prototyping systems.
- The top three tools used to support project teams are face-to-face meetings, teleconferences, and PERT/GANTT charts.

Areas of NPD seriously in need of improved management include:

- Idea management
- NPD project leadership and training
- Cross-functional training and team communication support
- Innovation support and leadership by senior management

The PDMA Best Practices Study compared results of the "best" performing companies versus the "rest" of the sample. Companies characterized as best were those that are in the top third of industry performance and simultaneously above the mean in program success, product sales, and profit success. A summary of results found by comparing the "best" versus the "rest" follows:

- The best have fundamentally different business strategies that are linked to their success. They are more likely to have first-to-market innovation strategies that result in a higher percentage of radical and next-generation projects in their project portfolio.
- The best use more formal processes for generating ideas.
- The best are more likely to put supporting organizational mechanisms and processes in place for managing collaborations with other firms, giving individuals from multiple functions the ability to work together as a team, supporting team leaders, and obtaining needed support from functional and senior managers.
- The best are more likely to test and implement many different kinds of NPD tools for marketing research, engineering design, technology, and team support.

A conclusion by the PDMA study was that the best "do not succeed by using just one new product development practice more extensively or better, but using a number of them more effectively simultaneously."

PDMA's Outstanding Corporate Innovator Award

In 1988, PDMA initiated a program called the Outstanding Corporate Innovator (OCI) award to recognize those organizations excelling at product development. Selection is based on meeting four criteria:

- A sustained record of success in launching new products over a five-year period
- Significant company growth delivered by the firm's successful new products
- A sound new product development process
- Unique and innovative features of the company's approach to product development that make it particularly suitable for the organization

Boike et al. (2005) examined the characteristics of OCI award winners, revealing a number of important characteristics and similarities across the set. The following notable best practices were indicated.

1. *A well-defined product development process unique to the company's market and technology environment.* This well-defined product development process reflecting the following attributes:

- Clear charter and strategy alignment for NPD
- Multiple phase gates
- Clear definition of milestones and phase activities
- Expected timelines for different class and/or complexity programs
- Ongoing monitoring of process performance with a goal of continually improving cycle time performance.

2. *A strong commitment to cross-functional teams as the fundamental organizational construct for executing NPD.* Companies rely heavily upon teams for completing NPD. The team structures customarily include the following features:

- Cross-functional roles and responsibilities
- Shared goals and objectives
- Co-location to the extent possible
- Team building and training

3. *Strong voice of the customer input.* Award-winning companies have made "customer focus" a high priority in their product development processes. They accomplish this by

- Continually refining insights into customer needs, behaviors, preferences, expectations, and economics, particularly separating needs and wants, so as to move beyond readily identifiable extensions to existing product forms
- Focusing value propositions on meeting those needs and achieving a superior customer experience
- Effectively capturing, analyzing, and disseminating an understanding of the customer throughout the organization
- Focusing resources and aligning measurement and reward systems on activities that maximize long-term customer value
- Employing the following best practice customer research techniques: customer surveys and research on desired product attributes and features; ethnographic studies of customer needs and behaviors; customer testing of new products prior to introduction; and extensive customer satisfaction monitoring and tracking.

4. *A robust process at the front end to drive innovation in the company's product portfolio.* Such a process seeks to identify and qualify new product concepts that can be supported with strong customer need and achievable technology and manufacturing.

5. *A strong linkage of NPD to the company's corporate strategy, therefore ensuring top management commitment.* All OCI companies' senior management view NPD as crucial to the company's growth and success.

While a clear set of common practices was defined across the population of OCI winners, the implementation details of these common practices did vary across the group, driven by their market, technology, and organizational environments. In many cases, the chosen solutions were quite distinctive, which implies an interesting best practice. That is, the unique solutions highlight that best practice companies mold their new product development process to the unique market, competitive, and technology situations facing their business.

For more information about PDMA and its research, see the PDMA website at www.pdma.org or call PDMA at 1–800–232–5241.

The Kahn, Barczak, Moss Best Practices Framework

In 2006, Kahn, Barczak, and Moss published a framework for organizing NPD best practices that comprised the six NPD management dimensions of strategy, portfolio management, process, market research, people, and metrics and performance evaluation, based on their review of new product development literature. Each dimension was described across four levels of sophistication, with each level of sophistication corresponding to a particular set of characteristics for poor or rudimentary practice (level one), better practice (level two), good practice (level three), and best practice (level four). In this manner, four general states of NPD practice can be illustrated for each of the six NPD dimensions so that an organization may characterize its own process relative to these four general states. If an organization does not characterize itself as using best practice on a particular dimension, then the characteristics portrayed by more sophisticated states would suggest a course for improvement. To date, the framework of Kahn, Barczak, and Moss (2006) has been found to be fairly robust and applicable worldwide. The six dimensions of the framework are discussed below.

Strategy represents defining and planning a focus for the NPD efforts of a strategic business unit (SBU), division, product line, or individual project. Cooper, Edgett, and Kleinschmidt (2002) clarify that strategy is important to guiding NPD activities and that almost 65 percent of companies report doing a good job of defining the strategy for their NPD efforts. Consequently, product development is viewed as a strategic, long-term endeavor. Organizations that look for future market opportunities and can recognize and identify customers' real or unarticulated needs are considered more sophisticated in terms of identifying a clear, new product strategy (Cooper, Edgett, and Kleinschmidt 2002).

Exhibit 14.1 portrays four levels of sophistication for strategy. Level-one companies do not set NPD goals, view NPD as very short-term and tactical, have prevalent pet projects, and make NPD decisions as part of the normal budget cycle (typically the annual budget process). Level-two companies have NPD goals that derive from the organizational mission, but such goals are obtuse, general, or not directly achievable. These organizations also identify products and programs for regular updating and modification. Level-three companies clearly align goals with their organizational mission and strategic plan and allow the mission and plan to identify or specify areas of opportunity, although market studies may provide some guidance in identifying particular priorities to pursue. Level-four companies embrace opportunity identification, which uses the mission and strategic plan to define opportunities but also responds to and highlights opportunities stemming from market changes and new technologies. Level-four companies reserve resources to pursue critical innovations and futuring (exploring the future) exercises and thereby truly view NPD as a long-term strategic endeavor.

Portfolio management represents the screening out of product concepts to identify the preferable product concepts with which to proceed. Work by Cooper, Edgett, and Kleinschmidt (2002) indicates that only 21.2 percent of companies report having a well-executed portfolio management system in place and that many companies rate their portfolio management as very weak in terms of the degree to which it is put in place. NPD organizations that are considered more sophisticated have a formal, systematic portfolio management approach, which results in better allocation of human and other resources. Sophisticated organizations also have portfolios containing a balanced percentage of radical or breakthrough types of projects and incremental projects (Cooper, Edgett, and Kleinschmidt 2002). Less sophisticated companies have unbalanced portfolios that favor incremental projects and an inefficient system for allocating resources.

Integrating these results, portfolio management practices are conceived as ranging from nonexistent portfolio management activities to a formal, systematic portfolio management process. As shown in Exhibit 14.2, level-one companies do not have a process for portfolio management, nor do they prioritize NPD projects; pet projects are the predominant driver behind project selection. Level-two companies prioritize NPD projects, predominantly stemming from decisions during the annual budgeting cycle; they have pet projects, although such projects would not dominate the portfolio landscape, and use a portfolio management process on existing products versus new

Exhibit 14.1

Strategy Dimension of the Kahn, Barczak, and Moss Framework

Level 1	Level 2	Level 3	Level 4
• No NPD goals	• Unclear NPD goals	• NPD goals are clearly aligned with organization mission and strategic plan	• Mission and strategic plan help define strategic arenas for new opportunities
• Short-term, tactical view of NPD	• Organizational mission and strategic plan drives NPD product selection	• Clearly defined and organization awareness of NPD goals	• Opportunity identification is ongoing and can redirect the strategic plan in real time in order to respond to market forces and new technologies
• NPD projects are identified during budget process and resources allocated accordingly	• NPD products, programs, and services are identified for regular updating	• Strategic plan identifies areas of opportunity	• There are strategic buckets of resources to facilitate innovation and futuring
• Funding drives NPD product selection	• Most NPD projects fit with mission, but some pet projects may not fit mission	• Pet projects are minimized	• Long-term, strategic view of NPD
• Pet projects are prevalent			

Source: Kahn, Barczak, and Moss (2006).

242

Exhibit 14.2

Portfolio Management Dimension of the Kahn, Barczak, and Moss Framework

Level 1	Level 2	Level 3	Level 4
• No process for undertaking portfolio management • No prioritization of NPD projects • No concern over types of NPD projects being developed • NPD projects may or may not be aligned with organization's mission and strategic plan • Pet projects are prevalent	• NPD project prioritization occurs during the annual budget process • A variety of NPD projects are supported with little to no regard for mix appropriateness • Most NPD projects are aligned with the organization's mission • Pet projects exist • A portfolio management process is used to manage existing offerings • The ability to secure funding drives NPD project selection and development • NPD concepts and project ideas are reviewed independently	• Resources can be made available should a new opportunity come onto the horizon (pop-up) • Trade-offs are made between project ideas within a department or SBU (projects are evaluated as a set within a particular group) • Very few, if any, pet projects exist unless approved by management • Trade-offs are made in an informal fashion to manage new offerings (done in a subjective fashion)	• A formal, systematic portfolio management process is in place • There is keen consideration for balancing the number of projects and available resources • There is a ranking or prioritization of projects • There is a balanced variety of projects • All projects must be aligned with the organization's mission or strategic plan • An idea bank exists

Source: Kahn, Barczak, and Moss (2006).

243

concepts. Level-three companies diminish the existence of pet projects and force a discipline around project selection. Resources are allocated to new ideas and opportunities that fit the mission, or strategy, of the organization. Level-four companies have keen consideration for balancing the number of projects and available resources in the course of a formal, systematic portfolio management process.

Process represents the NPD stages, corresponding activities, and gate criteria for moving products to launch. Cooper, Edgett, and Kleinschmidt (2002) found that "NPD advanced" organizations use a common, formal process with clearly defined stages and gates that are visible, documented, and used. Almost 47 percent of responding companies reported having clearly defined criteria to evaluate projects at each gate. Results also indicate that more than 40 percent of companies designate a process manager to own the process and ensure its use; 65 percent report having a process that was adaptable and scalable to different types of projects and situations (Cooper, Edgett, and Kleinschmidt 2002). These results are similar to a PDMA-sponsored study conducted by Griffin (1997) where 60 percent of profit organizations indicated using a stage-gate process for NPD, whereas 39 percent indicated no formal process at all.

As shown in Exhibit 14.3, level-one companies do not subscribe to any NPD process, nor do they reflect a discipline for managing NPD development activities. Level-two companies use an informal, decentralized process where different functional groups employ their own tailored process with limited documentation. Product champions are critical to moving projects through the process of level-two companies. Level-three companies establish a common, documented NPD process and are disciplined in adhering to this process, both of which factors cut across organizational groups. Product champions play a role in NPD but are not necessary for project success. Level-four companies establish for the entire organization a formal stage-gate process that is highly visible and well documented. Personnel in level-four companies are disciplined in using the NPD process and are aware of the go/no-go criteria for each review. Though formal, the process in level-four companies is flexible and adaptable to meet the needs, size, and risks of individual project situations.

Market research includes application of activities for sensing, learning about, and understanding customers, competitors, and macroenvironmental forces in the marketplace. Overall, sophisticated organizations employ a variety of market research techniques so that the customer can be involved throughout the development process (Griffin 1997). These techniques include concept testing, both internal and external product testing, and market testing to determine product definition and customer response (Cooper, Edgett, and Kleinschmidt 2002). Leading organizations provide adequate resources to sup-

Exhibit 14.3

Process Dimension of the Kahn, Barczak, and Moss Framework

Level 1	Level 2	Level 3	Level 4
• No NPD process exists • There is a flurry of NPD activity without any discipline surrounding the management of NPD development activities • Criteria for evaluating the NPD projects are not defined • There is no NPD process owner or NPD process champion	• Informal, decentralized NPD process exists where different groups use their own tailored process • Limited documentation on the NPD process • The process can be readily circumvented by anyone • A few standard criteria are used for evaluation of NPD project activity • Idea generation is structured and formal • Different processes exist for ideas coming from internal and external sources • Minimal testing performed • Product champions are critical to NPD success	• A common NPD process cuts across organizational groups • Documentation on the NPD process is available • Idea database is maintained • Time critical projects may skip stages of process • Product champions play an important role, but are not mandatory • One individual or group can be readily identified as the process manager • There is an apparent NPD discipline	• One formal stage-gate process is employed for the entire organization • The NPD process is quite visible and well documented • Personnel are very disciplined in using the process to develop all new offerings • Go/no-go criteria are clear and predefined for each review gate • The NPD process is flexible and adaptable to meet the needs, size, and risk of individual projects • There is an intranet for NPD process documentation

Source: Kahn, Barczak, and Moss (2006).

245

port the market research function, gathering a variety of market information to learn customers' current and unarticulated needs, problems, and benefits; customer reaction to the proposed product and price sensitivity; market size and potential; expected sales revenue; and competitive situation (Cooper, Edgett, and Kleinschmidt 2002).

Four levels of sophistication for NPD market research are suggested in Exhibit 14.4. Level-one companies do not perform market research, relying on anecdotal evidence that suggests an internal orientation toward product development focused on current problems and needs. Level-two companies use market research in a reactive fashion to clarify an issue that may arise. These companies wait until a project begins before initiating a market research study, since funding for such market research will be tied to the project itself. They also rely heavily on pilots, or product testing, for obtaining feedback from customers. Level-three companies are more proactive in using market research, as they have a formal, budgeted market research group that helps to develop the product definition. Level-three companies use concept, product, and market testing across projects, although not all projects will undergo the same types of testing. Level-four companies have ongoing market research and make it an integral part of the NPD process. The purpose of such research is not only to help in defining the product, but also to anticipate or identify future customer needs and problems. Concept, product, and market testing are common to all NPD projects.

The people dimension encompasses human resources and team-related initiatives. Cooper, Edgett, and Kleinschmidt (2002) found that leading organizations rely greatly on cross-functional teams throughout the NPD process and are likely to have a centralized NPD function at the corporate or divisional level where NPD specialists work full-time on such activities.

Exhibit 14.5 suggests a continuum from department silos to cross-functional teams. Level-one companies are characterized as functionally divided with strong departmental silos and individualistic NPD. Level-two companies begin to dedicate individuals to NPD activities but rely strongly on a committee approach for NPD activities and decisions. Level-three companies rely on department liaisons via multifunctional teams, using a project team leader to shepherd the project, but not all projects are under the auspices of an NPD team leader. Level-four companies use cross-functional teams to underlie the NPD process and have a clear structure for identifying project team leaders. Level-four companies also have ongoing training to manifest and sustain organizational NPD awareness.

Metrics and performance evaluation pertain to how NPD performance is measured, tracked, reported, recognized, and rewarded. The work of Cooper, Edgett, and Kleinschmidt (2002) demonstrates that sophisticated organiza-

Exhibit 14.4

Market Research Dimension of the Kahn, Barczak, and Moss Framework

Level 1	Level 2	Level 3	Level 4
• No market research performed; predominantly anecdotal evidence used instead • Focus on current organization needs and problems • Customer or user is uninvolved in NPD process • No concept, product, or market testing undertaken • No studies done to understand marketplace	• Market research is reactive in nature • Secondary research is performed once a project begins • Market studies are performed once a project begins • No market research function; primary market research is outsourced • Pilot testing is predominant form of testing • No real evaluation of testing results • Subject matter experts are used for macroenvironmental research	• Market research used to help develop product definition • A formal market research function exists in the organization • Concept testing, product testing, and market testing are used in some, but not all, NPD projects • Results of testing are formally evaluated • Market research is budgeted	• Product definitions are based on market research with customers and other stakeholders • Customer or user is an integral part of the NPD process • Market studies are ongoing • Concept, product, and market testing is consistently undertaken and expected with all NPD projects • Ongoing market research is used to anticipate and identify future customer needs and problems • Market research has an integral relationship with NPD activity

Source: Kahn, Barczak, and Moss (2006).

247

Exhibit 14.5

People Dimension of the Kahn, Barczak, and Moss Framework

Level 1	Level 2	Level 3	Level 4
• NPD is performed by individuals • Prevalent department silos • No project leaders • Personnel take on too many projects • No identifiable NPD group	• NPD is decentralized within each business unit or department • Champions shepherd projects and are a mainstay of project success • Full-time employees dedicated to NPD • No NPD teams, but cross-functional meetings are used to discuss new ideas and projects • NPD is committee-focused • Subject matter experts, volunteers, and possibly a board of advisers influence opportunity identification and concept generation stages	• Department liaisons compose established NPD teams (multifunctional teams are used) • Identifiable new product managers within business unit or department • Each project has a project leader • Champions exist for each project, but are not necessary for project success • Not all projects go through NPD group; some projects are simply handled by department managers • Some NPD training	• Cross-functional teams underlie the NPD process • Each project has a core team that remains on the project from beginning to end • NPD is team-focused • Clearly identifiable project leaders • An NPD group exists and is dedicated to just NPD work • Use of project management software and techniques to manage projects • Ongoing NPD training and NPD awareness

Source: Kahn, Barczak, and Moss (2006).

248

tions have defined go-kill gates and specific gate criteria, with an emphasis on strategic criteria such as fit with core capabilities, market need, and financial objectives. These organizations are also likely to gauge how well the project meets specific NPD goals such as market share, customer satisfaction, time to market, sales volume, and customers' attitude toward the brand.

Exhibit 14.6 presents a continuum that ranges from no standard criteria or metrics to use of standard criteria and multiple reviews. Specifically, level-one companies are characterized as having no standard criteria for evaluating NPD projects or standard criteria for evaluating their overall NPD efforts. Level-two companies use general criteria as guiding principles with an emphasis on revenue or customer volume, but the evaluation process is mostly informal in nature. Level-three companies employ scoring models and checklists and a team approach for evaluating NPD projects and the overall NPD process. Level-three companies use a formal set of business analyses across a series of gate-review points, with middle to upper management involved in the decision-making process. Level-four companies have a standard set of criteria for evaluating NPD projects and their overall NPD efforts. A distinction of level-four companies is the use of an evaluation team, which is charged with the task of NPD evaluation, and the storage and tracking of metric data for possible latter analyses.

To apply the best practices framework in the course of an NPD process audit, a product planner would map the respective company's NPD process characteristics onto the framework based on review with and evaluation of NPD staff, team members, third parties, or a combination. The level of sophistication for a particular dimension would be where the majority of characteristics typifying that organization are found. Naturally, an organization may reflect a number of varied characteristics, but experience suggests that one level of sophistication will usually be prevalent. For example, a company might be profiled as 334211 across the six dimensions and could then compare itself against the ideal case of 444444 or the best practitioner in the industry, for example 434322. This comparison serves as a diagnostic for indicating where the organization should focus its attention; in this example, the respective company could seek to improve its NPD performance in order to match the best practitioner on the first, fifth, and sixth dimensions. Experience suggests that many companies are characteristically level one or partially level two when it comes to NPD sophistication. These companies generally do not have an NPD process; do not prioritize NPD projects or use a portfolio management approach; have a predominance of pet projects; lack standard criteria for evaluating NPD projects and the overall NPD effort; take a short-term, tactical view of NPD; and do not use market research to its potential, if at all. Such a company contrasts with a true level-four company that has a

Exhibit 14.6

Metrics and Performance Measurement Dimension of the Kahn, Barczak, and Moss Framework

Level 1	Level 2	Level 3	Level 4
• No standard criteria for evaluating projects • No standard criteria for evaluating the overall NPD effort • Projects are never killed	• There are some general guiding principles for evaluating objects • Revenue or members served is the predominant metric for NPD project success • Some initial screening criteria used but very informal in nature • One person does all evaluations • Some projects may be dropped or killed	• Scoring models and checklists are used • Team approach is used to evaluate and make final decision on NPD projects • Projects can be stopped or killed at any time • Formal business analysis is undertaken • Business plans must be approved by directors or vice presidents • Multiple review points • Board of directors must approve really new ideas and projects and/or big projects	• There is a standard set of criteria for individually evaluating NPD projects • There is a standard set of criteria for evaluating the overall NPD effort • Multiple reviews and reviewers are used to evaluate NPD projects and NPD progress • There is a group charged with the task of evaluation • An evaluation software tool is employed • Metric data is tracked and stored • Metric data can be readily accessed for analysis

Source: Kahn, Barczak, and Moss (2006).

formal NPD process including portfolio management, visible gates, proactive market research, cross-functional teams, and standard criteria to support NPD as a strategic initiative. Transitioning from level one to four should not be viewed as easy or immediate. Companies might be able to rapidly transition from level one to two. However, as sophistication increases, it will likely take longer to transition from level two to three and even longer to transition from level three to four. For some companies and industries, level three may be acceptable due to diminishing returns from expending resources to secure all level-four characteristics.

Kahn, Barczak, and Moss (2006) have recognized limitations with the framework. They specifically note concerns with inclusivity, equality, and maturity. Inclusivity refers to whether or not the six dimensions are the only elements to contribute to NPD best practice. Key elements separately indentifying the fuzzy front end, life cycle management, commercialization, and launch are conspicuously missing. Equality refers to whether there is equal weighting among the dimensions. Some researchers argue that particular dimensions, such as NPD process and strategy, are more important to NPD success than others. Cooper and Kleinschmidt (1995) find that of nine factors that drive new product program performance, a high-quality new product process is most important, followed by a clearly articulated new product strategy. Maturity refers to the framework defining level four as perfection. In some cases, level four might not be attainable or advisable, especially in turbulent and uncertain contexts that require flexibility, creativity, and innovation. Indeed, some researchers have suggested that a curvilinear relationship between maturity and at least several dimensions may persist, where maturity is necessary up to a certain point, after which the introduction of more flexible, informal initiatives would be needed for stimulating more innovative new product development and commercialization. Radically new NPD projects, for example, would require less structure, more exploration, and more process flexibility than incremental projects due to their nature.

The Continued Search for Product Development Best Practices

Akin to the findings of Boike et al. (2005) and other researchers, an emerging consensus is that product development best practices will vary from firm to firm, evolving over time and with changes in the marketplace (Murray, O'Driscoll, and Torres 2002). Therefore, there is no "one best way" to achieve high performance but rather different routes to the same end goal. Loch (2000) argues that while the stage-gate process serves as the NPD backbone, company survival depends on how well that company adapts to specific environments and so there is no one "best practice" NPD process. Companies essentially need to develop a customized NPD project portfolio and a corresponding mixture of processes, which together meet strategic innovation needs across incremental projects, really new product projects, and radical innovation projects (Garcia and Calantone 2002); companies also need to emphasize process flexibility so that the process can continually adjust to the organization's needs and desires (Davidson, Clamen, and Karol 1999).

Kahn et al. (2010) empirically investigated the concerns underlying the best practices framework proposed by Kahn, Barczak, and Moss (2006). Based on a sizable sample comprising practitioners from the United States, United Kingdom, and Ireland, their results indicate that seven dimensions, not the above-cited six, seem more likely dimensions for product planning practice. These seven dimensions are strategy, process, research, project climate, company culture, metrics and performance measurement, and commercialization. Among these dimensions, practitioners in all three countries rated strategy the highest in importance; project climate and metrics rated lowest in importance. Further analysis examined the specific characteristics at each level of sophistication per dimension. The results show that practitioners appear able to distinguish what constitutes poor versus best practice, but the distinguishing of middle-range practices between good and better characteristics was not as clear. The best practices implications from Kahn et al. (2010) are:

- Managers should emphasize strategy when undertaking NPD efforts.
- Managers should consider the fit of their projects with company strategy.
- There appear to be clearly some poor practices that managers should avoid.
- There appear to be some best practices to which managers should ascribe.

Exhibit 14.7 shows which practices were clearly distinguished as poor practice and which practices were clearly distinguished as best practice.

Good Luck

It would be remiss to overlook the fact that luck does play a role in product planning success in conjunction with implementing the aforementioned best practices. Luck includes market timing, market response, and serendipitous revelations. Yet simply relying on luck alone will not ensure continued product planning success. The greatest propensity for sustained, long-term success is achieved through a systematic approach to product planning as discussed and prescribed in this book and as best practice research exemplifies. The hope is that this book has made such

Exhibit 14.7

Poor Versus Best Practices for Product Planning

Poor practice	Best practice
Commercialization	A standard protocol for planning a launch exists within the company
Marketing budget decisions can dramatically change up to the point of launch	The launch team is cross-functional in nature
	Cross-functional teams make decisions concerning manufacturing, logistics, marketing, and sales
	Logistics and marketing work closely together on new product launch
	Customer service and support are part of the launch team
	A project postmortem meeting is held after the new product is launched
Company Culture	
NPD is not a management priority	Top management supports the NPD process
All NPD ideas come from within the company	The company actively works with customers to develop new solutions
Management is primarily focused on operational efficiency and cost savings	
Metrics and Performance Measurement	
No standard criteria for evaluating NPD projects exist	
No standard criteria for evaluating the overall NPD effort exist	
One person does all NPD project evaluations	
Projects are never killed	
Process	
Criteria for evaluating NPD projects are not defined	A common NPD process cuts across organizational groups
Limited documentation on the NPD process exists	Go/no-go criteria are clear and predefined for each review gate
Minimal testing (concept, product, market) performed	The NPD process is flexible and adaptable to meet the needs, size, and risk of individual projects
No NPD process exists	The NPD process is visible and well documented
There is no discipline in using the organization's NPD process	An IT infrastructure with appropriate hardware, software, and technical support is available to all NPD personnel
There is no NPD process owner or NPD process champion	A clear NPD process exists

(continued)

Exhibit 14.7 *(continued)*

Not all NPD personnel have access to the same IT tools (software, hardware)
Projects are not reviewed at completion
The NPD process can be circumvented without management approval

Project Climate

No identifiable NPD group	Each project has a core cross-functional team which remains on the project from beginning to end
No project leader	Each project has a clearly identifiable project leader
NPD personnel are involved in too many projects	NPD activities between functional areas are coordinated through formal and informal communication

Research

Customer or user is uninvolved in NPD process	Concept, product, and market testing is consistently undertaken and expected with all NPD projects
Little if any market research is undertaken	Customer or user is an integral part of the NPD process
No real evaluation of testing (concept, product, market) results is undertaken	Results of testing (concept, product, market) are formally evaluated
No market studies are undertaken to understand marketplace	

Strategy

Most NPD projects fit with mission, but some pet projects that do not fit mission exist	Clearly defined and organizationally visible NPD goals
No NPD goals	The organization views NPD as a long-term strategy
The organization views NPD only as a short-term tactical initiative	Mission and strategic plan help define strategic arenas for new opportunities
Unclear NPD goals	NPD goals are clearly aligned with organization mission and strategic plan
A variety of NPD projects are supported with little or no regard for mix appropriateness	NPD projects and programs are reviewed on a regular basis
No concern over types of NPD projects being developed	Opportunity identification is ongoing and can redirect the strategic plan in real time to respond to market forces and new technologies
No prioritization of NPD projects	There is a ranking or prioritization of projects
No process for undertaking portfolio management	There is keen consideration for balancing the number of projects and available resources
NPD projects may or may not be aligned with organization's mission or strategic plan	
Pet projects are prevalent	
All trade-offs among NPD projects are made informally with no set criteria	

an impression on its readers and distilled their understanding of the extensive, diverse, and impactful nature of product planning.

Discussion Questions

1. What is a best practice?
2. What better or best practices does the APQC study suggest for product planning?
3. What better or best practices does the PDMA OCI program suggest for product planning?
4. What best practices does the Kahn, Barczak, and Moss (2006) framework suggest for product planning?
5. Based on the discussion of Chapter 14, how might a company improve its product planning efforts?

References

Adams-Bigelow, Marjorie E. 2005. "First Results from the 2003 Comparative Performance Assessment Study (CPAS)." In *The PDMA Handbook of New Product Development*, 2nd ed., ed. Kenneth B. Kahn, 546–566. Hoboken, NJ: John Wiley.

Barczak, Gloria, Abbie Griffin, and Kenneth B. Kahn. 2009. "Trends and Drivers of Success in NPD Practices: Results of the 2003 PDMA Best Practices Study." *Journal of Product Innovation Management*, 26 (1), 3–23.

Boike, Douglas, Thomas Hustad, Stan Jankowski, Sally Evans Kay, John Moran, Albert Page, and Norman Parker. 2005. "Lessons Learned from Outstanding Corporate Innovators." In *The PDMA Handbook of New Product Development*, 2nd ed., ed. Kenneth B. Kahn, 527–545. Hoboken, NJ: John Wiley.

Camp, Robert. 1989. *Benchmarking: The Search for Industry Best Practices That Lead to Superior Performance*. Milwaukee, WI: ASQ Quality Press.

Cooper, Robert G., Scott J. Edgett, and Elko J. Kleinschmidt. 2002. "Improving New Product Development Performance and Practices." Benchmarking Study by American Productivity & Quality Center.

———. 2004a. "Benchmarking Best NPD Practices—I." *Research-Technology Management*, 47 (1), 31–43.

———. 2004b. "Benchmarking Best NPD Practices—II." *Research-Technology Management*, 47 (3), 50–59.

———. 2004c. "Benchmarking Best NPD Practices—III." *Research-Technology Management*, 47 (6), 43–55.

Cooper, Robert G., and Elko J. Kleinschmidt. 1995. "Benchmarking the Firm's Critical Success Factors in New Product Development." *Journal of Product Innovation Management*, 12 (5), 374–391.

Davidson, Jeffrey M., Allen Clamen, and Robin A. Karol. 1999. "Learning from the Best New Product Developers." *Research-Technology Management*, 42 (4), 12–18.

Garcia, Rosanna, and Roger Calantone. 2002. "A Critical Look at Technological Innovation Typology and Innovativeness Terminology: A Literature Review." *Journal of Product Innovation Management*, 19 (2), 110–132.

Griffin, A. 1997. *Drivers of NPD Success: The 1997 PDMA Report*. Chicago: PDMA.

Kahn, Kenneth B., Gloria Barczak, Ann Ledwith, John Nicholas, and Helen Perks. 2011.

"An Examination of New Product Development Best Practice." *Journal of Product Innovation Management*, in press.

Kahn, Kenneth B., Gloria Barczak, and Roberta Moss. 2006. "Establishing a NPD Best Practices Framework." *Journal of Product Innovation Management*, 23 (2), 106–116.

Loch, Christoph. 2000. "Tailoring Product Development to Strategy: Case of European Technology Manufacturer." *European Management Journal*, 18 (3), 246–258.

Murray, John A., Aidan O'Driscoll, and Ann Torres. 2002. "Discovering Diversity in Marketing Practice." *European Journal of Marketing*, 36 (3), 373–390.

Power, Christoper, Kathleen Kerwin, Ronald Grover, Keith Alexander, and Robert D. Hof. 1993. "Flops." *Business Week*, August 16, pp. 76–82.

Urban, Glen L., and John R. Hauser. 1993. *Design and Marketing of New Products*. 2nd ed. Englewood Cliffs, NJ: Prentice-Hall.

Index

About the Author

Kenneth B. Kahn, PhD, is a professor of marketing and director of the da Vinci Center for Innovation at Virginia Commonwealth University in Richmond. His teaching and research interests concern product development, product management, and demand forecasting of current and new products. He has authored over forty articles and the books *Product Planning Essentials* (2000) and *New Product Forecasting: An Applied Approach* (2006). He also is senior editor of *The PDMA Handbook on New Product Development* (2nd ed., 2004).